GÖTTINGER ORIENTFORSCHUNGEN

I. REIHE: SYRIACA

Herausgegeben von
Martin Tamcke

Band 38

2010

Harrassowitz Verlag · Wiesbaden

Gotteserlebnis und Gotteslehre

Christliche und islamische Mystik im Orient

Herausgegeben von Martin Tamcke

2010
Harrassowitz Verlag · Wiesbaden

Bibliografische Information der Deutschen Nationalbibliothek
Die Deutsche Nationalbibliothek verzeichnet diese Publikation in der Deutschen Nationalbibliografie; detaillierte bibliografische Daten sind im Internet über http://dnb.dnb.de abrufbar.

Bibliographic information published by the Deutsche Nationalbibliothek
The Deutsche Nationalbibliothek lists this publication in the Deutsche Nationalbibliografie; detailed bibliographic data are available in the internet at http://dnb.dnb.de.

Informationen zum Verlagsprogramm finden Sie unter
http://www.harrassowitz-verlag.de

Kreuzberger Ring 7c-d, 65205 Wiesbaden, produktsicherheit.verlag@harrassowitz.de

Gedruckt auf alterungsbeständigem Papier.

ISSN 0340-6326
ISBN 978-3-447-06426-2

Inhalt

Vorwort

Das Beieinander von Christen und Muslimen ist nicht eine Erscheinung erst der letzten Jahre. Seit es den Islam gibt, von der ersten Stunde an, war dessen Existenz zugleich bestimmt vom Beieinander der beiden Weltreligionen. Wohin immer er sich ausbreitete, fast immer waren die Christen schon da oder kamen auch dorthin. Es gibt kein Land, indem es nur Muslime geben würde, immer sind Christen in der einen oder anderen Weise auch präsent. Schaut man auf die Kernregionen dessen, was heute als islamische Welt betrachtet wird, so ist auch dort dieses Beieinander auffällig, auch wenn das Christentum dort aktuell sehr unter Druck gerät. Vielfältige Untersuchungen haben dieses Beieinander vorrangig historisch in den Blick genommen. Das Beieinander erweist sich bei näherem Zusehen dann nicht als einfaches Nebeneinander, selten als Miteinander, oft aber als ein bewusster oder unbewusster Austausch zwischen beiden Weltreligionen.

Es ist unbestritten, dass Blüte und Kunstfertigkeit der arabischen Poesie den Anlass gaben für eines der herausragenden Werke der syrischen Poesie in Zeiten der syrischen Renaissance, dem *Paradies von Eden* des Ebedjesus.[1] In diesem Werk ging es darum, der arabischen Poesie die syrische als gleichwertig, wenn nicht gar als kunstfertiger gegenüber zu erweisen. Doch die gegenseitige Beeinflussung war nicht nur eine sprachliche. Auch inhaltlich ist das Bei- und Nebeneinander der beiden Weltreligionen ein Geben und Nehmen der einen von der anderen und der anderen von der einen. Dabei waren muslimische Theologen anfangs bewusst oder unbewusst im Empfangen stärker, späterhin waren es die Christen.

Oft waren es erste Beobachtungen ganz äußerlicher Art, die die Aufmerksamkeit auf die Gemeinsamkeiten beider Religionen lenkten. Dazu gehörte seit schon früh das Feld der Mystik.[2] So überraschte Jean Gouillard die Leser der von ihm erarbeiteten *Philokalie*, dem grundlegenden Lehrbuch zur Praxis und Theologie des Herzensgebetes auf der Grundlage von Vätertexten, damit, dass er im Anhang einen Text aus dem *Tanwir al-qulub* des Scheichs Muhammed Amin al-Kurdi al-Shafi i al-Naqshbandi (gest. 1332) mit veröffentlichte. Gouillard hatte geschickt dem Anhang jüngere Texte vorgeschaltet, die bereits aus christlicher Sicht Bezug nahmen auf die ähnlich geartete Praxis bei den Sufis. Doch sprechen die Verfasser dieser Texte in

1 Zum Werk und Person: Martin Tamcke, Art. ʿAbdīšo Bār Brīḵa und Art. Paradaisā da-'ḏen, in: Kindlers Literatur Lexikon, Band 1, 3. völlig neu bearbeitete Auflage, Stuttgart/Weimar 2009, 21; vgl. außerdem Martin Tamcke, Ebedjesus (ʿAbdiso Bar Berika), in: Markus Vinzent, Theologen. 185 Porträts von der Antike bis zur Gegenwart, Stuttgart 2004, 97–98.

2 Vgl. Martin Tamcke (Hg.), Mystik – Metapher – Bild. Beiträge des VII. Makarios-Symposiums, Göttingen 2007.

deutlich abweisender Form über die ihrer eigenen so ähnlichen Praxis der muslimischen Nachbarn, sprechen von einer widernatürlichen und unfrommen Wirksamkeit der muslimischen Pseudo-Mönche. Sie benennen die mit ihnen sozusagen im religiösen Wettbewerb stehenden Muslime eindeutig: Diese seien muslimische „Derwische, die sich im Kreise drehten, indem sie mit der Zunge schnalzten, geiferten und wie ihr Lehrer Mohammed alle möglichen Blasphemien ausstießen."[3] Das nur Ungefähre und der abweisende Ton zeugen scheinbar davon, dass hier sich ein Graben des Dissenses auftut. Doch dass in den Lehrtexten zum Herzensgebet, in diesem Kernstück mystischer Frömmigkeit der Ostkirche, auch auf die Praxis der muslimischen Mystiker Bezug genommen wird, zeugt zugleich von einem Bewusstsein für die als Gefahr gewertete und empfundene Nähe der Praxis in der anderen Religion im eigenen Umfeld. Gouillard hingegen schätzte die Texte der Sufis zu ihrer Praxis der Anrufung des göttlichen Namens, dem *dhikr*, als den christlichen Texten gegenüber höherwertig ein. Die Aufnahme des Textes in seine Ausgabe der *Philokalie* sei nicht so zu werten, als würde da nur ein zusätzlicher „Leckerbissen" geboten. „Denn keiner der überlieferten christlichen Texte kann es sowohl in didaktischer Hinsicht wie im Umfang und in der Präzisierung der Einzelheiten mit diesem Text aufnehmen. Seine symbolische Topographie der Zentren genügt, um die vagen Begriffe von der Erforschung des Herzens bei Pseudo-Simeon zu erhellen; seine Atemtechnik ist weit genauer. Andererseits bietet dieser Text zahlreiche frappante Parallelen mit der christlichen Tradition, besonders im Hinblick auf das Denken an den Tod und die absolute Notwendigkeit eines Lehrmeisters. Diese Feststellungen wollen keineswegs den Hermetismus gewisser Betrachtungen verbergen, noch die Abweichungen bagatellisieren. Aber es fällt schwer, sich den Gedanken aus dem Kopf zu schlagen, dass ein gemeinsamer Untergrund für diese Methode da sein muss oder dass wenigstens ein gemeinsames psychologisches Gesetz besteht, das sich nach den gegebenen Umständen ganz natürlich auswirkt."[4] Das Verhältnis von ostkirchlicher Mystik zu der der Sufis konnte Gouillard also einerseits durchaus komplementär sehen, andererseits die Parallelen betonen. Zuletzt leitete ihn aber der vage Gedanke nach dem beiden Gestalten der Mystik vorauslaufenden gemeinsamen Grund. Tatsächlich hat hier ein nicht unwesentlicher Teil der komparatistischen Forschung zu beiden Gestalten der Mystik angesetzt. Einerseits bot noch die Dissertation von dem auf der Konferenz anwesenden finnischen Kollegen Seppälä einen entsprechenden Forschungsansatz. Andererseits erwies sich bald, dass etwa für die Zeit der syrischen Renaissance davon auszugehen ist, dass islamische Mystiker von christlichen, syri-

3 Jean Gouillard, Gebet des Herzens. Kleine Philokalie. Eingeführt von Gebhard Frei, Zürich 1957 (Originalausgabe: Petite Philocalie de la Prière du Cœur, Paris 1953), 228. Zu Frei als Rezipienten des Herzensgebetes: Martin Tamcke, Im Geist des Ostens leben. Orthodoxe Spiritualität und ihre Rezeption im Westen, Frankfurt 2008, 95–99.

4 Gouillard, 237.

schen Mystikern rezipiert wurden.[5] Dies ließ sich etwa bei Barhebräus schon sehr bald zeigen. Und natürlich bewegt schon der äußerliche Umstand, dass viele ostsyrische Mönchsmystiker in Mesopotamien wirkten, wo ebenfalls viele der frühen Sufis ihre Lehren verbreiteten. Aber solche ersten Beobachtungen weisen lediglich die Richtung zu dem heute von der Forschung relativ intensiv bearbeiteten Feld.

Aus laufenden Arbeiten in diesem Feld erwuchsen die Beiträge dieses Bandes. Sie basieren auf Vorträgen, die auf der Konferenz „Gotteserlebnis und Gotteslehre: Christliche und islamische Mystik im Orient“ (Göttingen, 18.–19. April 2008) gehalten wurden. Die Konferenz wurde finanziert aus Mitteln des Göttinger Graduiertenkollegs „Götterbilder – Gottesbilder – Weltbilder“ (gefördert von der Deutschen Forschungsgemeinschaft), aus Mitteln des Instituts für Ökumenische Theologie und Orientalische Kirchen- und Missionsgeschichte in Göttingen und durch Mittel, die über die Erasmus-Kooperationen (besonders mit der Türkei, namentlich Ankara, Sakarya, Marasch, Istanbul) eingeworben wurden. Allen finanziellen Unterstützern sei für ihr Engagement zum Zustandekommen der Konferenz herzlich gedankt. Besonders die Kollegen aus dem türkischen Marasch trugen durch ein abendliches Konzert mit Musik aus der Sufi-Tradition zum Gelingen der Atmosphäre bei. Die Beiträge der meisten türkischen Kollegen werden an anderer Stelle publiziert. Der Plakat- und Programmheftentwurf zur Konferenz stammte von Sven Grebenstein. Die Bearbeitung der Beiträge für den Druck besorgte schließlich Dr. Egbert Schlarb. Im übervollen Tagungsraum vollzog sich die Arbeit nicht nur theoretisch interreligiös, sondern als ein reales Miteinander von Forschern aus beiden Religionen am gemeinsam interessierenden Phänomen.

5 Einen Überblick zu den Texten bietet – ohne intensivere Beachtung der jüngeren Forschung – Georg Günter Blum, Die Geschichte der Begegnung christlich-orientalischer Mystik mit der Mystik des Islam, Wiesbaden 2009.

An Important Concept in Muslim and Christian Mysticism: the Remembrance of God, *dhikr Allah – 'uhdōnō d-Alōhō*

Herman Teule

1. Introduction

Both the Greek and the Syriac Fathers have a long tradition of reflection on the concept of the Remembrance of God, the *Mnême Theou*[1] or the *'Uhdōnō d-Alōhō*, which semantically corresponds to what the Muslim tradition denotes as *dhikr Allah*. Some modern authors prefer to translate *'Uhdōnō d-Alōhō*, as "recollection of God", which is less appropriate for the later tradition, as will be demonstrated below. One of the representatives of this later tradition is Gregory Abū'l-Faraj Barhebraeus (* Malatya 1226, † Marāgha 1286), who discusses the Remembrance of God in two of his writings, the *Book of the Ethicon*[2] and the *Book of the Dove*[3], in a surprisingly original way.

Both works were written at the end of his life, the first in 1279, in the city of Marāgha (modern Iranian Adhorbaycan), the second, after the *Ethicon*, probably in Northern Iraq. Both works are intimately related to each other. The first is one of the few spiritual works composed in Syriac for secular people, *'olmōyē*, those who live in the world: it deals with a variety of subjects, such as rituals and ascetical practices, *canonical* or *ritual prayer, almsgiving, fasting, the pilgrimage* – comparable to four of the five pillars of Islam – or spiritual attitudes, such as love, compassion, hope, unselfishness, etc. In the second Memrō of this work, the author also devotes attention to trading – how to be an honest merchant –, to hospitality or to issues such

1 For this concept in the Greek patristic tradition, see Hermann Josef Sieben, MNHMH ΘEOY, in: DSp 10 (1980), 1407–1414.

2 Ethicon seu Moralia Gregorii Barhebraei, ed. by Paul Bedjan, Paris and Leipzig 1898, re-edition: Piscataway/NJ 2007; Herman Teule, Gregory Barhebraeus. Ethicon Memrā I, CSCO 534–535, Louvain 1993; Herman Teule, Gregory Barhebraeus. Ethicon Memrā II, CSCO (forthcoming).

3 Liber columbae, ed. by Paul Bedjan, Paris and Leipzig 1898, re-edition: Piscataway/NJ 2007 and a number of recent editions, cf. Hidemi Takahashi, Barhebraeus. A Bio-Bibliography, Piscataway/NJ 2005, 212–214. For an English translation, see Arent J. Wensinck, Bar Hebraeus's Book of the Dove together with some chapters from his Ethikon, Leiden 1919. A new French translation with identification of the sources is currently being prepared for the Series Sources Syriaques (Antélias-Beirut, Université Antonine).

as how to behave during meals or in the bathhouse.[4] The *Ktobō d-yawnō*/*Book of the Dove* was written for solitaries and monks who live in *šelyō*, in solitude, outside the monastery and therefore have no spiritual leader (*mdabbrōnō*) or *shaykh* to supervise their spiritual development. Basically, it gives a selection from the *Ethicon*, but, of course, only those themes which are relevant for monks and, hence, omits the rules for honest trading or correct behaviour in the bathhouse. On the other hand, it adds a centurion, a selection of a hundred mystical and hermetical sayings, intended for the monks to meditate upon, which are not found in the Ethicon. Such *centuria*, "centuries", are known from the Christian tradition, – we could think of the *Kephalaia gnostica* by Evagrius of Pontus, which were known to Barhebraeus, John of Dalyata or Isaac of Nineveh[5] – but I would also suggest that the idea of ending the *Book of the Dove* with a series of such sayings owes as much to the contemporary Sufi tradition as to the Christian. We only have to think of the by the end of the 13th century popular Ḥ*ikam*, the "words of wisdom" by a contemporary of Barhebraeus, Ibn 'Atā' Allah,[6] who was not the only Sufi author to compose such hermetical sayings,[7] designed to help the novice to attain to the knowledge (gnosis, *ida''tā, ma'rifa*) of God.

Both works of Barhebraeus make extensive use of previous sources: Christian works, both Greek and Syriac, on the one hand and Arabic-Muslim and even Persian sources, on the other. The Greek writings, such as those by Evagrius of Pontus (today, the Amasaya-region), Basil of Caesarea (Kayseri) or Gregory of Nazianze (southern Cappadocia) were all read in extant Syriac translations. The other sources were, in the first place, the *Ihya 'ulūm al-Dīn* by Al-Ghazālī, a work on psychology by Ibn Sina, probably excerpts from his *Šifā'*[8] and the *Akhlāq-i Nāṣiri* by Nāṣir al-din Ṭūṣī.[9] One could characterize the *Ethicon* as a sort of patchwork: it consists of hundreds of pieces of texts brought together, but in the same way that patchwork is a piece of art in itself which cannot be reduced to its individual components. The *Ethicon* is really a new composition, which, in its best passages, can be characterized as

4 Herman Teule, A Christian Muslim Discussion. The Importance of Bodily and Spiritual Purity. A Chapter from Memro II of Barhebraeus' Ethicon, in: Syriac Polemics, ed. by Wouter J. van Bekkum, OLA 170, Leuven 2007, 193–203; Herman Teule, La vie dans le monde. Perspectives chrétiennes et influences musulmanes. Une étude de Memro II de l'Ethicon de Grégoire d'Abū l-Farağ Bar'Ebrōyō, ParOr 33 (2008), 91–104.

5 See Herman Teule, Christian Spiritual and Ascetical Sources in Barhebraeus' Ethicon and the Book of the Dove, in: Journal of Eastern Christian Studies 60 (2008), 333-354.

6 Ibn'Atā' Allāh (m. 709/1309) et la Naissance de la Confrérie Sādilite. Edition critique et traduction des Hikam, ed. by Paul Nwyia, Dar el-Machreq and Beirut 1972, English translation: Ibn 'Ata' Allah's Sufi Aphorisms, transl. by Victor Danner, Classics of Western Spirituality, New York 1978.

7 Annemarie Schimmel, Mystische Dimensionen des Islams. Die Geschichte des Sufismus, Köln 1985, 356–357.

8 Cf. Ethicon III, 1–2 (Bedjan, 203–205).

9 For a general overview of Barhebraeus using Muslim models, see Takahashi, Barhebraeus. Bio-Bibliography, 96–99.

a – Christian! – synthesis of Muslim and Christian texts on the spiritual, ethical and mystical life (which makes it an important work).

2. *'Uhdōnō and Dhikr*. A Passage from the *Ethicon*

In the present paragraph, I give the text of a passage on the Remembrance of God, found in the third Memrō of the *Ethicon*. Generally speaking, this Memrō discusses the theme of cleansing the soul from shameful passions, such as gluttony, hypocrisy, pride, i.e. a list of vices which partly corresponds to the catalogue of passions, formulated by Evagrius. In the second chapter of this Memrō, the author devotes a paragraph to the issue of "staying in the cell" (*mawtbō da-b-qlōytō*), in which he describes the way, after training in the community of the Brethren, a person who has been deemed worthy of solitary life should perform his prayers.[10]

ܘܡܟܐ ܕܓܡܪܬܐ ܐܚܝܕܐ ܒܐܝܕܗ: ܒܡܘܬܒܐ ܕܒܥܘܕܪܢܐ ܐܒܘܪܐ: ܒܬܪ ܕܢܦܠܚ ܝܥ̈ܠܬܗ
ܕܥܕ̈ܢܝܬܐ: ܘܢܦܠܚ ܦܘܠܚܢܘܗܝ ܪܘܚܢܝܐ: ܒܛܝܒܘܬܐ ܐܦ ܒܥܘܬܐ ܘܥܘܗܕܢܐ ܘܩܪܝܢܐ ܘܗܪܓܐ ܐܝܟ: ܕܒܦܘܣܩܐ
ܗ̇ܘ ܕܒܡܐܡܪܐ ܩܕܡܝܐ ܒܨܝܢ: ܗܟܝܠ ܡܢ ܗ̇ܝ; ܕܡܪܝܐ ܡܪܝܐ: ܘܠܐ ܡܕܡ ܢܪܛܢ. ܥܕܡܐ ܠܗ̇ܝ;
ܕܐܦ ܠܐ ܢܙܝܥ ܣܦܘ̈ܬܗ: ܬܩܘܐ ܗ̇ܝ ܡܠܬܐ ܥܠ ܠܫܢܗ: ܘܢܬܐܡܨ ܥܠ ܗܕܐ ܥܕܡܐ ܕܢܬܠܥܐ
ܗܘ ܫܡܐ ܡܢ ܠܫܢܗ ܘܒܠܒܗ ܒܠܚܘܕ ܢܦܘܫ ܥܘܗܕܢܗ. ܐܚܪܝܐ ܐܦ ܡܢ ܠܒܐ ܡܬܠܚܝܐ
ܕܡܘܬܗ ܕܫܡܐ ܘܪܘܟܒ ܐܬܘ̈ܬܗ: ܘܒܣܟܠܗ ܒܠܚܘܕ ܦܫܝܛܐ ܫܪܟ ܒܡܚܫܒܬܐ. ܘܗܘ ܣܟܠܐ
ܟܕ ܡܬܩܒܥ ܒܢܦܫܐ ܡܫܪܪܐܝܬ: ܡܫܪܝܐ ܕܬܐܡܪ ܒܪ ܚܘܒ ܡܪܗ̇ ܠܐ ܡܣܬܝܟܢܐܝܬ: ܘܠܗ
ܢܫܠܡ ܟܠܗ̇ ܒܗ, ܕܐܚܪܢܝ ܠܐ ܦܠܗ ܥܠ ܟܠܗ̇.

> "When after completing his Prayer of the Hours,[11] (the solitary), during his stay in his small cell, with the help of Grace also performs his spiritual exercises which are supplication, remembrance, reading and meditation, as we have already investigated in the first Memrō, he should not murmur anything else but only "O, Lord, Lord", until this word remains on his tongue, even if he does not move his lips. And in this (state), he should persevere until this name disappears from his tongue and only its remembrance remains in his heart. Next also the image of the name will disappear from the heart as well as the composition of its letters. Only its mere understanding remains in (his) thinking. And when this understanding is solidly fixed unto the soul, it begins to burn with desire of the Lord infinitely and it will give itself to Him wholly, without thinking of anything else."[12]

10 Ethicon III, 2.10 (Bedjan, 232).

11 Or: his ecclesiastical prayers, according to the reading of one manuscript, which reads ܥܕ̈ܬܢܝܬܐ for ܥܕ̈ܢܝܬܐ (see Bedjan, 232).

12 Cf. Wensinck, Bar Hebraeus's Book of the Dove, XCIII.

3. Commentary

It is strange that this passage which, as appears from the context, is explicitly destined for the *iḥidōyē* (solitaries) living outside the community, the intended readership of the *Book of the Dove*, is lacking in this latter work.

A few things are striking in this passage: first, supplication – *bo'utō* – is reckoned among the ascetical practices which follow the ecclesiastical prayers, i.e. the Prayer of the Hours, *ṣlutō*, seven times a day. This distinction between *ṣlutō* and *bo'utō* is not accidental, but based on a traditional Muslim distinction between *ṣalāt*, the ritual prayer, in a certain way comparable to the monastic "Prayer of the Hours", and *du'ā'*, which has been translated by Annemarie Schimmel as "freies Gebet", free, supererogatory and unprescribed prayer, but which, in a literal sense, is, of course, the prayer of supplication, in which one asks God for things that are useful for one's spiritual life.[13] Various Muslim authors describe *du'ā'* as different from *ṣalāt*,[14] and it seems probable that Barhebraeus, in imitation of them, describes *bo'utō*, not in the chapter of Memrō I which is devoted to prayer, but in the paragraphs devoted to ascetical exercises.[15] He seems to be the only Syriac author to make this distinction.

In the passage under discussion, remembrance is considered to be one of these ascetical practices. It consists of the repetition of some verses from the Psalms or the Canticles and is extensively described in Memrō I, which will be discussed in paragraph 5.2 below. According to the fragment above, this remembrance is followed by a condensed form of vocal prayer, consisting of the name of God, *Moryo*, *Moryo*, which, in the second stage, should eventually lead to a deeply interiorized Remembrance, called remembrance in the heart, where the repetition of the name/word *Moryo* is no longer necessary. The passage is too brief to allow us to determine whether the remembrance in the heart is to be distinguished from a remembrance on an even more interiorized level, that of the soul. Or, in other words, whether Barhebraeus follows a distinction, popular in certain Sufi circles, between different levels of interiorized, non-vocal *dhikr*.[16]

4. The Remembrance of God in the Syriac Tradition

Before further analyzing this fragment, in order to understand Barhebraeus and the original step he takes when describing the idea of Remembrance of God as an asce-

13 Schimmel, Mystische Dimensionen, 223–225; Herman Teule, Vormen van gebed in het werk van Barhebraeus, in: Voor de mens die er nog in gelooft. Overwegingen bij psalmen, liederen en gebeden. Aangeboden aan Leo Meulenberg, ed. by Gian Ackermans et al., Theologisch Cahier 52, Nijmegen 1998, 127–136, esp. 132–133.

14 Cf. Louis Gardet, Du'ā', in: Encyclopaedia of Islam 2 (^{2}2009), 617–618.

15 Ethicon I (Teule), 24–36 (21–32), esp. 27–31 (24–28).

16 Schimmel, Mystische Dimensionen, 243.248.

tical practice of repeating his name, we also have to consider some other passages where our author discusses the *'Uhdōnō d-Alōhō*, as well as to pay some attention to this notion in the writings of the spiritual fathers of his own Christian tradition.

For a discussion of the latter issue, I shall limit myself to those authors whose writings were known to Barhebraeus. As a matter of fact, it is a concept which occurs in many more Syriac ascetical writings, originally Syriac ones, such as the works of Dadišo‘ Qaṭrāyā, Shubḥālmaran, or those translated from Greek, such as Mark the Hermit, Basil the Great and others.[17]

Of the authors known to Barhebraeus, I mention the following:[18]

4.1 Evagrius of Pontus

Evagrius is one of Barhebraeus' favourite spiritual fathers; in the *Ethicon*, he gives quotations from no less than 12 different writings.

In the works of Evagrius, the Remembrance of God is not a central theme. We only find a few passing allusions to it in some minor treatises. In the brief text *On Fasting*, we find that the *'Uhdōnō d-Alōhō* is the result of a number of ascetical practices, such as *aksnōyutō* (*xeniteia*), living in solitude, etc. and Evagrius emphasizes that there are fixed times for reading and for the Prayer of the Hours, but that "the Remembrance of God" is a matter of the ascetic's whole life, which suggests that this concept has to be distinguished from the ascetical practices.[19] Remembrance is permanent, for which reason some later authors, such as John of Dalyātā, will explicitly add *amminā* to the notion of *'uhdōnō*.[20]

There is an interesting passage in the treatise *On instruction* (*'al martyōnutō*). However, it is not so easy to determine what Evagrius means here: on the one hand, he says: "Remembrance of God cannot establish itself in the soul which is occupied with the necessities of living in society, but is promoted by a virtuous life and a number of ascetical practices, such as spiritual reading, prayer and *aksnōyutō*".[21] From this passage, one is inclined to conclude that the *'uhdōnō* is a spiritual attitude, which is the result of a number of ascetical practices, such as in the fragment from the treatise on fasting, and not an ascetical exercise itself. But in another section of the same treatise (no. 4), he states that asceticism (*'anwōyutō*) consists of "taking little food and sleep, of reading, performing prayers, *'enyōnō d-mellat Alōhō* – which might be another expression for prayer –, and the Remembrance of God",[22]

17 See Sebastian Brock, Isaac of Nineveh (Isaac the Syrian). 'The Second Part', Chapters IV–XLI, CSCO 554–555, Louvain 1995, 135 (transl., note 4).

18 See Teule, Christian Spiritual Sources in Barhebraeus' Ethicon and the Book of the Dove, cf. above, note 5.

19 See Evagriana Syriaca. Textes inédits du British Museum et de la Vaticane, ed. and trans. by Joseph Muyldermans, Louvain 1952, Treatise De jejunio, nr 7, 115–116.151; nr 11, 116.152.

20 Cf. Nadira Khayyat, Jean de Dalyatha. Les Homélies I–XV, Sources syriaques 2, Antélias 2007, 100–101.

21 Muyldermans, Evagriana syriaca, 126.157 (nrs 2 and 3, abbreviated).

22 Ibid.

which in this way would be reckoned among the ascetical practices. Unfortunately, Evagrius does not enlarge on this.

In another passage, quoted by Barhebraeus,[23] Evagrius says: "As life vanquishes death or light expels darkness, thus the remembrance of God destroys sin", which does not allow us to draw conclusions about his conception of remembrance.[24]

And finally, a short quotation in the *Kephalaia gnostica*, a work known to Barhebraeus, again suggests that remembrance is to be interpreted as a permanent staying with God, a spiritual attitude.[25]

4.2 The Egyptian Fathers

Besides Evagrius, Barhebraeus also had a great veneration for the other Fathers of the Egyptian desert, whose words were available to him in the *Paradisus Patrum*, the Syriac translation of the Stories and *Apophthegmata* of the Fathers of Egypt, made by the East-Syrian monk 'Enanišo', which was extremely popular reading in the West Syrian monasteries, especially in later times. In the *Ethicon*, he gives more than a hundred quotations from this work.[26]

In the *Book of Paradise*, the expression Remembrance of God is rather rare and does not seem to be linked with a practice of prayer, for instance: "A Brother asked Father Timotheus and said to him: I see myself that my remembrance is always before God. The Elder said to him: that your thinking is with God is not a great thing; it would be a great thing for a man to consider himself below all creation"[27] or "Let us put God before our eyes continually; remember death and Christ".[28] This latter apophthegma of Anthony is characteristic of the other passages – about fifteen in the *Paradisus Patrum*[29] – which refer to the Remembrance of God as a spiritual attitude. The Egyptian Fathers, of course, practiced the so-called *monologistos euchê*, a simple, short prayer, consisting of several words and frequently repeated,[30] but this

23 Ethicon IV, 13.1 (Bedjan, 448).

24 This citation by Barhebraeus remains unidentified. On the interpretation of this passage, see infra, par. 5.

25 Les six centuries des "Kephalaia Gnostica" d'Evagre le Pontique. Edition critique de la version syriaque commune et édition d'une nouvelle version syriaque intégrale avec une double traduction française, ed. by Antoine Guillaumont, ParOr 28.1, Paris 1958, 168 (S^1 IV,73): "Anyone whose nous is at all times with the Lord, whose thumos is full of His remembrance...".

26 Paradisus Patrum, ed. by Paul Bedjan in: Acta Martyrum et Sanctorum VII, Paris and Leipzig, 1897; The Book of Paradise of Palladius, ed. by Ernest A. Wallis Budge, Lady Meux Ms. Nr 6, Vol. 2, London 1904. English translation: Ernest A. Wallis Budge, The Stories of the Holy Fathers; The Wit and Wisdom of the Christian Fathers of Egypt, London 1934.

27 Bedjan, Paradisus Patrum, 632; Budge, Wit and Wisdom, 148.

28 Bedjan, ibid., 776; Budge, ibid., 260.

29 Lucien Regnault, Les sentences des Pères du désert III, Sablé-sur-Sarthe 1976, 375 (Index analytique).

30 Cf. Lucien Regnault, La prière continuelle "monologistos" dans la littérature apophtegmatique, in: Irénikon 47.4 (1974), 467–493.

prayer was not known as *Mnêmê Theou*, which was basically a state of prayer for them and not a practice.[31]

4.3 Isaac the Syrian

Isaac the Syrian (Isaac of Nineveh) mentions the Remembrance of God in several homilies, belonging to the well known classical "First Part" of his writings, edited by Bedjan as *De Perfectione religiosa*,[32] the "Second Part", recently discovered by Sebastian Brock,[33] and his *Chapters of Knowledge*.[34] Barhebraeus knew and used all three works.

Isaac's ideas on the *'Uhdōnō d-'Alōhō* are not easy to study, since we only have relatively short passages, allusions rather than systematic elaborations, scattered over different homilies.

In Homily XXXV of the First Part, he says: "When the Remembrance of God is stirred in the mind of (the person who seeks Gods), straightway his heart is kindled by the Love of Him and his eyes pour forth abundant tears. For love is wont to ignite tears by the recollection of the beloved ones".[35]

Remembrance is here stirred in the mind or intellect (*taš'itā*). It is clearly an "intellectual" activity, it is "thinking of God" in the same way as a person can think of his loved ones. Thus, it is a spiritual attitude, a state of mind or awareness of God.

In another passage (Homily XLV), Isaac makes a comparison with wine: "when the power of wine enters the members (of the body), it makes the intellect oblivious to the precise (nature) of all things; and when the Remembrance of God takes possession of a pasture in the soul, it causes every memory of visible things to vanish from the heart."[36]

And finally, a last passage from the First Part: "Remember God that He too might always remember you … Do not forget Him, your mind being distracted with futile concerns … Seat yourself before the Lord continually, keeping the remem-

31 Régnault, Prière continuelle, 484; Irénée Hausherr, Noms du Christ et voies d'oraison, OrChrA 157, Rome 1960, 150–159 and passim. Cf. the apophthegma by Abbā Poemen, quoted by Barhebraeus and discussed infra, par. 5.1.

32 Paul Bedjan, Mar Isaacus Ninivita. De Perfectione religiosa, Paris and Leipzig, 1–581; The Ascetical Homilies of Saint Isaac the Syrian, trans. by Dana Miller, Boston 1984 (the translation is from the Greek version, but takes into account the Syriac original). Earlier, but still valuable translation by Arent J. Wensinck, Mystic Treatises by Isaac of Nineveh. Translated from Bedjan's Syriac Text with an Introduction and Registers, VNAW Nieuwe Reeks XXIII.1, Amsterdam 1923.

33 Brock, Isaac of Nineveh (cf. supra note, 15).

34 Italian translation by Paolo Bettiolo, Isacco di Ninive. Discorsi spirituali, Comunità di Bose 1985, ^{2}1990. Edited Syriac text not yet available.

35 Bedjan, De perfectione religiosa, 261 (transl. Miller, 183, slightly adapted; Miller translates: Recollection of God).

36 Ibid., 324–325 (transl. Miller, 231, slightly adapted).

brance/memory of Him in your heart, lest, having lingered outside His memory, you are unable to speak boldly when you enter in before Him".[37]

In the Second Part, we again find mention of the continual *'Uhdōnō d-Alōhō*, which is the *result* of prayer, reading the scriptures and psalmody (Homily XXX)[38]. In another passage (Homily V: "Grant me Lord, that I may be made holy by praising You, and be made pure by the remembrance of You"), remembrance seems an activity like praising, but no precisions are given.[39]

In the *Kephalaia gnostica* (IV 74), Isaac only says that purity cannot be kept in confusion and the *'Uhdōnō d-Alōhō* by occupying oneself with external matters.[40]

The conclusion to this paragraph is that, in most passages of Isaac's works, the *'Uhdōnō d-Alōhō* is a state of constant awareness of God and not an ascetical practice.[41]

4.4 John Klimakos

Barhebraeus is the first Syriac author to make extensive use of the *Ladder* of John Klimakos.[42] For John, the *Mnêmê Theou* belongs to the activities of the intellect and comes close to the notion of continual prayer.[43] In the Ladder, however, there is also the notion of the *Mnêmê Iêsou*: "let the remembrance of Jesus be united with your breath and then you will know the value of stillness", a famous passage which has sometimes been interpreted as a first reference to a form of Jesus prayer that was to be developed in the later hesychast movement, so a technique of prayer. Apart from the fact that this is reading too much into this particular passage,[44] at least it is not a conclusion drawn by Barhebraeus, who ignores this fragment.

4.5 John of Dalyātā

Barhebraeus also had great admiration for John Sābā or John of Dalyātā, whose homilies are frequently quoted in his Ethicon. John probably devoted more attention to the concept of *'Uhdōnō d-Alōhō* than any other Syriac author. "Remembrance of God" is even the title of one of his letters (Letter 50)[45] and an important theme in his

37 Ibid., 72–73 (transl. Miller, 48).

38 Brock, Isaac of Nineveh, 123 (transl. 134–135).

39 Ibid., 7 (transl. 9).

40 Bettiolo, Isacco di Ninive. Discorsi spirituali, 219.

41 According to Hausherr, Isaac does not appear to devote attention to a systematic use of set prayers (see his Noms du Christ, 211–215), but the practice of repeating short prayers is not entirely absent from Isaac's work, see Placide Deseille, Saint Isaac le Syrien. Discours ascétiques, St Laurens en Royans 2006, 90.93.

42 Herman Teule, L'Echelle du Paradis de Jean Climaque dans la tradition syriaque. Premières investigations, ParOr 20 (1995), 279–293; Teule, Christian Spiritual Sources in the Ethicon of Barhebraeus, cf. supra, note 5.

43 Cf. John Chryssavgis, John Climacus. From the Egyptian Desert to the Sinaite Mountain, Aldershot 2004, 126.227.

44 Ibid., 230–231.

45 La collection des lettres de Jean de Dalyatha. Edition critique du texte syriaque inédit, trans.,

homilies. His ideas have been analyzed by Robert de Beulay[46] and, more recently, by Nadhira Khayyat, in the introduction to her edition of the first part of John of Dalyātā's Homilies.[47]

Both scholars emphasize that, for John, the Remembrance of God is essentially a practice: *dubbārā, pulḥānā*, which would suggest that it is one of the ascetical works. As a matter of fact, this *dubbārā* is a movement of interiorization, the concentration of the mind or the intellect on itself, which has two aspects, an active and a more passive one. The active one resembles the movement of interiorization which one can also detect in the fragment by Barhebraeus. John of Dalyātā creates a rich imagery to describe this movement: it is a descent into the depth, an elevation of the spirit towards the bosom of the Lord, a knocking at the door of God's abode, but it never indicates a practice of prayer; the more passive aspect can be characterized as a state of the mind, without movement, waiting at the door of the heart. It is highly significant that a passage on the Remembrance of God, taken from his Homilies, could, without any problem, be inserted into (the Greek version of) Isaac of Nineveh's treatises, where the recollection of God, as seen above, is a state rather than a practice of prayer.[48]

The analyses by Beulay and Khayyat demonstrate that John of Dalyātā was definitely not one of Barhebraeus' sources for his interpretation of the Remembrance of God.

4.6 Barhebraeus

In the passage quoted above, the Remembrance of God is clearly a form of ascetical practice, the repetition of *Moryo, Moryo*, which should eventually lead to an inner movement of prayer. On account of this vocal aspect, Wensinck chose to translate it as "invocation".[49]

However, there are a number of other passages in Barhebraeus' works which have to be taken into consideration.

4.6.1 In the fourth Memrō of the *Ethicon*, dealing with the acquisition of virtues, such as hope, love, confidence, etc., i.e. the positive counterpart of the third Memrō, the eradication of passions and vices, he devotes an entire chapter to "the Remem-

---

intro. and notes by Robert Beulay, ParOr 39.3 (1978), 462–463. For an English translation of the letters, see Mary Hansbury, The Letters of John of Dalyatha, Texts from Christian Late Antiquity 2, Piscataway/NJ 2006.

46 Robert Beulay, L'enseignement spirituel de Jean de Dalyatha. Mystique syro-oriental du VIIIe siècle, ThH 83, Paris 1990, esp. 122–142.

47 Khayyat, Jean de Dalyatha. Les Homélies I–XV, 51–57.

48 Cf. Miller, The Ascetical Homilies, 85; cf. CXIII and XCI. Cf. Khayyat, Homilies, 100–101. The passage in the text of Isaac speaks of the mind that "comes out" from the Remembrance of God and enters into the remembrance of the world. John of Dalyātā speaks of "coming out" (mapaqtā) from the knowledge of God.

49 Wensinck, Bar Hebraeus's Book of the Dove, XCIII.

brance of God and the Meditation on His wonderful Creation" (chapter 13).[50] Again, it has no parallel in the *Book of the Dove*, which, in this case, too, is difficult to explain, since the whole context is monastic and even eremitic.

The structure of this chapter is the usual one. It begins with an introductory paragraph containing a number of quotations of the "Fathers", followed by the analysis of the subject matter of this chapter, which, in fact, is meditation, *hergō*, rather than remembrance, which is only dealt with superficially.

As proof of the importance of meditation, he quotes Abba Poemen: "Cut off the desire of your lust through the Remembrance of God, and you will find rest".[51] This passage is not very helpful in determining how Abba Poemen and Barhebraeus interpreted the Remembrance of God. It is, however, linked to another apophthegma, attributed to an anonymous *sōbō* or spiritual Father, who, when asked how a monk should live, answered: "He should live alone, in solitude, in order that his thinking is exclusively with God". Apparently, *'uhdōnō* is related to thinking or meditation.

Barhebraeus also gives a quotation of Evagrius: "As life vanquishes death or light darkness, so does the Remembrance of God destroy sin". That Barhebraeus quotes this fragment by Evagrius, which is not clear in itself, as a testimony to a spiritual interpretation of the remembrance, becomes clear from the fact that he links it to the following passage: "As soon as a man is aroused by a movement of wonder about having been called into existence by God, he is filled with sweetness and, in wonder, he is silenced. Without words, he praises God: Glory to your Grace, O God, that you brought me into existence..., etc." Does the absence of words suggest a transition from a vocal *'uhdōnō* to an interiorized one, as in the fragment quoted in paragraph 2? In a third quotation of Evagrius, he says: "the highest perfection is that your thinking is not cut off from God".

In the same introductory paragraph, we find a quotation by John of Dalyātā: "More than ascetical labours, the Remembrance of God eradicates the passions from the heart. In this respect, nothing is more effective." Thus, remembrance is not reckoned among the ascetical works and is linked with wonder about God.

The last quotation is ascribed to Mar Isḥāq, Isaac of Nineveh: "The thinking of a person, whose soul has tasted the sweetness of divine consolation, is always focused on the love he feels in himself. His heart is widened by the Remembrance of God. It is as if he were already in heaven".

With these quotations, Barhebraeus proves that, in Memro IV, his interpretation of *'Uhdōnō d-Aloho* is the classical one of the Syriac tradition: a state of mind related to wonder and to meditation. It is not an ascetical practice. For this reason, the rest of this chapter is entirely devoted to meditation, more specifically, on God's

---

50 Ethicon IV. 13 (Bedjan, 447–466).

51 Cf. Budge, The Wit and Wisdom, 265 (nr. 223). This apophthegma seems to be absent from the Paradisus Patrum, as edited by Bedjan, 783, which corresponds to 202 or has been relegated to a different section or chapter.

creation, by which the Remembrance of God is established in the intellect of the meditating person.

4.6.2 Before turning back to the fragment of the third Memro, where *'uhdōnō* is an ascetical practice which consists of repeating the name of God, we have to discuss the passage on the Remembrance of God, to which Barhebraeus refers in the passage translated above. It is found in *Ethicon*, Memrō I, chapter 3, which is devoted to the ascetical practices of supplication, spiritual reading, remembrance and meditation.[52] This time, it has an equivalent in the *Book of the Dove*.[53] Here, the *'Uhdōnō d-Alōhō* is truly an ascetical practice and should consist of reciting *ten verses* – the number is important – from the two Canticles of the Three Children of the House of Henanya in the Book of Daniel. These are to be repeated three, seven or forty times, depending on time and strength. In this paragraph, remembrance is just another word for a form of vocal prayer and is not so different from the *bo'utō*, supplication, which also has to be repeated and which, in its most reduced form, – the one Barhebraeus prefers – consists of the formula: "Have mercy on me on the day of Your Judgment, O Jesus, full of Love". According to this description, supplication and remembrance are works which are to be put into practice by both lay-people and ascetics. In the Chapter on Travelling, which he reckons among the ascetic exercises – it is related to the concept of *aksnōyutō*, being a foreigner to everything in this world –, he still adds that the Remembrance of God belongs to the spiritual characteristics of a journey and may consist of the recitation of psalms.[54]

Thus, we have two interpretations of *'Uhdōnō d-Alōhō*: the first as an ascetical practice, the second as a state of mind, the first leading to the second, at least according to the fragment presented in paragraph 2 of this article.

As said above, *'uhdōnō* as an ascetical practice is new and not found in earlier Christian sources, at least not in those works known to Barhebraeus. This, of course, raises the question of the sources. For the description of the Remembrance of God in the first memrō, the ten verses from the Canticles in the Book of Daniel, these are not difficult to find. The whole description of the four ascetical works of invocation, remembrance, spiritual reading/recitation and meditation is a Christian adaptation of comparable passages in Book IX of the first part (quarter) of the *Iḥyā' 'ulūm al-dīn* by Abū Ḥāmid al-Ghazālī (d. 1111), in Barhebraeus' times still a most popular work, commented upon by different Muslim authors.[55] *'Uhdono* here translates *dhikr*, which, in the corresponding passage of the *Iḥyā'*, only seems to mean the

52 Ethicon I (Teule), 27–36 (translation, 24–32).

53 Dove, (Bedjan), 540–541; Wensinck, Bar Hebraeus's Book of the Dove, 22–23.

54 Ethicon I (Teule), 119 (translation, 102): "during his journey, the (traveller) shall occupy himself with the Remembrance of God; if he knows psalms, he shall recite them..."

55 I use the following edition: Iḥyā' 'ulūm al-dīn, Cairo, A.H. 1337 (4 vol.).

repetition of ten *kalimāt*,[56] repeated as in the case of Barhebraeus, three, seven or more times.

For the fragment in Memro III, Wensinck sees a relationship with the *Ḥikam* of Ibn 'Atā' Allah, mentioned above, who expresses the similar idea, that in the highest state of *dhikr* the invocation itself has disappeared, but the agreement is too general to speak of a direct influence. It is highly improbable that Barhebraeus would already have known the work of Ibn 'Atā' Allah, who was a younger contemporary and worked in Cairo. Again, the direct source is Ghazālī, who, in his third Book of the *Iḥyā'*, Chapter II, devoted to "the training of the soul, the correction of morals (*tahdhib al akhlāq*) and the healing of sicknesses of the soul", also describes the practice of *dhikr* as follows:[57]

فيجلس ويقول مثلاً الله الله او سُبحان الله سُبحان الله او ما يَراه الشيخ من الكلمات. فلا يزال يواظب عليه حتى تسقط حركة اللسان ونكون الكلمة كأنها جارية على اللسان من غير تحريك.
ثم لا يزال يواظب عليه حتى تسقط الأثر عن اللسان وتبقى صورة اللفظ في القلب. ثم لا يزال كذلك حتى يمحى عن القلب حروف اللفظ وصورته وتبقى حقيقة معناه ...

> "And he (the murīd, the novice) should sit down and say, for example, 'O God, God' or 'Praise to God, Praise to God' or other verses, according to the opinion of the Sheikh. And he should persevere in this until the movement of his tongue falls still and it seems as if that word were flowing on his tongue without being put into movement.
> Then he should persevere in this until the (last) trace (of it) falls from the tongue and only the image of what was said stays in the heart. He should remain in this (state) until the letters and the image of what was said are erased from his heart and only the reality of its meaning remains."[58]

There is no doubt that Barhebraeus used this passage. He could allow himself to do so, since, as we have seen, there was a long tradition in Christian monastic and mystic circles of, to use a Sufi terminology, *dhikr qalbī* or *sirri*, the remembrance of the heart or the intimate self, a non-vocal remembrance, seen as a state of awareness of God. There was also a tradition of saying short prayers, which was, however, not normally called remembrance and which, generally speaking, did not receive much attention in the works of the authors we have discussed. It is his contact with Ghazālī and maybe his observation of the practice of *dhikr* in certain Sufi circles which brought Barhebraeus to this, for the Christian tradition original description.

---

56 Iḥyā' I, 302.

57 Iḥyā' III, 66.

58 Cf. Wensinck, Book of the Dove, XCIII–XCIV; Louis Gardet, Un problème de mystique comparée: la mention du nom divin (dhikr) dans la mystique musulmane, Part I, in: Revue thomiste 52 (1952), 642–679; Part II, in: RThom 53 (1953), 197–216, esp. I, 643; Kojino Nagamuro, Al-Ghazālī. Invocations & Supplications. Kitāb al-adhkār wa'l-dakawāt. Book IX of the Revival of the Religious Sciences, Iḥyā' kulūm al-dīn, translated with an introduction and notes, Cambridge 1990 (revised edition, first ed. 1973), xxvi.

6. Concluding Remarks

First, we know that Barhebraeus' *Ethicon* became extremely popular, judging from the many manuscripts, copied by both East and West Syrian scribes, and the three different classical translations into Arabic, not to speak of the modern one, etc.[59] Did this also mean that the prayer described in this fragment, as well as the systematic repetition of the ten verses taken from the Canticles of the Three Children from the Book of Daniel, ever became a practice in West Syrian monasteries? A definite answer is not possible on account of our defective knowledge of the later development of West Syrian monastic life or spirituality. From some soundings in the few writings that are known to us: the *Elfō ruḥōnōytō* (the Spiritual Boat) by the 15th century mystic author, Mas'ūd of Ṭūr 'Abdin,[60] or the *Urḥō d-Quštō* (the Way of Truth) by Abū'l-Ma'āni, living in the same century,[61] it does not seem that the *'Uhdōnō* as described by Barhebraeus has ever been a current work of devotion.

Secondly, the fact that Barhebraeus could use passages on prayer, praying techniques, and, more generally, on mysticism from a seminal work of Islamic piety, means that, for him, some aspects of the Muslim traditions in the field of spiritual life were recognizable and acceptable.[62] It seems to me that in the present day discussions about interfaith dialogue, this aspect should be more taken into consideration.

59 Takahashi, Bio-Bibliography, 201–209; Teule, Ethicon, XI–XVII (translation).

60 Cf. B. L. van Helmond, Mas'oud du Ṭour 'Abdin. Un Mystique syrien du XVe siècle. Etude et texte, BMus 14, Louvain 1942, esp. 40*–43* (translation: 68*–70*), the end of this treatise, which is devoted to asceticism.

61 Cf. Rudolf Macuch, Geschichte der spät- und neu-syrischen Literatur, Berlin-New York 1976, 14–15, with thanks to Mr. Hanna Ibrahim, Université Libre de Bruxelles, Brussels, (preparing a PhD-thesis on Abū'l-Ma'ānī), who kindly provided me with the original Syriac text and French translation.

62 Especially since also in the works of Ghazālī and other spiritual authors, the most important interpretation of *dhikr* is, of course, the spiritual and not the vocal one, the latter leading to the first or being an auxiliary method for it, see Nagamuro, Al-Ghazālī, xx–xxviii; Schimmel, Mystische Dimensionen, 243–253; Gardet, Problème de mystique comparée I, 662–679.

The Virtue of Continence (*al-'iffah*) and the 'Perfect Man' (*al-insān al-kāmil*): An Islamochristian Inquiry in Abbasid Religious and Philosophical Circles

Yaḥyā ibn 'Adī and Elias of Nisibis in Defense of the Christian Practice of Lifelong Celibacy

Sidney H. Griffith

I

In the intellectual milieu of Baghdad from the ninth to the eleventh centuries, thinkers such as the Muslims Abū Bakr Muḥammad ar-Rāzī (850–925) and Abū Naṣr Muḥammad al-Fārābī (870–950), along with the Christians Yaḥyā ibn 'Adī (893–974) and Elias of Nisibis (975–1046), were much concerned with the proper behavior (*adab*) that befitted a person bent on the pursuit of what Yaḥyā ibn 'Adī called "true science and godly wisdom."[1] Appropriate virtues were commended in treatises such as Yaḥyā ibn 'Adī's *Reformation of Morals (Tahdhīb al-akhlāq)*,[2] and Aḥmad ibn Muḥammad Miskawayh's (932–1030) work of the same name.[3] Somewhat earlier, the philosopher Abū Yūsuf Ya'qūb ibn Isḥāq al-Kindī (d. 870), in a very popular treatise *On the Art of Dispelling Sorrows*, had commended a philosophical view of life designed to provide comfort and consolation in the midst of the travails of this world.[4] So popular in the Arabic-speaking world did this treatise become that no fewer than three Christian writers were subsequently moved in response to write books on the same theme in which they brought Christian views on the subject to the fore.[5] It was inevitable then that in the course of these and other contemporary, reli-

1 Yaḥyā used this expression in his Colloquy on Sexual Abstinence and the Philosophical Life; see Vincent Mistrih, Traité sur la continence de Yaḥyā ibn 'Adī: Édition critique, SOC.C 16 (1981), 1, 3–4, 33, 2–3, 34, 5–7.

2 See Yaḥyā ibn 'Adī, The Reformation of Morals, ed. Samir Khalil Samir, trans. Sidney H. Griffith, Eastern Christian Texts I, Profo/UT 2002.

3 Constantine K. Zurayk (ed.), Tahdhīb al-akhlāq li Abi 'Alī Aḥmad Muḥammad Miskawayh, Beirut 1966; idem (trans.), The Refinement of Character, Beirut 1968; Mohammed Arkoun (trans.), Miskawayh (320/21–420), Traité d'éthique, 2nd ed. Damascus 1988.

4 See Abū Yūsuf al-Kindī, Le moyen de chaser les tristesses; et autre texts éthiques, intro., trans., and notes, Soumaya Mestiri and Guillaume Dye, Paris 2004.

5 See Sidney H. Griffith, The Muslim Philosopher al-Kindī and His Christian Readers: Three

gious and philosophical discussions about the pursuit of happiness and the cultivation of those spiritual exercises conducive to the achievement of a full and fully human life that the topic of sexual continence would soon arise.

Meanwhile, in the works of contemporary Sufi writers, the commendation of ascetical practices (*zuhd*)[6] suitable for the attainment of that 'self-renunciation' (*fanā'*) that leads one to 'abiding' (*baqā'*) in the presence of God, including a due measure of control over the human appetites, received considerable attention in the discussions of the early Muslim ascetics, whose practices seem often to have mirrored aspects of current Christian asceticism.[7] They focused their attention on how one might work toward leading the life of the 'perfect man' (*al-insān al-kāmil*) here below. This theme of living life toward the goal of human perfection had deep roots, already prior to the rise of Islam, in the spiritual worldview of the Syriac-speaking Christians, who were the dominant Christian presence in the environs of Baghdad and beyond in Abbasid times. Syriac spiritual writers often spoke of 'the perfect ones' (*gmîrê*), whom they distinguished from mere 'hearers' of the word of God and the teachings of the Church, as those whose spiritual and ascetical discipline had achieved a measure of 'perfection' (*gmîrûtâ*) that went well beyond the ordinary, and not least in the practices of virginity, celibacy and other measures of sexual continence.[8] Among these Christians, the apogee of moral perfection in sexual continence was thought to be achieved precisely in the practice of lifelong celibacy, a way of life for the single, unmarried person, or 'monk' (Syriac, *îḥîdāyyâ*, i.e. 'single one') who lived in imitation of the 'single' way of life of Jesus of Nazareth, confessed by Syriac-speaking Christians to be the 'single' Son of God.[9]

This ideal of lifelong celibacy as the moral or ascetic practice characteristic of Christian monasticism marked the parting of the ways between Christian and Muslim ascetics in the Abbasid period.[10] It was no doubt the rejection of this practice that lay behind the popularity among Muslim thinkers in the third Islamic century of the famous prophetic *ḥadīth*, 'There is no monasticism (*rahbāniyyah*) in Islam'. It was in just this period, from the ninth to the eleventh centuries, that according to Louis Massignon, in reaction to the Qur'ān's and some earlier Muslim scholars' apparent if limited appreciation of Christian monasticism, and in the context of the

---

Arab Christian Texts on 'The Dissipation of Sorrows, BJRL 78 (1996), 111–127.

6 See Leah Kinberg, What is Meant by Zuhd, StIsl 61 (1985), 27–44.

7 See James A. Bellamy, Sex and Society in Islamic Popular Literature, in: Afaf Lutfi al-Sayyid-Marsot (ed.), Society and the Sexes in Medieval Islam (Giorgio Levi Della Vida Conferences, 6; Malibu/CA 1979), 23–42; Ofer Livne-Kafri, Early Muslim Ascetics and the World of Christian Monasticism, Jerusalem Studies in Arabic and Islam 20 (1996), 105–129.

8 See, e.g., this language used in Robert A. Kitchen and Martien F.G. Parmentier (trans.), The Book of Steps: The Syriac Liber Graduum, CistSS 196, Kalamazoo/MI 2004.

9 See Sidney H. Griffith, Asceticism in the Church of Syria: The Hermeneutics of Early Syrian Monasticism, in: Vincent Wimbush and Richard Valantasis (eds.), Asceticism, New York 1995, 220–245.

10 See Livne-Kafri, Early Muslim Ascetics, 110–111.

then burgeoning Sufism and its ascetical and mystical practices in the ninth and tenth centuries, that the 'no monasticism' *ḥadīth* gained prominence among those contemporary Muslims who were opposed to what they regarded as Muslim asceticism and Sufism's innovations in traditional Islamic life.[11] In the 'sectarian milieu' of the time, in the mix of the Jewish, Christian and Muslim currents of thought that seem often to have mutually played the foil for the development of doctrines in the three communities, the Christian esteem for celibacy became a significant point of contention. It was one of the most startling Christian practices indicative of a radical clash of religious anthropologies between Christians and Muslims.

Indeed, from the Christian perspective, the clash of moralities between Christians and Muslims in sexual ethics was already apparent in the apologetic and polemical tracts written by Christians in the earliest Islamic period. In the context of their discussion of the ways to recognize the true religion, Christian controversialists regularly rejected Islamic ideas about marital and sexual morality and Islamic visions of the nature of the blessings of Paradise. Arguing on the grounds that Muslim teachings and practices in this area pandered to man's lowest instincts, Christian polemicists charged that Islamic views were too corporeal, insufficiently spiritual, to qualify as being worthy of the highest dignities of mankind. Therefore, already in the view of these early Christian polemicists in the Islamic milieu, the bodily values inherent in the Islamic moral and eschatological vision yielded the conclusion that Islam could not be the true religion, in which the one God, creator of all things, wanted to be worshipped.[12] In due course, the ascetical practice of lifelong celibacy, and the Christian defense of it, became the focal point for Islamochristian discussions about the body and the sacred, and that personal discipline necessary for both the philosophical life and religious perfection.

In this essay we shall consider two treatises on the virtue of continence, written in Arabic by two Christian scholars who lived in Abbasid times: Yaḥyā ibn 'Adī (893–974), the 'Jacobite' logician, and Elias bar Shīnāyā (975–1046), the 'Nes-

---

11 See Louis Massignon, Essay on the Origins of the Technical Language of Islamic Mysticism, trans. Benjamin Clark, Notre Dame/IN 1997, 98–104. See also Edmund Beck, Das christliche Mönchtum im Koran, StOr 18 (1946), 3–29; Sara Sviri, Wa-Rahbānīyatan ibtadaʿūhā: An Analysis of Traditions concerning the Origin and Evaluation of Christian Monasticism, Jerusalem Studies in Arabic and Islam 13 (1990), 195–208. See further, Christopher Melchert, The Transition from Asceticism to Mysticism at the Middle of the Ninth Century C.E., StIsl 83 (1996), 51–70; idem, Early Renunciants as ḥadīth Transmitters, The Muslim World 92 (2002), 407–418.

12 See the selection of quotations from Christian writers on this theme in Paul Khoury, Matériaux pour servir à l'étude de la controverse théologique islamo-chrétien de langue arabe du VIIIe au XII siècle (4 Vol.s Religionswissenschaftliche Studien, 11:1–4), Würzburg und Altenberge 1989–1999, Vol. I, 190–380. On this theme developed systematically see the discussion of Theodore Abū Qurrah's treatise on discerning the true religion in Sidney H. Griffith, Faith and Reason in Christian Kalām: Theodore Abū Qurrah on Discerning the True Religion, in: S. Kh. Samir and J.S. Nielsen, Christian Arabic Apologetics during the Abbasid Period (750–1258), SHR LXIII, Leiden 1994, 1–43.

torian' metropolitan of Nisibis. Both of them wrote in response to Muslim objections to the Christian ideal of lifelong sexual continence, and both of them commended the practice of celibacy in dialogue with views put forward by prominent Muslim intellectuals. After describing their treatises, the essay will conclude with a brief reflection on the contrasting, indeed the clashing religious anthropologies which the Christian and Muslim ascetic ideals reveal.

II

Yaḥyā ibn ʻAdī seems to have been the first Christian scholar living in the Islamic milieu and writing in Arabic systematically and specifically to have defended at some length the practice of celibacy against objections coming from Muslims. We find his work on the subject in a tri-partite text on sexual abstinence and the philosophical life, which records a colloquy between Yaḥyā and several Muslim interlocutors about the legitimacy and verisimilitude of the distinctly Christian rationale for lifelong celibacy.[13] We shall hereinafter refer to this composite work as the 'Colloquy on Sexual Abstinence'.

In the 'Colloquy', Yaḥyā commends celibacy as a practice suitable for one who is devoted to the life of reason, which, in another work, he describes as the goal of the 'complete' or 'perfect man' (*al-insān al-kāmil/at-tamm*). In his essay on *The Reformation of Morals*, Yaḥyā set the agenda for the 'perfect man' as follows:

> To direct his attention to the study of 'true science'; to make it his aim to grasp the 'quiddities' of existing things, to disclose their causes and occasions, and to search out their final ends and purposes. He shall not pause in his labor at any particular end without giving some consideration to what is beyond that end. He shall make it his badge of honor, night and day, to read books on morals, to scrutinize books of biographies and of conduct. He shall devote himself to implementing what virtuous people have bidden to be implemented and what the sages who have gone before have advised to be made habitual. He shall also acquire a modicum of the discipline of grammar and rhetoric and be endowed with a measure of eloquence and oratorical felicity. He shall always frequent the sessions (*majālis*) of scholars and sages and continually associate with modest and abstinent people.[14]

13 See the text, with a French translation, published in Yaḥyā ibn ʻAdī, Traité sur la continence (Vincent Mistrih, ed. and trans.), SOC.C 16, Cairo 1981. See the discussion by Sidney H. Griffith, Yaḥyā ibn ʻAdī's Colloquy on Sexual Abstinence and the Philosophical Life, in: James E. Montgomery (ed.), Arabic Theology, Arabic Philosophy: From the Many to the One; Essays in Celebration of Richard M. Frank, OLA 152, Leuven 2006, 299–333.

14 Yaḥyā ibn ʻAdī, The Reformation of Morals, 94, §4.

Obviously, Yaḥyā here envisions the 'perfect man' as a philosopher. But it is also clear in *The Reformation of Morals* that he considers 'scholars' (*ahl al-'ilm*), 'monks' (*ar-ruhbān*) and 'ascetics' (*az-zuhhād*) altogether to be in pursuit of that goal. He says of them:

> What is to be considered good for them is clothing of hair and coarse material, traveling on foot, obscurity, attendance at churches and mosques and so forth, and an abhorrence for luxurious living.[15]

It is with these high ideals about 'the perfect man' in the background that in January of the year 964 AD, as he tells us, Yaḥyā ibn 'Adī engaged in a colloquy with several interlocutors on the subject of the Christian ideal of celibacy, and the 'Colloquy on Sexual Continence' is the surviving textual record of the conversation. The text comes down to us in three parts: a brief treatise (*maqālah*) that Yaḥyā had composed in affirmation of the practice of abstaining from procreation; a record of Yaḥyā's rejoinders to objections to his treatise contained in a communication from one of his friends to another one, concluding with three further questions posed by Yaḥyā; and finally a copy of his interlocutor's answers to the questions, along with Yaḥyā's rebuttal and further clarifications of his position.[16]

A. Yaḥyā's Initial Treatise

At the very beginning of his treatise in defense of the practice of lifelong celibacy, while he defends it on philosophical grounds, Yaḥyā ibn 'Adī speaks of the Christian promoters (*dā'ī n-naṣārā*) of this practice and of the 'opponents of the Christians' (*al-mukhālifū li n-naṣārā*), making it clear that this was an interreligious issue for him as much as it was a philosophical one. In the course of his remarks he refers to Socrates, Plato, Aristotle, Alexander the Great, Porphyry and the Arab philosopher Abū Yūsuf Ya'qūb ibn Isḥāq al-Kindī (d. c. 866), but as the colloquy with his interlocutors develops, there is also mention made of the prophets, the Messiah, and even an allusion to Muḥammad without explicitly naming him.

Yaḥyā introduces the topic by observing that scholars (*ahl an-naẓar*) have different opinions about what he calls in Arabic *at-tafarrud*,[17] that is to say 'being alone' or 'staying single'. The Arabic term is an apt translation of what one suspects is the Syriac expression in the back of Yaḥyā's mind, *îḥîdāyûtâ*, the word that in the works of the classical Syriac writers such as Ephraem the Syrian or Jacob of Serug describes the practice of those who forego marriage in imitation of Jesus of Nazareth,

15 Yaḥyā ibn 'Adī, The Reformation of Morals, 60, §43.

16 For a full discussion of the 'Colloquy', see Sidney H. Griffith, Yaḥyā ibn 'Adī's Colloquy On Sexual Abstinence and the Philosophical Life, in: James E. Montgomery, Arabic Theology, (note 13), 299–333. See also Thérèse-Anne Druart, An Arab Christian Philosophical Defense of Religious Celibacy against Its Islamic Condemnation: Yaḥyā ibn 'Adī, in: Nancy van Deusen (ed.), Chastity: A Study in Perception, Ideals, Opposition (Presenting the Past, Vol. 1), Leiden 2008, 77–85.

17 See Yaḥyā ibn 'Adī, Traité sur la continence, 14, §1.2 (Arabic) and 65 (French).

the Father's 'single son' i.e., the monks.[18] Yaḥyā repeatedly speaks of this practice as one's "avoiding any involvement in seeking to procreate," in order to enhance the exercise of one's reason in the effort to acquire "true science and godly wisdom."[19] He says that the adversaries of the Christians maintain that such a practice is contrary to what God intended when He equipped mankind with the means to procreate and that to abstain from procreation is a practice "at variance with God, inimical to Him and loathsome to Him."[20]

The treatise unfolds in two parts, in the first of them Yaḥyā repeats four lines of argument against the Christian practice of celibacy, including his rebuttal to them. In the second part he puts forward and defends his own position. The four premises on the basis of which, according to Yaḥyā, the adversaries conclude that the practice of lifelong celibacy is 'detestable' (*maqīt*) to God are as follows. First, they argue that since all agree that God is wise, He would not have done anything futile and profitless. He created man with the power to generate offspring, the profitable benefit of which is the survival of the human species and the stability of the world. Therefore, whoever would prevent human reproduction is opposed to God's will. Second, since the existence of anything is better than its non-existence, to do something detrimental to it is wrong. So anything that would frustrate the continuance of the human species, such as abstaining from procreation, would be detrimental to it and would therefore be wrong. Third, out of His 'bountiful goodness' (*al-jūd*), the 'bountifully good' (*jawād*) God wills the continued existence of the human species. Therefore, anyone who would pose an obstacle to what God wills, such as proposing to abstain from procreation, would clearly be acting in opposition to God. And fourth, granting the principle that existence is better than non-existence, it follows that whoever contributes to the increase of something good is good and whoever contributes to its decrease is bad. So, those who have children are good and those who espouse perpetual abstinence from procreation are bad and inimical to God.

Yaḥyā then offers a rebuttal to each of the four objections and as a professional logician, his principal argument is that, as he puts it, "all their syllogisms inevitably comprise false premises." He argues in reply to the first objection that God in His wisdom did not create man just to procreate; He created him to pursue happiness, i.e., to acquire 'true science and godly wisdom', and to maximize the circumstances in his life that are conducive to this goal. For those who are capable of sexual continence, therefore, to abstain from procreation so as not to be distracted from their goal in life is commendable behavior. In reply to the second objection, Yaḥyā argues that one who does something God wants even more than He wants procreation, as he says is the case with one abstaining from indulging the desire to procreate in the rational pursuit of happiness, that person is in no way at variance with God's will. As for the third objection, Yaḥyā points out that not everyone has the wherewithal to

18 See Sidney H. Griffith, ibid. 220–245.
19 See Yaḥyā ibn 'Adī, ibid. 14 §1.3–4 and 65 (French).
20 Ibid. 14, §1.9 (Arabic) 65–66 (French).

practice lifelong sexual abstinence, so the question is moot. But he goes on to say that even if, *per impossibile*, everyone did abstain, if God nevertheless wanted the human race to continue, "He could create individual human beings, just as He created the first father for humankind, Adam."[21] But Yaḥyā is very clear on the point that celibacy is in fact not a real option for everyone. Finally, Yaḥyā counters the fourth objection with the observation that there are in fact situations in which more of a good thing is not better, nor is it less bad. Ultimately, along with his faulting of the logical adequacy of the premises of his adversaries' arguments, Yaḥyā argues that it would not in fact be good for someone to engage in procreation if he were a person capable of foregoing it easily, and without harm to himself, for the sake of the pursuit of happiness, i.e., the pursuit of 'true science and godly wisdom'.

In the second part of his treatise, Yaḥyā positively sets out the view he says the Christians are concerned to defend, a view he expresses as follows: "To be singly concerned to pursue happiness and to refrain from being distracted from it in pursuit of procreation."[22] He begins by stating what he considers to be an unassailable premise, namely that "the intellect is the most estimable [faculty] with which man is endowed."[23] And the intellect is naturally directed to the acquisition of 'true science and godly wisdom'. In human life as we know it, Yaḥyā then claims, "the most extreme and the highest degree of hindrance"[24] to the achievement of the intellect's natural goal is to be found in family life and child rearing. Therefore, reasons Yaḥyā, the practice of lifelong celibacy is not only not reprehensible in God's sight, but it is a positive good. So, then recalling the premise that "everything that helps the acquisition of virtue is good, and everything which impedes the acquisition of the most virtuous virtue is bad,"[25] and that whatever is bad is displeasing to God, Yaḥyā concludes that "everyone who brings children to birth in pursuit of progeny, when to do so is devoid of virtue, is detestable to God (*maqīt 'inda Allāh*)."[26] For Yaḥyā, having children is devoid of virtue when people who otherwise are perfectly capable of practicing sexual abstinence without adverse effects on themselves fail to do so. In the end, one readily recognizes that Yaḥyā has now reversed the charge that at the beginning of his treatise he says the adversaries of the Christians advanced against the Christian commendation of the practice of celibacy, namely that such a practice is detestable to God..

B. The Rejoinders

Yaḥyā ibn 'Adī's treatise caused a flurry of discussion among its readers. When one reader wrote to another reader about his reservations, a copy came into Yaḥyā's

21 Yaḥyā ibn 'Adī, Traité sur la continence, 20, §18.7 (Arabic) and 74 (French).
22 Ibid. 22, §24.2 (Arabic) and 77 (French).
23 Ibid. 22, §25 (Arabic) and 77 (French).
24 Yaḥyā ibn 'Adī, Traité sur la continence, 24, §30.2 (Arabic) and 80 (French); 25, §32.3 (Arabic) and 81 (French).
25 Ibid. 25, §34.2 (Arabic) and 82 (French).
26 Ibid. 25, §34.9 (Arabic) and 82 (French).

hands; he composed a précis of it and refuted the author's arguments. The reader had argued that on the principle, 'virtue stands in the middle', the reasonable man would conclude that moderation in sex and procreation was more virtuous than lifelong celibacy. What is more, the reader had proposed that given the nobility of the human species, it would be better for there to be more rather than fewer human beings, a circumstance that he argued would better serve the well-being of the temporal order. Yaḥyā replied that the principle that 'virtue stands in the middle' cannot be used as a premise in a valid argument because it cannot be taken absolutely. Then, reaffirming his position that the pursuit of 'true knowledge and godly wisdom' is the highest human goal, and recalling his conviction that the vicissitudes of parenthood, when "devoid of any virtue to bring one nearer to God,"[27] constitute an obstacle to that pursuit, Yaḥyā concludes that one cannot then argue that moderation in procreation is preferable to abstention from it altogether.

The question that then confronted Yaḥyā was, when is procreation devoid of any virtue to bring one nearer to God? His answer reflects Yaḥyā's dependence on the thought of his teacher, the philosopher Abū Naṣr al-Farābī. Yaḥyā wrote:

> [The pursuit of procreation] is devoid of any virtue to bring one closer to God when it is devoid of any intention to generate a prophet, a just king, a distinguished priest, or a skillful physician, or any intention to eliminate an illness, or to take precautions against falling into a sickness, which would prevent anyone whom it would afflict from achieving the acquisition of the highest degree of true knowledge of which he is capable.[28]

As for a larger number of people being preferable for the well-being of society, Yaḥyā says that this would not be the case if the larger number negatively affected the pursuit of wisdom. And he brought his reflections to an end with three questions for the reader of his treatise. They may be paraphrased as follows: which of two men is the most virtuous, one who labors all his life for 'true wisdom and godly knowledge', abstaining from procreation so as to attain as much knowledge as possible, or one who is preoccupied with expending as much as is humanly possible on having children? Which of two historical eras is the best, and which of two populations is happiest, those in which most people are concerned with the acquisition of knowledge, without giving much thought to procreation or those in which people have as many children as possible, with no time left for the pursuit of knowledge? Which is the best and happiest of human conditions, that in which the number of wise men who do not procreate exceeds the number of unwise procreators, or the reverse?

---

27 Yaḥyā ibn 'Adī, Traité sur la continence, 35, §58.5 (Arabic) and 95 (French).

28 Ibid. 35, §59.2–3 (Arabic) and 96 (French). Later in his reflections Yaḥyā again mentions what he considers to be worthy intentions for procreation; he lists them slightly differently several times and he speaks of them as the six values or worthy purposes that justify having children; he finds them exemplified in the lives of Socrates and Aristotle. See the fuller discussion in Griffith, Yaḥyā ibn 'Adī's Colloquy on Sexual Abstinence, 327–332.

Yaḥyā's reader wrote in response to Yaḥyā's reactions to the reader's reservations about Yaḥyā's original treatise, and he answered the three questions. The reader's answers, as Yaḥyā summarized them, reiterated the reader's reliance on the principle that 'virtue stands in the middle'. And in his conclusion the reader posed a question of his own, in which he neatly sketched the two opposed views about how sexual continence should, in his opinion, be practiced in a virtuous life. He asked which of two hypothetical individuals, both endowed with the highest human potential, best depicted the human ideal. He describes the first one of them in language which clearly envisions the vocation of a Christian monk or ascetic, whose life is characterized by a lonely, celibate search for wisdom in solitude in the wilderness, amidst hardship and deprivation. The reader says that in his opinion this man's career is "a life that hampers and holds its protagonist back from every virtue."[29] He mentions that in this destitute situation such a person misses the opportunity for access to what the reader calls "philosophical knowledge and its utilization."[30] The second highly favored individual, by way of contrast, lives his life in community with others. He seeks knowledge wherever he can find it, especially "from reading established books which, over the courses of the ages, the most virtuous men have spent their lifetimes writing, augmenting and enhancing."[31] Such a man has "wealth, offspring, slaves and a wife."[32] The reader says that in his opinion this man's career is "a humane, rich life, the best of lives, the basis of which is the right ordering of the mind."[33] In the reader's opinion such a life was that of Socrates, Plato and Aristotle, and also the way of life of the prophets and law-givers, among whom, he says, only the Messiah was not married and even he did not require his disciples and apostles to be celibate. Among the latter, the reader mentions Simon, John and Luke as the best of the Messiah's disciples. But among all these, he says, "I think that Aristotle, Plato and Socrates, more than all the other practitioners of philosophy and the devotees of religion are the most virtuous in moral choice, and the most perfect in conduct and gentility."[34] Then, almost as an after-thought, he says, "Our prophet, may God's prayer be with him, is the most virtuous of prophets and his companions are the most virtuous of companions." [35]

In his rebuttal of the reader's position, Yaḥyā returns to the principle that 'virtue stands in the middle', which he had earlier said could not be a premise in a valid argument because it cannot be taken absolutely. Now he points out that the principle does not mean that one should be moderate in his indulgence of the appetites. Rather, he argues, the requisite moderation is to be predicated of the human being who controls the actions of his appetites. Accordingly, Yaḥyā says,

29 Yaḥyā ibn 'Adī, Traité sur la continence, 45, §92.1 (Arabic) and 110 (French).
30 Ibid. 45, §93.3 (Arabic) and 111 (French).
31 Ibid. 44, §91.6–7 (Arabic) and 110 (French).
32 Ibid. 45, §91.9 (Arabic) and 110 (French).
33 Ibid. 45, §93.1 (Arabic) and 111 (French; 45, §92.2 (Arabic) and 110 (French).
34 Ibid. 46, §96.3 (Arabic) and 112–113 (French).
35 Ibid. 46, §97.1 (Arabic) and 113 (French).

> The most virtuous way of life is to spend one's time gaining knowledge, to devote oneself to it according to one's ability, and not to be concerned with consorting with a wife, nor with having children, unless it would be to achieve one of the six purposes we have already prescribed.[36] It is to spend what goods one has by the labor of others for one's own well-being and nourishment, without which one could not maintain one's life in a manner which would suffice for devoting one's time to gaining knowledge. It is to spend the remainder on whatever would help one to achieve the maximum of knowledge, such as books and teachers and whatever else follows the same course, without being concerned to seek offspring, save for the six purposes.[37]

Yaḥyā brings his rebuttal, and his whole presentation of his colloquy with his colleagues and adversaries to a close by extolling Plato, Socrates and Aristotle as exemplars of the way of life he commends. But he says that in the matter of the exercise of the virtue of continence (*al-'iffah*), the Messiah was the most successful; he was a life-long celibate, who commended celibacy to his followers. And Yaḥyā reminds his readers and interlocutors, whom he certainly takes to be Muslims, that they too recognize the Messiah as one who was perfectly virtuous, especially in continence, courage, wisdom and justice.

III

The 'Nestorian' Elias of Nisibis lived a generation and more after the 'Jacobite' Yaḥyā ibn 'Adī, yet in his 'Letter on the Virtue of Continence' (*Risālah fī faḍīlat al-'afāf*)[38] Elias addressed many of the same topics already familiar from Yaḥyā's work, albeit that Elias wrote in his own style and much more obviously in dialogue with well-known Muslim thinkers of an earlier generation.

---

36 See the reference in note 28 above

37 Yaḥyā ibn 'Adī, Traité de la continence, 57, §120.4–7 (Arabic) and 127–128 (French).

38 The text is published in a non-critical edition by Georges Raḥma, Risālah fī faḍīlat al-'afāf, al-Machriq 62 (1968), 3–74 and in a critical edition, with a German translation, in the dissertation of Andreas Hau, Brief über den Vorzug der Enthaltsamkeit gegenüber dem Geschlechtsverkehr: Einführung, Übersetzung, Text, Bonn 1970. Hereinafter the text is cited according to both editions, albeit that in a number of passages, the editors have privileged different recensions, yielding somewhat different readings of the text. For more information on the text, see Samir Khalil Samir, Bibliographie du dialogue islamo-chrétien: Élie de Nisibe (Iliyyâ al-Naṣîbî) (975–1046), Islamochristiana 3 (1977), 257–286, 278–279. The writer is grateful to Grigory Kessel for giving him access to Hau's dissertation.

Elias addressed his letter to his brother,[39] Abū Sa'd Manṣūr ibn 'Îsā, who had written to Elias for help in how to think about a passage in the well-known *Kitāb al-Ḥayawān* by the famous, ninth-century *littérateur*, Abū 'Uthmān 'Amr ibn Baḥr al-Jāḥiẓ (d. 868/9). In that book, in the context of a disquisition on castration and its effects, al-Jāḥiẓ spoke at some length about the conscious 'desire for begetting' (*ṭalab al-walad*) that he said characterizes the sexual lives of human beings, by way of contrast with the simpler appetitive behavior of non-human animals. In the process, he brought up the case of an aged eunuch, the centenarian Abū Mubārak aṣ-Ṣābī, who, in spite of age and mutilation, nevertheless still felt sexual desire for women. And in reference to aṣ-Ṣābī's reported admission, al-Jāḥiẓ expressed it as his opinion that men do not have the ability "to withhold themselves from wanting, needing and desiring women." And, as if he had in mind the very controversy between Christians and Muslims on this issue, he goes on to say of male human beings that "God, who is most compassionate toward His creatures and most just toward His servants, is too exalted to encumber them with foregoing anything He had bestowed on their hearts and confirmed."[40]

It was just this passage that Elias said had amazed his brother, considering what the metropolitan called al-Jāḥiẓ's "haughty opposition to reason and revelation (*al-'aql wa l-shar'*) in it."[41] And Metropolitan Elias, who apparently did not think much of al-Jāḥiẓ's essays in general, went on immediately to say that he thought one should consider the passage in question on the same level as one thought of the famous writer's essay on misers and his essay on his preferment for mad men over intellectuals.[42] At this juncture, Elias announces his intention to refute al-Jāḥiẓ's position. But first he points out that while natural scientists claim that the desire for sexual intercourse arises from the kidneys, Jesus taught that "vicious thoughts come from the heart" (Mt 15:19) Elias then declares that neither sexual desire nor sexual indifference depend solely on the sexual organs themselves. And he claims that in the normally endowed man, even when an excess of seminal fluid wells up within him, nature will move it along and it will be ejected and sexual desire will thereby be lessened and weakened. As for eunuchs like aṣ-Ṣābī, Elias claims that castration has weakened them to the point that they lack the self control of the normal man and that is why they fail to govern their desires.

Following this prolegomenon, Metropolitan Elias structures the rest of his letter in four parts: a presentation of the ways in which the desire for women is in fact dispelled among men; a refutation in some detail of al-Jāḥiẓ's claims about the im-

---

39 It is clear that while he addressed it to his brother, Elias intended his letter to circulate more widely. At the end of it he prays that the peace of our Lord Jesus might "come upon you and upon all who read this letter of ours and profit from what it says and from reading it, and upon everyone who hears it and understands its meanings." Elias, Risālah, 74.

40 Abū 'Uthmān 'Amr ibn Baḥr al-Jāḥiẓ, Kitāb al-Ḥayawān (7 vols.), Cairo 1938–1945, Vol. I, 128.

41 Elias, Risālah, 15 (Raḥma) and 4 (Hau).

42 Ibid. The reference is to two other essays by al-Jāḥiẓ,

possibility of continence; an explanation of why sexual continence is better than marriage, albeit that marriage is permitted; and finally a section in which he presents the thoughts of monks, Sufis and sages on the subject of continence.

A. The Ways of Dispelling Desire

By far the longest part of the letter is devoted to Elias' listing and discussion of nine causes that he says will irrefutably neutralize and eliminate sexual desire. They are: a sound mind and a love of knowledge; the practice of religion and the fear of God; the advice of wise teachers; poverty, dire need, seeking relief for heart and body; jealousy and anger; sad songs and disquieting news; disdain, obsequiousness and self-promotion; an abundance of sorrow and strong determination; manliness, love of males and vain glory. The metropolitan is aware that his list is not comprehensive; at the end of his presentation of them he remarks that there are other means of dispelling sexual desire that he had not discussed. He mentions fear of punishment and falling into misfortunes, feelings of shame and the use of artifices in social relations, "as monks and ascetics do,"[43] he says, and there is even the use of drugs, just like people do to enhance their sexual potential. But in the end, Elias claims, "The aforementioned reports and sayings have shown that many factors dispel the love of women and the desire for intercourse; some are voluntary, some are enforced."[44] The truth of all of them, in his view shows that al-Jāḥiẓ's claim that continence is impossible is false.

As in the case of his book 'On Dispelling Sorrows' (*Kitāb daf' al-hamm*),[45] so here in the *Risālah fī faḍīlat al-'afāf*, albeit to a lesser extent, Elias evokes the names and careers of the sages and saints of old, their sayings and doings, to make his points. To demonstrate that a sound mind and a love of science dispel sexual desire, Elias cites the example of Socrates, whose disciples by a ruse disclosed that their master had a strong desire for fornication. The metropolitan says, "Since the mind of this man, this philosopher, his love for wisdom and knowledge, and his devotion to them, dispelled from him this vicious desire ..., it is therefore known that a sound mind and the love of knowledge will dispel desire."[46]

In the matter of the practice of religion and the fear of God as a practical preventative of lust, Elias tells the story of an observant monk sorely tempted by a prostitute sent to seduce him. But the monk overcomes the temptation and converts the prostitute. Elias cites his source for the story as the *Book of Paradise*,[47] and he

---

43 Elias, Risālah, 48 (Raḥma) and 50 (Hau).

44 Elias, Risālah, 49 (Raḥma) and 51 (Hau).

45 See Elia di Nisibi, Il Libro per Scacciare la Preoccupazione (Kitāb daf' al-hamm) (Tomo 1°, Testo arabo, Samir Khalil Samir, trad. e note, Anna Pagnini, Patrimonio Culturale Arabo Cristiano 9), Torino 2007.

46 Elias, Risālah, 23 (Raḥma) and 15 (Hau).

47 The Book of Paradise to which Elias refers is the Syriac recension of the Lausiac History of Palladius (c. 365–425), put together by the seventh century monk 'Anân Îshô' of Bêth 'Âbhê, for which see E. A. Wallis Budge (ed. and trans.), The Book of Paradise being The Histories

concludes, "It is therefore a known fact that the practice of religion and the fear of God can prevent one from indulging in morally repugnant desires."[48]

In order to show that advice from wise and learned men is sufficient to dispel sexual desire, Elias cites the example of Plato, who persuaded one of his disciples caught up in a foredoomed love affair, that an early separation from the beloved would be less painful than a later one. The metropolitan cites as his source for this information the book of the Muslim scholar, Abū Bakr Muḥammad ibn Zakarriyyā ar-Rāzī (850–925), called the *Book of Spiritual Medicine* and he concludes that the story shows that "admonitions, when they come from the hearts of the scholars to the lovers of knowledge, will dispel detestable desires."[49]

Elias once again finds a story about an Egyptian monk in the *Book of Paradise* to show that poverty and dire need can quench the desire for the pleasures of sexual intercourse. The monk desperately wanted to marry to fulfill his desires, so he devised a plan to determine if he could afford it. He made a wife of clay and installed her in his cell and put aside two-thirds of his earnings to support her and her children, reserving only a third for his own needs. But he found that increased labor only fatigued him, injured his health, and failed to yield sufficient means. So he concluded that marriage was not worth the price he would have to pay in order to indulge his desires; he remained a monk. Elias said the story "shows that poverty, dire need, and seeking relief for the heart and the body weaken repulsive desire."[50]

Again the *Book of Paradise* furnished Metropolitan Elias with a story to show that jealousy and righteous anger can dispel sexual desire. Elias cites the story of Anthony's disciple Paul, who as a married man discovered his adored wife *in flagrante delictu* with another man. In reaction, Paul went off to Anthony in the desert and sought to become a monk, a goal he achieved after enduring many trials and tests set by Anthony. According to Elias, Paul's story shows "that jealousy and righteous anger will dispel despicable desire and the love of women."[51]

As for the effects of sad songs and disquieting news, Elias recalls the story of Odysseus the Melode that he says was told in the annals of the kings of the Greeks and repeated by Diogenes the logician in his commentary on the *Eisagoge* of Porphry. According to the story, King Agamemnon engaged Odysseus to regale his wife and slave girls with sad and mournful melodies during his absence to prevent them from being tempted to have sex with anyone else in the king's absence. The metropolitan speaks at some length about the properties of music which can be used both to arouse and to allay sexual desire. He says that in the instance of Agamem-

---

and Sayings of the Monks and Ascetics of the Egyptian Desert by Palladius, Hieronymus and others, The Syriac Texts, according to the Recension (2 vols., Lady Meux Manuscript, no. 6), London 1904.

48 Elias, Risālah, 28 (Raḥma) and 23 (Hau).

49 Elias, Risālah, 30 (Raḥma) and 26 (Hau). See Abū Bakr Muḥammad ar-Rāzī, The Spiritual Physick of Rhazes (trans. Arthur J. Arberrym Wisdom of the East Series), London 1950.

50 Ibid. 32 (Raḥma) and 29 (Hau).

51 Elias, Risālah, 36 (Raḥma) and 35 (Hau).

non's ploy, Odysseus' music was in fact sufficient to prevent his wife from acceding to the wishes of her lover, until the lover killed the musician. Elias takes this story to prove the effects of music and he says, "For this reason, monks and religious devotees (*ar-ruhbān wa l-'ubbād*) employ melodies (*al-alḥān*) which induce submissiveness and promote sorrow."[52] And of course the metropolitan concludes that "when a man hears disquieting news or a sad melody, repulsive desire will vanish from his heart."[53]

In a very interesting story involving a highborn but illegitimate, young Muslim man named Abū l-Ḥasan ibn ukht 'Umar, by whose name one assumes he had already fathered a son, Ḥasan, but who refused even the Sultan's entreaties to marry, Metropolitan Elias both engages in some not too subtle, anti-Islamic polemic and presents a case for the claim that prideful disdain and self-importance effectively dispels sexual desire. For the young man's reason for refusing to marry in spite of the pressures put upon him to do so was that he had little desire for sexual relations with either women or men due to pride and disdainful human respect rather than for any religious reason. An intriguing aspect of the story is that his Muslim family and friends engaged the services of the Catholicos, Mār Ibrāhīm, to talk sense to the young man. After hearing his reasons, the catholicos said to the youth, "If you get married, your religion is upheld and your honor is preserved. If you do not marry, I do not believe that anything will emerge to weaken your religion or spoil your reputation."[54] Abū l-Ḥasan, for his part, is said to have preferred not "being burdened with a woman or with a youth,"[55] and the catholicos found him to be telling the truth and concluded that he should not be required to marry. So, Metropolitan Elias takes it as the point of this story that it shows that "disdain and self-importance can dispel wicked desire."[56] But what the modern reader notices is that the young Muslim, who is described in a demeaning way as "the son of the sister of Umar," is seen to have had a wide choice of sexual partners, including both men and women, and that for effective personal advice in the area of morality, he is made to have recourse to a Christian hierarch. From the Christian perspective, one senses in this account a none-too-latent polemic against current Islamic thought and practice.

From a story about the Buwayhid sultan, 'Aḍud ad-Dawlah (949–983), which Elias says was widely known among many people, the metropolitan tells of an episode in which the sultan ordered the death by drowning of a beautiful servant girl with whom the sultan had become infatuated.[57] His reason for this desperate action was his conviction that his infatuation for the girl was distracting him from the duties of government. So, out of anxiety for the affairs of state, and a strong personal

52 Ibid. 39 (Raḥma) and 38 (Hau).
53 Ibid.
54 Elias, Risālah, 41 (Raḥma) and 40 (Hau).
55 Ibid. 42 (Raḥma) and 41 (Hau).
56 Ibid. 42 (Raḥma) and 42 (Hau).
57 See this story discussed in J.C. Bürgel, Love, Lust, and Longing: Eroticism in Early Islam as Reflected in Literary Sources, in: Society and the Sexes in Medieval Islam, 104–105.

determination, he ordered her death. Elias remarks, again in words that one can only regard as containing an anti-Islamic polemical nuance, that "'Aḍud ad-Dawlah did not do what he did because of the practice of religion; his religious law did not prohibit serving girls."[58] The metropolitan then says that he cites the story to show that "great anxiety and strong determination can dispel vicious, detestable desire."[59]

Finally, Elias claims that engagement in the life of the *futuwwah* 'fraternities'[60], the love of males and the male practice of vying in braggadocio with one another, dispels sexual desire. He tells the story of a man who was the head of a 'fraternity' and who was infatuated with a particular youth, but he sent him away whenever he posed too strong an enticement because he felt that he really was the man most entitled to be the head of the group. In fact, the man went so far as to break all ties with the youth and to take measures that would ensure no contact with him whatever. The metropolitan says he heard this story from a preacher who was commending continence (*al-'iffah*) and *al-futuwwah*. And he comments that if a man has the ability to abstain from sexual desire for reasons like those of the man in the story, others, who had even more concrete reasons for continence, could certainly dispel sexual desire.

B. Refuting al-Jāḥiẓ

Metropolitan Elias says that some people might call into question the veracity of the accounts he has given to disprove the claim of al-Jāḥiẓ, quoting aṣ-Ṣābī, that it is impossible to dispel the love of women and the desire for sexual intercourse with them. But the metropolitan says that his sources are in fact more reliable than aṣ-Ṣābī and that even if they were to prove false about the persistence of desire *per se*, he still has a stronger case than al-Jāḥiẓ does regarding men's ability to resist sexual desire and not to put it into practice.

Furthermore, Elias says that even if al-Jāḥiẓ himself had neither a wife nor a concubine, by the force of his own logic, relying on the testimony of aṣ-Ṣābī that sexual restraint is impossible for man, he, al-Jāḥiẓ would then have had to have been a whoring profligate himself. And if that was not in fact the case, then al-Jāḥiẓ's own experience should be sufficient to impugn the soundness of aṣ-Ṣābī's testimony about the inevitability of sexual desire.

As for al-Jāḥiẓ's argument that "God, who is most compassionate ..., is too exalted to encumber [men] with foregoing anything He had bestowed on their hearts and confirmed,"[61] Metropolitan Elias says that people use this excuse when they think that if God did not positively enjoin them to renounce sex, and did not impose marriage on them, then they need not practice sexual continence. And the metropolitan goes so far as explicitly to say, "This belief is an 'act of faith' (*dīnan*) in the creed (*madhhab*) of Islam, which is the creed of al-Jāḥiẓ and of the rest of the 'fol-

58 Elias, Risālah, 44 (Raḥma) and 44 (Hau).
59 Ibid. 44 (Raḥma) and 45 (Hau).
60 See Claude Cahen, Futuwwa, in: EI, new ed., Vol. II, 961–965.
61 Al-Jāḥiẓ, Kitāb al-ḥayawān, Vol. I, 128.

lowers of the *Sharī'ah*' (*ash-shar'iyyīn*)."[62] And Elias goes on to say that when they put the sexual drive on the same level as the drive for food and drink, the flaw in the argument is that food and drink are necessary for survival, whereas sexual indulgence is not. Furthermore, the metropolitan argues, just because God permits marriage and makes it attractive to men, does not mean that it is wrong to forego it. Elias points out that 'in law and reason' (*fī sh-shar' wa l-'aql*) there are many good and permitted things which one might renounce in favor of something better, and he lists a number of them. One of the several examples he gives is the eating of meat; Elias says, "When a man gives it up voluntarily and as an act of religion, it is better in reason and law than doing it, albeit that doing it is good and licit."[63] His conclusion is that it is more than possible that God both permits something to His servants and also wants them to renounce it as choosing the better part, as is the case, he claims, with marriage.

C. Celibacy versus Marriage

Having cleared the ground, so to speak, for the purpose of advancing his main thesis, Metropolitan Elias says, "I am going to make it clear that abstaining from marriage is preferable to marriage."[64] He begins by reminding his readers that God has no where either commanded or forbidden marriage, and human reason has not dictated that it is commanded or forbidden to marry. Having taken this position, Elias then advances his reasons in behalf of the Christian practice of celibacy.

The metropolitan first, on physiological and psychological grounds, describes in some detail the pathological conditions that he claims result from marriage and sexual intercourse. He says, for example, that "engaging in intercourse quenches the innate heat and weakens the natural functions, reduces power and lessens the body's vivacity."[65] And he goes into some detail in describing just how these things happen. Contrariwise, he says that renouncing sexual intercourse is productive of the opposite effects; it enhances human life. "For this reason," says Elias, "the philosophers renounce intercourse and sexual desire and they keep their distance from women."[66]

For proof that from a scriptural point of view, renunciation is preferable to sexual intercourse, Elias appeals to passages in both the Old Testament and the New Testament in which ritual purity is commended. He first cites Moses' instructions to the Israelites at Mount Sinai, including the injunction, "Do not go near a woman." (Exodus 19:15) And then he quotes St. Paul's First Epistle to the Corinthians, "I wish all the people were like me, being in abstinence. If they cannot endure, let them marry. Marrying is better than burning with desire." (1 Cor 7:7–9)[67] And there is

62 Elias, Risālah, 51 (Raḥma) and 54–55 (Hau).
63 Elias, Risālah, 53. (Raḥma) and 56–57 (Hau).
64 Ibid. 54 (Raḥma) and 59 (Hau).
65 Ibid. 55 (Raḥma) and 62 (Hau).
66 Elias, Risālah, 56 (Raḥma) and 63 (Hau).
67 Ibid. 57 (Raḥma) and 64–65 (Hau).

even what seems to be a quotation from Muḥammad to state the case from the Islamic side; Elias says, "There is a saying of the 'master of the law of Islam' (*ṣāḥib sharī'at al-Islām*) about women: "Doing without them is better than putting up with them, and putting up with them is better than putting up with the fire."[68] Elias remarks that this is the same position as the one espoused by St. Paul.

Having established both philosophical and scriptural grounds for preferring abstinence to marriage, i.e., according to 'reason and law', as he constantly puts it, Metropolitan Elias turns to the question of the danger to the world of depopulation if everyone agreed to abstain from sexual intercourse. This concern arises on the part of those who think that marriage is to be preferred to continence because to marry is good in 'reason and law' and in God's sight. But if that were absolutely the case, says Elias, the more children one would have, the better off he would be. But if that were so, "God would distinguish His prophets and His messengers with a multitude of children, and those who oppose Him with few children and progeny. But we see prophets and messengers to be the people with the fewest children."[69] So Elias goes on to observe that there is no more reason to think that it is likely that everyone would adopt celibacy because it is good 'in reason and law' any more than everyone would be likely to adopt any other behavior that is good 'in reason and law', just because it is good in itself, or at least permissible. Therefore, the worry about the disappearance of the world's population is groundless.

The metropolitan then proposed an interesting exegesis of Genesis 1:28, where God is recorded as having said to the first couple He created, "Increase, multiply and fill the earth." Elias says it "was not a command ... It was only an invitation and an invocation of blessing," and he claims that the proof of it is that when He created the animals, the fish, the birds and the plants, He said the same thing, "Increase and multiply." But these creatures, unlike Adam and Eve, cannot be morally burdened, and so, Elias reasons, this fact shows that when God used the same phrase when addressing Adam and Eve, as He used with the lesser creatures, He could only have meant it as an invitation and a blessing. Therefore, the scripture passage cannot be used against the commendation of lifelong sexual continence.[70]

Some people argued that the retention of sperm in a man's body without discharging it would harm his health. Metropolitan Elias spent a lot of time on this topic in his *risālah*. After a lengthy discussion of the properties of sperm by comparison with other bodily humors, he alleges that unlike the situation with other bodily fluids, the retention of sperm is actually good for a man. Elias says, "What shows that there is no harm to the body in retaining the sperm is that we find the monks and those who abstain from intercourse stronger in their bodies and longer

68 Ibid. 58 (Raḥma) and 65–66 (Hau), where Peter is mentioned rather than Paul. Presumably the passage alludes to a ḥadīth report.
69 Elias, Risālah, 59 (Raḥma) and 68 (Hau).
70 Ibid. 61 (Raḥma) and 70–71 (Hau).

lived than whose who continue to engage in intercourse."[71] But the metropolitan admits that when intercourse and the ejaculation of sperm has become habitual, there may be some pain and discomfort when the practice is suddenly stopped, just as is the case, he says, with nursing mothers, when suddenly they stop nursing their children, they experience pain and discomfort in their breast. With time, he counsels, this pain then yields welcome benefits.

D. Corroborative Testimonies

Metropolitan Elias devoted the last pages of his *risālah* to the citation of quotations from noted sages, scholars, monks and philosophers, which would on the face of it support his contention, in answer to his brother's query, that not only is sexual abstinence possible for men, but that life-long celibacy is both a healthy practice and one conducive to both the philosophical and religious ways of life. He engages substantially with the work of Abū Bakr ibn Muḥammad ar-Rāzī (850–925), whom he had quoted earlier in the *risālah,*[72] he quotes several well-known monks, including one by name, Abraham bar Dashandad, about whom more is said in another essay in this volume.[73] And finally, Elias tells the story of a conversation between an unnamed monk and three Muslim Sufis (*thalāthah min ṣūfiyyati l-muslimīn*), quoted from what Elias calls the monk's account of his religious formation, *Kitāb inshā'ihi*. The conversation is a mini-debate about celibacy and marriage, about Christian asceticism and Islamic asceticism, such as one might imagine a Christian apologist having composed. In the form in which we have the account, quoted in Elias' *risālah*, it wants only a setting in an emir's *majlis* to be an example of a well known apologetic genre in Arab Christian writing.[74]

According to the story, once upon a time the monk was in the company of three Sufis; one after another they posed objections to him about the Christian practice of celibacy and he rebuts their challenges. To begin with, they said to him, "Monks are disobedient people who deserve Hell-fire (*an-nār*) due to their avoidance of marriage." The monk replied, "What is the virtue (*faḍīlah*) of marrying over renouncing marriage?"[75] One of the Sufis answered that the virtue is that marriage generates children who will worship God, and it multiplies the number of Muslims, and so one is rewarded. The monk then asks about children who become infidels and even kill Muslims, will their parents be rewarded? When the Sufi answered no, the monk took the debater's advantage to declare that in that case, since no sin on the parents' part

71 Elias, Risālah, 63 (Raḥma a) and 83–84 (Hau).

72 See n. 49 above.

73 See Grigory Kessel's contribution in this volume.

74 On this genre, see Sidney H. Griffith, The Monk in the Emir's Majlis: Reflections on a Popular Genre of Christian Literary Apologetics in Arabic in the Early Islamic Period, in: Hava Lazarus-Yafeh et al. (eds.), The Majlis: Interreligious Encounters in Medieval Islam, Studies in Arabic Language and Literature, Vol. 4, Wiesbaden 1999, 13–65.

75 Elias, Risālah, 69 (Raḥma) and 87 (Hau).

was attached to bearing bad children, neither should the parent of good children be rewarded. And the Sufi fell silent.

Another Sufi said to the monk, "The virtue of marriage is that a man seeks to procreate, in accord with how God has seen fit and has chosen [to create him], and neither the sins nor the rewards of his children attach to him."[76] The monk then elicited from the Sufi the admission that it is therefore wrong to have sex without the intention to procreate, and the Sufi said, "This is sound and it is the belief of the people of the truth."[77] So the monk concludes that since in marriage the fulfillment of desire often supercedes the intention to procreate, every man who has a wife is in fact a sinner, and his sin is greater than his reward. So the monk concludes that celibacy is preferable to marriage because there is sin in marriage, but no sin in not marrying. The Sufi fell silent.

The third Sufi said that the virtue of marriage lay not so much in procreation but in the satisfaction of desire, for which one thanks God. He said, "The virtue of marriage is that a man is comforted and he takes pleasure in intercourse and he provides the children with the means of subsistence, he takes delight in them and he thanks God for the pleasures He has given him in this world."[78] The monk said that if this is the case, there are people in the world who think that pleasure and escape from hardship, such that they would thank God for it, accrue to them precisely in not marrying, and he says that this is in fact the belief and practice of the monks. For, the monk says, "Our hearts are wider, our souls are more tranquil, our bodies are healthier and our providing a more ample opportunity for knowledge, fasting and prayer is greater."[79] By contrast, the monk goes on to say, marriage is a tiresome and burdensome business; deliverance from it is a great blessing, for which one can only thank God. And the Sufi said, "You have spoken the truth."[80] And so the mini-debate came to an end, with the Sufis admitting that the monks had the better part.

Metropolitan Elias brings his *Risālah* to an end with a few more recollections. A certain wise man was put off from seeking to satisfy his lust when his inamorata rehearsed for him the squalor of it all; a certain scholar reflects on how the desire for sex is strong for some and weak for others. Elias quotes a saying of Solomon from Proverbs 7:21–27, to the effect that women are traps for men, and he ends with several sayings attributed to Socrates. He states in the concluding paragraph of the *Risālah*:

> These sayings, and other which I cannot recall, show that abstinence from sexual intercourse is a virtue profitable to the body and the soul, beneficial now and in the future. this is what I wanted to make clear to you.[81]

---

76 Ibid. 70 (Raḥma) and 88 (Hau).
77 Elias, Risālah, 70 (Raḥma) and 88 (Hau).
78 Ibid. 71 (Raḥma) and 89 (Hau).
79 Ibid. 71 (Raḥma) and 90–91 (Hau).
80 Ibid. 72 (Raḥma) and 92 (Hau).
81 Elias, Risālah, 74 (Raḥma) and 95 (Hau).

IV

One thing that immediately occurs to readers of the treatises 'On Continence' by both Yaḥyā ibn 'Adī and Metropolitan Elias of Nisibis is their concern to defend the Christian practice of celibacy against the counter arguments of Muslims, who describe it alternatively as a practical impossibility, or as an affront to God. One may think that in the Islamic view, the practice of lifelong sexual abstinence is an instance in the sphere of Christian morality of that 'excessiveness' (*ghuluwun*) in religion (*dīn*) on the part of the 'People of the Book', of which the Qur'ān speaks more directly in its criticisms of Christian doctrine (e.g., IV *an-Nisā* 171 & V *al-Mā'idah* 77). Alternatively, in this context one may also think of celibacy as that aspect of Christian monasticism (*rahbāni'ah*), which the Qur'ān criticizes in God's name as being something which "they invented, for We did not prescribe it for them, seeking thereby to please God, they did not observe it properly." (LVII *al-Ḥadīd* 27)[82] On either view, the proper governance of the human sexual appetite emerges as one of the moral issues, alongside the more familiar doctrinal issues, that divide Christians and Muslims, albeit that historically the doctrinal questions have received more attention from both Christian and Muslim commentators.

In the heady days of the so-called era of 'Islamic humanism', when philosophy and the life of reason held the attention of many Christian and Muslim intellectuals in the milieu of Baghdad in Buyid times,[83] it is clear that scholars of both communities engaged in an on-going debate about the degree of sexual renunciation that was appropriate for those seriously interested in pursuing the philosophical life. Alternatively, in this same era, the times of Abū l-Qāsim Muḥammad al-Junayd (d. 910), Ḥusayn ibn Manṣūr al-Ḥallāj (d. 922), Abū Naṣr aṭ-Ṭūsī as-Sarrāj (d. 988) and Abū 'Abdu r-Raḥmān as-Sulamī (d. 1021), when Sufism was coming into its classical expression in many Islamic communities,[84] the role of marriage in the ascetic life was an important consideration. One may think of Yaḥyā ibn 'Adī's 'Colloquy on Sexual Abstinence' as presenting the Christian view of celibacy as an appropriate spiritual exercise for philosophers, while Elias of Nisibis' *Risālah* 'On Continence' makes the case for lifelong sexual abstinence more pointedly, and in greater physiological and psychological detail, as a preferable way of life for ascetics.

Among Muslim philosophers, there was some controversy over the requisite degree of the suppression of the natural desires that could be considered consistent with the determination to acquire knowledge and to practice virtue. One finds this

82 On these matters see Jane Dammen McAuliffe, Qur'ānic Christians: An Analysis of Classical and Modern Exegesis, Cambridge 1991.

83 See Joel Kraemer, Humanism in the Renaissance of Islam: The Cultural Revival during the Buyid Age (Leiden 1986); Lenn Evan Goodman, Islamic Humanism, Oxford 2003.

84 See Louis Massignon, La Passion de Husayn ibn Mansur Hallaj: martyr mystique de l'Islam, execute à bagdad le 26 mars 922: etude d'histoire religieuse, 4 vols., nouvelle éd., Paris 1975; English trans. Herbert Mason; Princeton/NJ 1982; Annemarie Schimmel, Mystical Dimensions of Islam, Chapel Hill/NC 1975.

discussion most readily in Abū Bakr ar-Rāzī's *Kitāb as-Sīrah al-Falsafīyah.* Here ar-Rāzī defends himself against a charge leveled against him by his adversaries to the effect that his lifestyle was not characterized by a sufficient degree of asceticism and the requisite suppression of the appetitive and irascible desires necessary to qualify him as a true philosopher. His response to his critics evokes the figure of Socrates, to whose example he appeals, making a distinction between two different phases of Socrates' life. In the first phase, according to ar-Rāzī, Socrates practiced an unreasonable degree of renunciation; foregoing gratifications which, again according to ar-Rāzī, when indulged in moderation would actually aid the acquisition of knowledge and the practice of justice. In the second phase of his life ar-Rāzī says that Socrates in fact renounced the extremes to which he had earlier been prone in his spiritual exercises and he lived more moderately. So ar-Rāzī says that he emulated the Socrates of the second phase of his life, disagreeing not with the manner of Socrates' self-discipline, but with the degree to which he practiced it in the first phase of his life, going so far then as completely to renounce having any progeny, ever fighting enemies and never attending entertainments. Ar-Rāzī went on to identify Hindus and Manichaeans as groups who in his opinion regularly espouse unreasonable and reprehensible ascetical practices. And in this connection he comes to the Christians. He says,

> What comes under this same heading, albeit far down the list, is what the Christians practice: living the monastic life and withdrawing into hermitages. Many Muslims too adopt the practice of staying in mosques, renouncing property, restricting themselves to a small amount of food, and then the mostdistasteful of it, to chafing clothing, and then to the coarsest of it. All of this on their part is an outrage against themselves; it causes them pain, while weightier pain than it is not dispelled by means of it. Socrates pursued a way of life like this in the first phase of his lifetime, but he abandoned it in the second phase of his life, as we mentioned earlier.[85]

On the face of it, ar-Rāzī's ideas would seem to be the very ones against which Yaḥyā ibn 'Adī argued so strenuously in his 'Colloquy on Sexual Abstinence." Similarly, as we have seen, Metropolitan Elias also developed his ideas on sexual continence first of all in response to another prominent Muslim thinker, Abū 'Uthmān al-Jāḥiẓ, who had questioned the very possibility of lifelong abstinence. And the Metropolitan also took issue with ar-Rāzī on the issue of the appropriate measure of sexual continence for a philosopher. But Elias, albeit that he, like ar-Rāzī, mentions Socrates and echoes other concerns of the philosophers, he seems, like Yaḥyā, more readily to evoke the monastic way of life prized among the Christians and to contrast it, in the matter of celibacy, with the sexual ethos of the Islamic milieu in which he and his brother lived, and with the ascetic practices of the Muslim Sufis.

85 Paul Kraus, Raziana I, in: Or. 4 (1935), 316 (300–334).

Finally, after reading the works of both Yaḥyā ibn 'Adī and Metropolitan Elias of Nisibis on continence, it seems fair to say that both writers commend this virtue, and in particular its practice within a commitment to lifelong celibacy, as a human value, fully in accord with reason and the good of the human family. This is an aspect of the matter that comes to light especially in passages in which the good of procreation is discussed, and God's will for the continuation of the human species. It is noteworthy that this is also the context in which the eminent Muslim theologian and Sufi thinker, Abū Ḥāmid Muḥammad al-Ghazālī (1058–1111), in his magisterial *Iḥyā 'ulūm ad-dīn*,[86] written at least a generation after the time Elias, discussed the same issues, including the advantages and disadvantages of marriage, and the decision for and against celibacy. One modern commentator has given it as his opinion that, "One gets the impression from reading Ghazzālī that he really would have preferred to make a stronger case for celibacy than he was able," and he goes on to say that elsewhere in the *Iḥyā*, al-Ghazālī "is quite insistent that the Sufi *murīd* (novice) avoid marrying at the beginning of his career because enjoying his wife will distract him from God." The commentator concludes his remarks on Ghazālī with the observation, "We can see that the question of celibacy versus marriage remained a live issue in Islam, but that the impetus to marry was always dominant." [87]

Notwithstanding the seemingly sympathetic views of al-Ghazālī a generation and more after their time, the Christian writers whose treatises we have been reading, were pressed by Muslim scholars of their own time and earlier to defend the distinctively Christian views of sexual continence. We have seen that they chose to do so largely on pragmatic and philosophical grounds, in view of their ideal of the 'perfect man' (*al-insān al-kāmil*), a category that allowed them to appeal to the interest among contemporary Muslim philosophers and Sufis in that same ideal. Yaḥyā ibn 'Adī, with his talk in *The Reformation of Morals* of scholars, monks and ascetics, churches and mosques, seemed even to hope that in the Islamochristian milieu of his time, philosophers in the several confessional communities could successfully commend a measure of mutual esteem even between the upholders of religious convictions that are inherently critical of one another. He says,

> Men are a single tribe (*qabīl*), related to one another; humanity (*al-insānīyah*) unites them. The adornment of the divine power is in all of them and in each one of them, and it is the rational soul. … Since their souls are one, and love is only in the soul, all of them must then show affection for one another and love one another.[88]

In the end, in the Islamochristian milieu of the tenth and eleventh centuries in Buyid times, it was not just some philosophic 'humanism' in the modern sense of the term that in Yaḥyā's view Christians and Muslims should share, but *al-insānīyah*, 'hu-

86 Abū Ḥāmid al-Ghazālī, Iḥyā 'ulūm ad-dīn, 4 vols., Cairo 1352/1933, Vol. II, 22 ff.
87 Bellamy, ibid. 33–34.
88 Yaḥyā ibn 'Adī, ibid.106, §5.14–15.

mane behavior', based on their views of the 'perfect man', a concept with both philosophical and mystical dimensions, having to do ultimately with fulfilling the will of the one Creator God for the human family.

Some Prominent Themes in the Writings of the Syriac Mystics of the 7th/8th Century AD (1st/2nd cent. H)

Sebastian Brock

The present contribution is primarily concerned with the writings of the monastic authors of the Church of the East writing in Syriac during the 7th and 8th centuries AD (1st–2nd cent. H), for the most part in what is today Iraq and western Iran; the main authors thus covered are (in approximate chronological order) Sahdona, Isaac of Nineveh, Dadisho', Shem'on d-Taybuteh, and John of Dalyatha. In the background, but rarely, if at all, cited below, are a number of earlier writers who were used by them; these fall into two categories: (1) Greek authors available in Syriac translation, notably Evagrius and the Macarian Homilies, both of the fourth century, the Egyptian monastic literature, of the fifth century, and the Dionysian Corpus of the early sixth century; and (2) Syriac authors, in particular Aphrahat and Ephrem of the fourth century, and especially John the Solitary of the first third of the fifth century. Furthermore, in order to avoid the discussion becoming too diffuse or general in nature, three specific topics have been selected: light, love, and humility; before turning to these, however, a little needs to be said about the tradition of "the interior person" in Syriac writers.

The Inner Person

The phrase ὁ ἐντὸς ἄνθρωπος, "the interior person", already occurs in Plato,[1] but more important for the Greek Christian tradition was Philo's use of a related phrase, ὁ ἀληθινὸς ἄνθρωπος, "the true person", and (above all) Paul's ὁ ἔσω ἄνθρωπος, "the inner person" (Rom 7:22, II Cor 4:16, Eph 3:16). The theme of "the interior person" was taken up among Greek writers especially by Origen in the early third century, and by the Syriac writers, Aphrahat and Ephrem, in the fourth century, and especially John the Solitary in the early fifth.[2] These authors developed the imagery

1 Plato, Republic 9, 588f.

2 The form found in the Peshitta New Testament (Rom 7:22, and Eph 3:16; cf. II Cor 4:16), is *barnasha dal-gaw,* lit. "the person who (is) within", but the adjectival *gawwaya* is also frequently found from Aphrahat (Homilies 4,10,13; 6,1) onwards. John of Apameia employs several further phrases, in particular *barnasha kasya*, "the hidden person" (John of Apameia [Johan-

of a set of "interior limbs", existing in parallel with the exterior ones; thus phraseology involving the "eyes", "ears" etc. of the "heart", the "soul", and the "mind" came to be developed, with the "heart" acting as the focal point of the interior person.[3] Here it is important to recall that in the biblical understanding the heart is the seat of the intellect as well as of the emotions; in other words, there is no distinction (as there is in modern English usage, going back to Bernard of Clairvaux in the Middle Ages) between "the heart" and "the head".[4] Thus in our texts the terms "heart“, "soul", "mind", "intellect", are often interchangeable, though in general one can say that authors using the term "heart" are more biblically oriented, while those employing "mind" or "intellect" are writing more in the Greek philosophical tradition.

Light

Ephrem already develops the analogy between the physical eyes and sight and the interior, or spiritual eyes and what they can see:[5] according to his understanding of optics, the physical eye is enabled to see by means of the presence in it of light, and so, by analogy, the interior, or spiritual eye of the heart/mind is enabled to see by means of the presence in it of faith. The analogy is developed by John of Dalyatha in the following way:

---

nes von Lykopolis]. Ein Dialog über die Seele und die Affekte des Menschen, ed. by. Sven Dedering, Arbeten utgivna med understöd av Vilhelm Ekmans Universitetsfond 43, Uppsala, 1936, 60.63.84–86 [The attribution to John of Lykopolis is incorrect].), based on I Pet 3:4, which is taken up later by both Isaac (Kephalaia I.77. Isaac of Nineveh [Isaac the Syrian]. "The second Part". Chapters IV–XLI, ed. and trans. by Sebastian Brock, CSCO.S 224–225, Louvain 1995 and Œuvres spirituelles II. 41 discours récemment découverts, trans. by André Louf, SpOr.Série Monachisme primitif 81, Bégrolles-en-Mauges 2003) and John of Dalyatha (John of Apameia, Ein Dialog, 12,3.10. Les Homélies I-XV, trans. by Nadira Khayyat, Sources Syriaques 2, Antélias 2007); and *barnasha ruḥana* "the spiritual person" (Hom. 14.20.65). Both these are equivalents of the later term, *b. metyad'ana* "the noetic person", based on Greek νοερός, which is first found in the sixth century.

3 See further, Sebastian Brock, The interior limbs, in: St Isaac of Nineveh and some other Syriac writers, The Memorial Volume for Robert Beulay, Antélias forthcoming.

4 Sahdona, Livre de la perfection. 1e partie, ed. and trans. by André de Halleux, in: Œuvres spirituelles 1, ed. by André de Halleux, CSCO.S 86–87, Louvain 1960. Livre de la perfection. 2me partie (Ch. 1–7), ed. and trans. by André de Halleux, in: Œuvres spirituelles 2, ed. by André de Halleux, CSCO.S 90–91, Louvain 1961. Livre de la perfection. 2me partie (Ch. 8-14), ed. and trans. by André de Halleux, in: Œuvres spirituelles 3, ed. by André de Halleux, CSCO.S 110–111, Louvain 1965. Lettres à des amies solitaires. Maximes sapientales, ed. and trans. by André de Halleux, in: Œuvres spirituelles 4, ed. by André de Halleux, CSCO.S 112–113, Louvain 1965. In Œuvres spirituelles 3,138, Sahdona speaks of the heart as "the sovereign of the thoughts".

5 For Ephrem, see Sebastian Brock, The Luminous Eye. The Spiritual World Vision of St Ephrem, Placid Lectures 1984, Rome 1985, rev. Reprint: Kalamazoo/MI 1992.

> "We cannot see each other's face without the intermediary of external created light. In the same way it is not possible for us to see what is hidden in our souls [lit. the hiddenness of our souls] and rejoice over the mysteries in them without the intermediary of the Creator's creative light"[6] (Letter 9,1)[7].

Elsewhere he explains that this spiritual vision is only possible "through the intermediary of the holy and divine light" (Hom. 6,3).

John of Dalyatha also uses the striking image of a baby emerging from the darkness of the womb into "the light of the world of Adam" (that is, of human beings), and both comparing and contrasting this with "when the children of God go out from the gloomy womb of repentance, [then] the glorious light of the New World [begins to] shine out on their countenance" (Letter 43,2).

"Repentance" (*tyabuta*, lit. "turning") is an important feature here: according to the standard understanding of Genesis 1–3, humanity ("Adam and Eve") were created in an unblemished state, possessing a "natural beauty"[8]. This "beauty", however, was lost at the Fall which is understood in the Syriac tradition primarily as an act of disobedience and misuse of the gift of free will. Thus according to this understanding, in its original state the soul possessed its own "natural beauty", in other words, the divine "image" in which human beings are created (Gen 1:26–7). Consequently the whole aim of the spiritual path is to try to return to this primordial state and to restore the lost, or sullied, "image"; for this process what is required is constant "repentance", or "turning/returning". Once something of the soul's "natural beauty" has been achieved, then it will begin to become aware of "divine light" shining out within itself.

In order to illustrate how this process works, many Syriac writers use the imagery of the interior mirror.[9] Here one needs to recall that mirrors in antiquity were of course not made of glass, but of metal, and in order to function properly they

---

6 Since both the adjectives with "light" can be taken in two different ways and it is likely that the author intended a *double entendre*, I have given a double translation of both: *nuhra barya/ barraya*, "created/external", while *nuhra baroya* can be either "the Creator's light" or "creative light".

7 La collection des lettres de Jean de Dalyatha, trans. by Robert Beulay, Patrologia Orientalis 39.3, Turnhout 1978 and The Letters of John of Dalyatha, ed. by Mary T. Hansbury, Texts from Christian Late Antiquity 2, Piscataway/NJ 2006.

8 Isaac of Nineveh (Kephalaia I.37) probably derives the phrase "beauty of soul" from Evagrius (Kephalaia, Suppl. 50), though its "natural beauty" is already a theme in Jacob of Serugh (Homiliae selectae Mar-Jacobi Sarugensis, ed. by Paul Bedjan, Homiliae selectae 1, Paris 1905, 282.287; for the East Syriac monastic writers, cf. Commentaire du livre d'abba Isaïe (logoi I-XV). Par Dadisho Qatraya (VIIe s.), ed. by René Draguet, CSCO.S 144–145, Louvain 1972, IX.5.

9 For further details on the use of this imagery, see, Sebastian Brock, The imagery of the spiritual mirror in Syriac literature, in: Journal of the Canadian Society for Syriac Studies 5 (2005), 3–17. Ephrem already makes considerable use of it; see Edmund Beck, Das Bild vom Spiegel bei Ephrem, in: OrChrP 19 (1953), 5–24, and Tanios Bou Mansour, La pensée symbolique de Saint Ephrem le Syrien, Bibliothèque de l'Université Saint-Esprit de Kaslik 16, Kaslik 1988, 61–71.

needed to be kept continuously in a high state of polish. This interior mirror, of "mirror of the self" as John of Dalyatha calls it (Letter 51,13), requires constant polishing, achieved through continuous repentance, or "turning" to God, along with the continuous "recollection of God". Thus John of Dalyatha writes:

> "The [human] mind, which seeks for God in itself, itself becomes a mirror in which God is seen by it" (Letter 50,19).

And earlier in the same Letter:

> "Gaze within yourself on God, [and see] how 'God is light' [I John 1:5]: by nature He is glorious light, many-rayed, and He manifests the light of His nature to those who love Him" (Letter 50,5).

The process envisaged here could be described as a succession of different stages:

(1) Humanity is created in the "image of God" (Gen 1:26–7). At this stage the image functions like a fully polished mirror, and so it fully reflects the divine light.

(2) At the Fall (the transgression of God's "tiny commandment", as Ephrem put it), involving the misuse of the gift of free will, the image/mirror no longer functions properly, being overlaid with rust and grime. This is seen as representing our present state, and the starting point for the following stage.

(3) The essential aim of the spiritual life should be the recovery of the lost or marred "image", a process for which constant "returning" to God and "recollection" of God is required, in cooperation with the assistance of divine grace; or, using the imagery of the mirror, the rusted mirror needs to be brought back into a state of high polish, so that more and more it reflects the divine light that falls upon it: in the course of the polishing the mirror becomes progressively more capable of reflecting the divine image in which the mirror was originally created. The process can equally be described as one whereby the soul's "natural beauty" (or "natural light", as John of Dalyatha describes it in Letter 50,5) is recovered. Since that natural beauty is a reflection of the divine beauty, the process is equally a theophanic one, revealing something of God.

Because, however, this "divine light" is so dazzling, it is also paradoxically described as "the dark cloud of (divine) light",[10] using imagery which goes back to Gregory of Nyssa on the experience of Moses on Sinai; in Syriac writers this is especially common in the Letters and Homilies of John of Dalyatha. John indeed goes so far on one occasion as to address God in a prayer as "O Dark Light" (Letter 46,3).

(4) The final stage comes when at least the internal mirror is fully polished, a stage which is only very rarely, and then only momentarily, reached in this life (as

10 The phrase *'arpella d-nuhra* already occurs in Sahdona (Livre, 2me partie (Ch. 1-7), de Halleux, 43 and Lettres, de Halleux, 83) before being taken up by John of Dalyatha, who quite frequently uses it: Letters 36,5; 47,6; Hom. 6,3.21; 11,1; 15,2.

several authors stress). Here it will be best to let John of Dalyatha speak for himself, describing what happens when "the stage of perfection" is reached:

> "When that person has approached prayer, he will see the brilliance of his own self, and the soul's natural beauty will shine out over it, and the soul will see itself as it [really] is, and it will see the Divine Light shining out in it and transforming the soul into the likeness of that Light. The likeness of its own nature is raised up before its sight, and it sees itself in the likeness of God, in that it is united with the formless Light, which is the Light of the Trinity which shines out in itself" (Hom. 6,15).

Love

That such an exalted stage should be made even a possibility for human beings is due to the overflowing nature of divine love. At one point John of Dalyatha exclaims:

> "Blessed is the soul which recognizes itself to be a mirror on which it can fix its eyes and see the radiance of Him who is hidden from all. [...] How great is Your love, O God, seeing that those who have tasted of the immensity of its sweetness have become disgusted by every (other) delight" (Letter 7,3).

Although John's writings display an astonishing fervour, it is two other Syriac authors, Sahdona and Isaac, who speak more specifically on the subject of love. Sahdona in fact speaks of "the light of the love of God" on a couple of occasions.

What, then, is divine love, and how does it compare with human love? Isaac stresses the contrast between it and human love:

> "Love which stems from creation is like a small lamp whose light is sustained by being fed with oil. Again, it is like a wadi fed by rainfall: once the supply that feeds it fails, the surge of its flow abates. By contrast, love whose cause is God, is like a spring welling up from the depths: its flow never abates, for God alone is that spring of love whose supply never fails" (Hom. 53[11]).

Elsewhere Isaac emphasizes that love is the basis for *all* God's actions:

> "In love did He bring the world into existence; in love does He guide it during this its existence in time; in love is He going to bring it to that wondrous transformed state, and in love will the world be swallowed up in the great

11 Mar Isaacus Ninivita de perfectione religiosa, ed. by Paul Bedjan, Paris and Leipzig 1909, 382 and Mystic treatises by Isaac of Nineveh, trans. by Arent J. Wensinck, VNAW 23, Amsterdam 1923, Reprint Wiesbaden 1969, 256.

> mystery of Him who has performed all these things; in love will the whole course of the governance of creation be finally comprised."[12]

Once it has been discovered, this divine love has a transformative effect, as Isaac explains:

> "When we have found [divine] love, we eat the heavenly Bread and we are sustained without labour and without weariness. [...] This is the love from which the debauched have drunk – and they became sober, from which sinners have drunk and they forgot their ways of offence," (etc.) (Hom. 43)[13].

The aim for human beings should be to reciprocate this love of God, or, using the mirror imagery, to reflect it. Thus Isaac explains:

> "The purpose of prayer is for us to acquire the love of God, for in prayer there can be discovered all sorts of reasons for loving God. [...] Love proceeds from conversing with Him" (Hom. 63)[14].

The love of God cannot, however, be acquired simply by human effort, for it is a gift, for which one needs to ask:

> "Anyone who wishes to attain to a taste of our Lord's love should *ask* Him that this door be opened."[15]

In all these monastic authors there is the underlying theme of the constant need for cooperation between the human and the divine: God is understood as providing the initial opportunity, but the individual human being needs to respond at each stage, so that the progress of the spiritual life can be seen as taking the form of a spiral that proceeds upwards with every positive response on the part of the individual.

The effects for the person who truly reflects the divine love are dramatic. Three particular images tend to be used in the attempt to describe this.

(1) In two verses in the Song of Songs (2:5 and 5:8) the "Beloved" is said to be "*wounded* by love", and this phrase is frequently used by the Syriac writers in this context. The translation "wounded" is in fact the rendering of the Septuagint, whereas the Peshitta has "sick with love"; the phraseology of the Septuagint, however, will have become familiar to the East Syriac monastic authors through the Syriac translation of Gregory of Nyssa's Commentary on the Song of Songs, which dates from c. AD 500.

(2) The imagery of inebriation is also rather frequently found, making use of the paradoxical theme of "sober drunkenness".[16] This was taken over by Greek writers

12 Isaac, Brock, ch. 38,2.

13 Isaacus, Bedjan, 317 and Treatises, Wensinck, 211f.

14 Isaacus, Bedjan, 439 and Treatises, Wensinck, 294f.

15 Isaac, Brock, ch. 35,5.

16 For this theme in Syriac, see further: Sebastian Brock, Sobria Ebrietas according to some Syriac texts, in: ARAM Periodical 17 (2005), 185–191.

such as Origen and Gregory of Nyssa from Philo, but it also features at an early date in Syriac tradition, as testified by the Odes of Solomon, which perhaps belong to the second century:

> "I drank [from the fountain of the Lord] and I became drunk with the living immortal water – but my drunkenness was not that of ignorance" (Odes of Solomon 11:6–8).

Imagery of this sort is especially frequent in the East Syriac monastic writings. Thus, for example, Isaac says in one of the homilies in the recently recovered "Third Part" of his works:

> "In the case of those who are inebriated with wine, their mind forgets all about the harm being done to their souls. Whereas let *us* become inebriated with the love of God, and in our inebriated state we will forget the things below, here on earth, that are subject to corruption."[17]

For Sahdona, this divine love is the motivating force behind, and an essential part of, the ascetic life. In the following passage he combines the imagery of "sober drunkenness" with that taken from the Song of Songs:

> "Those who love God and are wounded by desire for him are like people who are inebriated" (On Perfection, I.ch.III, v.148–150)[18].

(3) The third prominent way of describing divine love is to employ bridal imagery. The theme of Christ as the Bridegroom and the Church, or the individual soul, as the Bride is remarkably common in Syriac writers, and one of the most frequent terms for the Kingdom of Heaven in the liturgical texts of all the Syriac Churches is "the heavenly Bridal chamber"[19]. Perhaps surprisingly, it is the sparse New Testament allusions that serve as the source of this imagery for early Syriac writers, and not the Song of Songs, the influence of whose language was not felt to any extent before the sixth century.

A short passage from Sahdona will serve as an example of this imagery:

> The monk "who has separated himself from the world, or rather, died to the world, [...] has betrothed his soul to Christ, the heavenly Bridegroom" (Letter 4,26)[20].

In passing it is worth noticing that Isaac seems to be deliberate in his avoidance of bridal imagery, despite the frequency of passages where he describes the effect of

17 Discorsi ascetici. Terza collezione, trans. by Sabino Chialà, Magnano 2004, ch. 6,56.

18 Livre. 1e partie, de Halleux, 70f.

19 The origin of this usage seems to be a variant reading in the Parable of the Wise and Foolish Virgins (Mt 25:1–10); see further, Sebastian Brock, The Bridal Chamber of Light: a distinctive feature in the Syriac liturgical tradition, The Harp 18 (2005), 179–191.

20 Lettres, de Halleux, 29.

divine love. Instead, he makes use of another important image connected with the theme of love, namely, that of "fire".

On several occasions Isaac points out that one of the consequences of the acquisition of divine love, is with regard to other human beings:

> "the person whose interior mirror effectively reflects God's love will thereby also reflect God's love for all human beings [indeed, all creation]: Out of the love of God you will arrive at perfect love of [your fellow] human beings."[21] And once someone has arrived at the love of God, "with this love of God he will draw close to perfect love of fellow human beings."[22]

As Isaac goes on to point out, this includes sinners:

> "In the case of someone who has been held worthy to taste divine love, that person customarily forgets everything else by reason of its sweetness. [...] Such a person's soul gladly draws near to a luminous love of humanity, not distinguishing between [good and bad] people, for he is never overcome by the weaknesses to be found in people, nor is he ever upset."[23]

Likewise Sahdona exhorts:

> "Let us be abundant in our love towards everyone – towards both the good *and* the bad, towards both the upright *and* the wicked – in imitation of God, who causes the sun of His kindness to shine on both the good and the bad; who causes the rain of His grace to descend on both the upright *and* the wicked [cf. Mt 5:45]. [...] Let us manifest our love overflowingly on those who love us *and* on those who despise us, so that we hold in honour the 'image of God' [hidden in everyone], embracing both righteous *and* sinners, seeing that they are all created in the image of God" (On Perfection, II.4.51)[24].

Or, as Isaac puts it succinctly, "Love sinners but reject their works" (Hom. 5)[25]. Isaac's contemporary Simeon the Graceful says much the same thing, introducing the images of light and the mirror:

> "We have learnt from experience that, when [divine] grace visits us, the light of the love of our fellow human beings which is shed on the mirror of our heart is such that we do not see in the world any as sinners or evil people."[26]

---

21 Isaac, Brock, ch. 10,29.

22 Ibid., ch. 10,33.

23 Ibid., ch. 10,36.

24 Livre 2[me] partie (Ch. 1-7), de Halleux, 49.

25 Isaacus, Bedjan, 79 and Treatises, Wensinck, 54.

26 Early Christian Mystics, ed. and trans. by Alphonse Mingana, Woodbrooke Studies 7, Cambridge 1934, 35.298.

When the interior mirror of the heart/soul is so highly polished that it can reflect God's "equal love"[27] for everyone, good or bad, such a person sees everything and everyone from God's perspective, and no longer from a human perspective.

This divine love, while always profoundly compassionate, nevertheless remains, as it were, impassible, not subject to hurt or suffering caused to it by human wickedness. On the other hand, its "light" simply shows up all the evil and wrongdoing that hides in the darkness of sin. As Isaac points out, it is the realisation of having sinned against divine love that causes the true anguish and torment of Gehenna:

> "The pain which grips the heart as a result of sinning against love is even sharper than all the torments that exist. [...] The power of love works in two ways: it torments those who have sinned – just as happens among friends here on earth, but to those who have observed love's obligations, love gives delight. So it is with Gehenna: the contrition that comes from love is the harsh torment; but in the case of the children of heaven, delight in this love inebriates their souls" (Hom. 27)[28].

Humility

A further consequence of attaining to the stage of reflecting divine love is the acquisition of a profound humility: "Wherever the sign of love [...] is present, there is a profound humility which rises up from the inner mind" (Hom. 5)[29]. Sahdona says very much the same thing when he states that "repentance is the child of love"[30], and (in turn) "repentance is the mother of humility"[31].

According to Isaac, humility of heart can come from two very different situations: (1) a realisation of one's own sin, and (2) the recollection of the majesty of God and of the immensity of his love.[32] It will be the latter which produces what he terms "true", or "perfect", or "profound humility". Elsewhere Isaac asks, "What is perfection?", and the answer he gives is "profound humility" (Hom. 74)[33].

Isaac devotes the final discourse (Hom. 82) of the First Part of his writings to the subject of "true humility". In this panegyric – for such it is – of true humility the starting point is provided by the model given by God himself. Thus Isaac begins his discourse:

> "I wish to open my mouth, my brethren, and speak about the exalted subject of humility. I am full of fear, being someone who is aware that he is going to

27 Thus Isaac, Brock, ch. 38:5.
28 Isaacus, Bedjan, 201 and Treatises, Wensinck, 136.
29 Isaacus, Bedjan, 80 and Treatises, Wensinck, 55.
30 Livre 2me partie (Ch. 8–14), de Halleux, 29.
31 Ibid., 46.
32 Isaac, Brock, ch. 18,6.
33 Isaacus, Bedjan, 507 and Treatises, Wensinck, 341.

> speak about God in the course of his words. For [humility] is the garment of the Divinity, seeing that the Word who became human, put it on and spoke with us in this [garment], by means of our body. And everyone who is truly clothed in this [humility] is an imitator of Him who descended from on high, covering up the radiance of His majesty" (Hom. 82)[34].

John of Dalyatha, who likewise devotes a whole discourse to the topic of humility, similarly speaks of humility as the "garment" of the divinity (Letter on Humility, 3).

Thus, for Isaac, God himself has provided human beings with the model for profound humility by his condescension (in the good sense of that word), stooping down, as it were, to speak to humanity on its own level. This sort of humility is totally different from what is normally thought of as humility.

"A person who is perfect in humility is someone who does not need to find a reason to make his mind humble, [...] [for] he possesses humility as something natural" (Hom. 82)[35]. In the case of such a person, it is a matter of *being*, rather than of doing; and this, ultimately is the result of a divine gift, made possible thanks to that person's openness to the divine Spirit. The model of the cooperation, or to use the Greek term, *synergeia*, that is required on the part of human beings is indicated by Isaac when he states that "God is compassionate and eager to give – but He desires that we give him the opportunity" (Hom. 24)[36].

One of the paradoxical features accompanying this "profound humility" is that a person sees everyone else – including the worst sinners – as better than himself. Thus Dadisho' says that such a person "considers himself inferior to everyone, and more sinful than everyone – even adulterers, plunderers and murderers. Such humility is a gift that comes after ascetic labours."[37]

Evidently what is understood here is that such a person as it were underpins all others, including even murderers, by taking upon himself the sins of others as an expression of his sharing in what Isaac calls "the stink of Adam".[38]

Conclusion

In this paper I have attempted to show briefly how, in the thought of some of the great East Syriac monastic writers, the three themes of light, love, and humility are closely interlinked, even though on the surface they might not seem to be. The key linking element between light and love is the image of the interior mirror within

34 Isaacus, Bedjan, 574 and Treatises, Wensinck, 384.

35 Isaacus, Bedjan, 579 and Treatises, Wensinck, 387.

36 Isaacus, Bedjan, 181 and Treatises, Wensinck, 132.

37 Commentaire, Draguet, 47.

38 The underlying idea would seem to be connected with the theme of the saint who acts as a "pledge" for someone else, an example of which is to be found in the History of Eulogios the Stonecutter, which forms part of the cycle of narratives surrounding Abba Daniel of Sketis.

each human person, which properly ought to reflect the image of God in which every individual is created according to Gen 1:26–27. This the interior mirror can only do, if it is properly polished – and then, the more highly polished it is, the better will it effectively reflect the light of God's love. Since this divine love is all–embracing, the person who reflects it will come to perceive *all* creation, and thus including all human beings, both good and bad, from the perspective of God, and no longer from an ordinary human perspective. Such a person, awed at the immensity of the divine love, then reflects and imitates that divine love, which has come down to the human level, by responding with its own profound humility, thus underpinning, as it were, the rest of humanity.

The East Syrian Monk Simon the Persecuted and his Book of Chapters

Gerrit J. Reinink

In the thirteenth century, probably somewhere in its two last decades, a monk named George Washnaya was wandering around in Northern Iraq, visiting East Syrian communities and monasteries. In these travels he propagated a new and stunning message: everything is God by nature; there are no angels, souls and demons, neither is there Jesus Christ, nor a resurrection for the bodies; further, there is no sin for the sinners, and the Christian sacraments of baptism and eucharist are of no use.[1]

One of the monasteries visited by George was the monastery of 'Abdisho' of Kum, in the neighbourhood of the town of Amadia in Northern Iraq. The abbot of this monastery, Isho', was anything but taken with George's ideas, and without delay he threw the heretic out of his monastery. However, one of Isho''s monks, Simon called 'the Persecuted' (*rdīpā*), judged that these physical measures taken against George were not sufficient, and he determined that the man should also be eliminated intellectually. Simon decided to write a work against George under the title *On the Union*, after the example of the homonymous standard work of East Syrian Christology, written by Babai the Great some seven centuries earlier.[2]

Simon's *On the Union*, which is still unpublished, is an interesting witness of the cultural, religious and intellectual climate in thirteenth-century Northern Iraq, in particular in connection with the revival of radical Evagrian ideas; it seems that the latter not only attracted Syrian Orthodox monks but even some members of the Church of the East.[3] But Simon's work is also important for another reason. It offers

1 These words present Simon the Persecuted's summary of George's views in his work On the Union (see below note 2). For a discussion of the background, origin and possible source of George's ideas, see Gerrit J. Reinink, "Origenism" in Thirteenth-Century Northern Iraq, in: Gerrit J. Reinink and Alexander C. Klugkist (eds.), After Bardaisan. Studies on Continuity and Change in Honour of Professor Han J. W. Drijvers, OLA 89, Leuven 1999, 237–252.

2 Reinink, Origenism, 238. This information is provided by Simon's introduction, which is preserved in the manuscript Cambr. Or. 1317. In the other manuscript of On the Union accessible to me, Mingana Syr. 544, the introduction is not preserved owing to the loss of several folios. For the influence of Babai's On the Union on Simon's work, see ibid, 242.245–246.

3 For the role of the Maphrian Gregory bar Hebraeus (1264–1286) in the finding of a copy of the Book of the Holy Hierotheos together with its commentary composed by Theodosius, the Patriarch of Antioch (887–896), for the benefit of a monk of the monastery of Mattai near Mosul, and for Gregory's own commentary on the Book of the Holy Hierotheos, see now Karl Pinggéra, All-Erlösung und All-Einheit. Studien zum „Buch des heiligen Hierotheos" und seiner Rezeption in der syrisch-orthodoxen Theologie, Sprachen und Kulturen des christlichen Orients

an interesting example of the medieval 'Nachleben' of Babai's heritage, involving reworking and adaptation, and the enrichment of its ideas with materials from other important sources.[4] Simon the Persecuted certainly deserves a more prominent place in any 'new Baumstark'.[5]

This upwards revaluation would be all the more justified, if we may assume that Simon was the author of another sizeable work, one that is a typical representative of monastic literature and mysticism. In the paragraph on Simon d-Taybuteh, an East Syrian monastic writer from the end of the seventh century, Anton Baumstark mentions a work 'asketischen Inhaltes in 7 BB [books] zu je 100 Sentenzen', which was composed by Simon, one of the 'sons' of Rabban Isho'.[6] Baumstark's source of information here was Addai Scher's description of the manuscript *Mosul 97*.[7] Although Baumstark had his doubts about Scher's identification of this Simon with Simon d-Taybutheh,[8] he accepted Scher's opinion that Simon's tutor Rabban Isho' must be identified with Isho', who, according to the *Book of Chastity* of Isho'dnah of Basra[9], was a pupil of Aphnimaran, who lived in the seventh century.[10] For that reason, Baumstark situated Simon, the author of the book of the sayings in *Mosul 97*, also in the seventh century.[11]

As we shall see, the Simon who was one of the sons of Rabban Isho', is, in fact, none other than Simon the Persecuted, the author of the work *On the Union*, and

10, Wiesbaden 2002, 169–177. In the article mentioned in note 1 (above) I suggested that George Washnaya's views were derived from the Book of Hierotheos rather than from George's reading Evagrius's works directly and independently (251).

4 See Gerrit J. Reinink, The Quotations from the Lost Works of Theodoret of Cyrus and Theodore of Mopsuestia in an Unpublished East Syrian Work on Christology, in: E. A. Livingstone (ed.), StPatr XXXIII, Leuven 1997, 562–567; idem, A New Fragment of Theodore of Mopsuestia's Contra Magos, Muséon 110 (1997), 63–71; idem, The Book of Questions of Cyrus the Greek, in: René Lavenant (ed.), Symposium Syriacum VII, OrChrA 256, Rome 1998, 453–461.

5 Anton Baumstark, Geschichte der syrischen Literatur, Bonn 1922, 210: „Völlig dunkel bleibt vollends ein Š. ‚der Verfolgte', dessen Name ein erhaltenes Werk über die Inkarnation trägt."

6 Ibid.

7 Addai Scher, Notice sur les manuscrits syriaques conservés dans la bibliothèque Chaldéen de Mossoul, Revue des Bibliothèques 17 (1907), 252.

8 For this reason, it is strange that Baumstark, Geschichte, 210, note 4, mentions Cambridge Add. 2023 as a manuscript which contains a quotation or short abstract from the work in Mosul 97. The quotation in the Cambridge manuscript is indeed attributed to Simon called 'd-Taybutheh', whereas the work in Mosul 97 does not carry this identification. Possibly the quotation in Cambridge Add. 2023 indeed derives from a work of Simon d-Taybutheh; cf. W. Wright and S.A. Cook, A Catalogue of the Syriac Manuscripts Preserved in the Library of the University of Cambridge 2, Cambridge 1901, 611. For an introduction to Simon d-Taybutheh's spirituality, see Seely Beggiani, Introduction to Eastern Christian Spirituality. The Syriac Tradition, London-Toronto 1991, 82–89.

9 Cf. Jean Baptiste Chabot, Le livre de la chasteté composé pas Jésusdenah, évêque de Baçrah, Rome 1896, 38–49 (transl.), 58 (ed.).

10 Scher, Notice, 252, n. 1. For Aphnimaran, see Baumstark, Geschichte, 204; Jean Maurice Fiey, Assyrie chrétienne 2, Beirut 1965, 742–747.

11 Baumstark, Geschichte, 210.

Rabban Isho' is indeed the same person as Isho', the abbot of the monastery of 'Abdisho' near Amadia in Northern Iraq. Thus, Simon the Persecuted is reported to have also written a book of *Kephalaia* or sentences in the literary tradition of Evagrius Ponticus, Babai the Great and Isaac of Niniveh.[12]

The manuscript *Mosul 97* seems today to have disappeared without a trace.[13] According to Scher, the manuscript contained three texts: 1. The *Capita scientiae* of Simon (seven *mēmrē* each of them containing one hundred *Capita* – the first two *mēmrē* are missing in this manuscript); 2. an explication of these *Capita*, divided into five 'discours'; 3. a philosophical and theological book on God and His providence, consisting of two parts, with eight and eighteen chapters respectively. Scher considered Isaac of the monastery of Isho', who wrote a *Book of Chapters*, to be the author of this text, and he identified this Isaac with none other than Isaac of Niniveh.[14]

I do not know whether there exist other manuscripts containing the contents of *Mosul 97*. But, if not, we may consider ourselves fortunate that this work of Simon the Persecuted is today not wholly inaccessible. Excerpts from it, under the title of the *Book of Chapters*, have been preserved in the manuscript *Mingana Syr. 18*.[15] In what follows below, I investigate the following two questions with respect to the

12 For the Syriac translations of Evagrius's Kephalaia Gnostica, see A. Guillaumont, Les "Kephalaia Gnostica" d'Évagre le Pontique et l'histoire de l'Origénisme chez les Grecs et les Syriens, Patristica Sorbonensia 5, Paris 1962, 200–258; for Babai's Commentary on Evagrius's Kephalaia Gnostica, see Geevarghese Chediath, The Christology of Mar Babai the Great, Kottayam-Paderborn 1982, 32; W. Frankenberg, Euagrius Ponticus, AWGW.PH, N.F., Band XIII. 2, Berlin 1912; for the Kephalaia in Isaac's works, see Sebastian P. Brock, The Wisdom of St. Isaac of Nineveh, Texts from Christian Late Antiquity 1, Piscataway/NJ 2006, XII, 26–32; Paolo Bettiolo, Isacco di Ninive. Discorsi spirituali. Capitoli sulla conoscenza, Preghiere, Contemplazione sull'argomento della gehenna, Altri opusculi, Communità di Bose 1990 (Italian translation of the Kephalaia).

13 Cf. William F. Macomber, New Finds of Syriac Manuscripts in the Middle East, in: W. Voigt (ed.), XVII. Deutscher Orientalistentag von 21. bis 27. Juli 1968 in Würzburg. Vorträge, Teil 2, Sektion 4, ZDMG Suppl. I, Teil 2, Wiesbaden 1969, 475; Alain Desreumaux, Répertoire des bibliothèques et des catalogues de manuscrits syriaques, Paris 1991, 194.

14 Scher, Notice, 252: "Or ce livre est tiré du Ve volume d'Isaac de Ninive"; cf. Baumstark, Geschichte, 224. Isaac is not mentioned as the author of this part of the Mosul manuscript. Scher concluded from the correspondences between the third text and Isaac's Book of Chapters that Isaac was the author of this part of Mosul 97. The Book of Chapters composed by Isaac, 'monk of the monastery of Rabban Isho'', is preserved among others in the manuscript Notre-Dame des Semences 70; cf. Baumstark, Geschichte , 224, note 4; J. Vosté, Catalogue de la bibliothèque syro-chaldéenne du couvent de Notre-Dame des Semences près d'Alqoš (Iraq), Rome-Paris 1929, 29. Fiey, Assyrie chrétienne 2, 746, suggests that the Rabban Isho' mentioned in the title of the Book of Chapters in Notre-Dame des Semences 70 was the third abbot of the monastery of Mar Aphnimaran, who lived in the eighth century, and that the monk Isaac, author of this Book of Chapters (not to be identified with Isaac of Niniveh) was a contemporary of his. For other manuscripts of Isaac's Book of Chapters, discovered by Grigory Kessel, see below.

15 Described by A. Mingana in his Catalogue of the Mingana Collection of Manuscripts 1, Cambridge 1933, col. 53–56.

contents of this latter manuscript. In the first place, I attempt a better understanding of the literary structure and character of Simon's *Book of Chapters*. In the second place I discuss in particular the quotations in *Ming. Syr. 18* which were derived from the works of the exegete and theologian *par excellence* of the East Syrian tradition: Theodore of Mopsuestia. The role of Theodore in this manuscript has an additional significance, since it presents fresh materials from the lost works of Theodore.

Mingana Syr. 18 was written in 1883 by the well-known copyist Stephen Rais, in the monastery 'of the Virgin Mary' (i.e. *Notre-Dame des Semences / Our Lady of the Seeds*) in Alqosh.[16] In the preface, Stephen explains why he decided to transcribe some sections from the *Book of Chapters* (*ktābā d-rēšē*) 'from the writings of our sublime father and philosopher Mar and Rabban Simon, the anchorite and monk from the monastery of Mar Isho''(f. 1v). Stephen was impressed by Simon's poetic and rhetorical style and thought that it would be useful for his 'Christian brothers' to write some of the treatises (*mēmrē*) which the *Book of Chapters* contained. Furthermore, the monk and priest Jeremiah also urged him to copy out some of the work's enigmas and sweet treatises. This task was not so easy, Stephen says, since the manuscript which he had at his disposal was a very old, but undated, codex from the monastery of Isho'.[17] The condition of the manuscript was bad and its letters were difficult to read. Only after he had studied the letters and the handwriting for a year did Stephen copy out about ten quires from the manuscript (ff. 1v–2r). *Mingana Syr. 18*, therefore, represents a selection of passages from the *Book of Chapters*, and comprises only a small part of its 'Vorlage'; moreover, it does so in a rather confusing way.

The extracts begin with the postscript of the seventh *mēmrā of the Chapters*, apparently the seventh and last collection of hundred *Chapters* or sentences (f. 2v). Thereafter comes the introduction of the explication of the *Chapters*, which corresponds with the introduction of the second text in Scher's description of *Mosul 97* (ff. 2v–3r).[18] This is immediately followed by an introduction, which announces Simon's explication of places from the first *mēmrā of the Chapters* (f. 3r), and a quotation from the words of Simon the Persecuted himself, who informs us about the request of his brothers Joseph and Isho' to give some explication of the secret meaning of

16 Stephen Rais is the copyist of several manuscripts of the library of the monastery of Notre-Dame des Semences in Alqosh; cf. Vosté, Catalogue, 38.69–70.205.235.316. The manuscripts of this library are now in the library of the Chaldean monastery in Baghdad; cf. J. Isaac, 'Les manuscrits syriaques du couvent des moines chaldéens à Bagdad-Iraq', in: Han J. W. Drijvers, René Lavenant, Cornelia Molenberg, and Gerritt J. Reinink (eds.), IV Symposium Syriacum 1984, OrChrA 229, Rome 1987, 453–455; P. Haddad and J. Isaac, Syriac and Arabic Manuscripts in the Library of the Chaldean Monastery Baghdad. Part I Syriac Manuscripts, Baghdad 1988.

17 The information concerning the provenance of the manuscript is in the colophon (f. 51r).

18 Scher, Notice, 252. It is clear that Scher's second text is not a separate work, but that it is simply the second part of Simon's Book of Chapters.

the *Chapters* (ff. 3r–3v). What follows is an explanation, apparently by Simon himself, of the thematic arrangement of the *Chapters* in three parts in the fifth section (*pelgūtā*) of the *Book of Chapters* (f. 3v).[19] In addition, a collection of sentences *stricto sensu* is presented – presenting sayings bearing the numbers 72–100, 31, and then 39–42 (ff. 4r–8v). On f. 8v there appears a new title, which introduces the following as being taken from the sixth section (*pelgūtā*) and its last *mēmrā*. This section begins with an introduction which is explicitly attributed to Simon, in which he expounds the misunderstanding of some people who, from the weak and human words concerning God in the Scriptures, draw false conclusions regarding His essence (ff. 8v–9r). Simon then proceeds to explaining the preceding *Chapters*. The manuscript offers the explanations of ten *Chapters*, treating themes related to the definition of God's essence and His relation to the Creation, in which the eternity and unchangeableness of God's will and design play a central role. In this part we find four quotations from the works of Theodore of Mopsuestia (ff. 9v–24v). A poetical *mēmrā* according to the metre of 7+7 syllables is the next item. The poem 'on things which are useful to consider in times of temptations' is attributed to Mar Isaac (ff. 24v–26v).[20] After three extracts, of which the first and longer one deals with the ways of reason (ff. 26v–35r), the final part of the extracts in *Mingana Syr. 18* follows. This part is introduced by the following title: *Chapters of theoria, the record of which is useful for the recollection of the mind and for the motion towards the truth regarding the divine nature and its dispensation and the mystical knowledge (existing) in the things made by it, so that the mind shall ascend by the motion of these things to the divine nature through the vision of its mysteries.* What follows are extracts from explanatory *mēmrē*, which in succession bear the numbers 1, 2, 5, 6, 8 and 3. In this part we find five quotations from Theodore's works (ff. 35r–51r). The colophon on f. 51r reports that the *mēmrē* on the *Chapters of theoria* were composed by Simon the anchorite from the monastery of Mar Isho', and that they were taken from an old codex in the handwriting of the same monastery by Stephen Rais in 1883.

As far as we may surmise on the basis of the materials, which in a rather confusing way were extracted by Stephen from that old codex, the *Book of Chapters* composed by Simon the Persecuted was divided into at least six sections, called *pelgwātā*, which were subdivided into separate treatises, called *mēmrē*. The first part of the work contained seven *mēmrē*, each of them consisting of one hundred chapters or sentences, called *rēšē*. The remaining part consisted largely of explanations and clarifications of, and digressions on, the thoughts, ideas and dark sayings of the sentences, sometimes taking the format of more elaborated treatises on the relevant

19 According to Simon some chapters deal with the life and works of the Lord, some with the hidden knowledge of the eternal Essence, the Creation and the eschatological future of the Creation, some with the perfect spiritual knowledge and the hidden *theoriai* received by the saints.

20 Mingana, Catalogue, col. 55, attributes this *mēmrā* to Isaac of Niniveh, but this seems doubtful. The poem is also found in the Book of Chapters attributed to Rabban Isaac of Mar Isho', which was the source of the text on ff. 8v–51r in the Mingana manuscript (see below).

themes, such as the divine providence, the properties of God and God's relation with the Creation, etc.

This conclusion, however, is not without problems. Grigory Kessel (Marburg University), who at present is preparing a study on the literary heritage of Simon d-Taybutheh, drew my attention to the close textual correspondences between the part *Mingana Syr. 18* (ff. 8v–51r) and the *Book of Chapters* attributed to Isaac of the monastery of Rabban Isho'.[21] Kessel found at least four manuscripts, in which Isaac's treatise is preserved, and he compared the contents of one of these (*BL Or. 9378*) with *Mingana Syr. 18*. It appeared that the part ff. 8v–51r in the Mingana manuscript (which is attributed here to the last *mēmrā* of the sixth section of Simon the Persecuted's *Book of Chapters*) almost completely corresponds with Isaac's *Book of Chapters* (as already suggested by Scher with regard to the anonymous third text in *Mosul 97*). Kessel thinks that the 'Vorlage' of the scribe of *Mingana Syr. 18* contained Isaac's *Book of Chapters* anonymously (like the third text in *Mosul 97*), and that it was Stephen Rais, the scribe of *Mingana Syr. 18* who (wrongly) connected Simon's name with this part of the Mingana manuscript.

If this conclusion is right, we must assume that only a very small part of Simon the Persecuted's *Book of Chapters* is preserved in *Mingana Syr. 18*, ff. 1v–8v. This means that the first part of Simon's *Book of Chapters* indeed contained seven *mēmrē,* each of them consisting of hundred chapters or sentences, and that its second part included Simon's explanation of these chapters, which were classified, as also Scher indicated, into five sections. Extracts of the first part of Simon's work are found in *Mingana Syr. 18*, ff. 4r–8v, and of its second part in *Mingana Syr. 18*, ff. 2v–4r. For practical reasons I shall in the following section of this article call the source of Theodore's quotations the *Book of Chapters* of Isaac, in spite of the fact that *Mingana Syr. 18* attributes all of them to Simon the Persecuted.

With regard to the contents of the extracts in *Mingana Syr. 18* I concentrate, as already indicated, on one aspect, namely the content and function of the nine explicit quotations from the works of Theodore of Mopsuestia.

In the first part of Isaac's *Book of Chapters* Theodore is adduced in the explanations of the second, fourth, fifth and eighth chapters. Chapter 2 deals with the question, whether God is unchangeable or perhaps changeable in His mind (*tar'ītā*) and nature (*kyānā*). Through selecting the quotation of Theodore from the first volume of his *Commentary on Genesis*, Isaac wants to argue for, and to elucidate, the un-

---

21 I am most grateful to Dr. Kessel for sharing this important information with me. For this Isaac of Mar Isho', see Jean-Baptiste Chabot, 'Isaac de Rabban Isho, moine nestorien', Muséon 59 (1946), 345–351; idem, Notice sur deux manuscrits contenant les oeuvres du moine Isaac de Rabban Isho' et du métropolitain Ahoudemmeh, Notices et extraits des manuscrits de la Bibliothèque Nationale et autres bibliothèques 43, Paris 1965, 43–50. Is there a connection between the three Isho''s mentioned in our texts: the monastery of Isho' of the manuscript which was the 'Vorlage' of Mingana Syr. 18, Isho' the abbot of Simon the Persecuted and Isaac of Mar Isho'? Could Isaac be an (older?) authority of the same monastery of Isho'?

changeableness of God's mind (*tar'ītā*).[22] Theodore, here, calls attention to the eternal will of God, who does not think things which He had not thought before, and who does not introduce into the Creation any correction, which did not exist in His mind (*tar'ītā*) before. Everything belonging to the Creation, including the deeds and thoughts of men, and not only in one generation (that of the house of Adam) but in all ages, is concluded in God's eternal foreknowledge.[23]

Also from the first volume of Theodore's *Commentary on Genesis* – to be precise, from the beginning thereof – comes the quotation in Chapter 4 on the question, whether God created the Creation in eternal love or not.[24] The short quotation affirms this question: it is from much goodness and abundant love that God came to the construction of the Creation.[25]

Chapter 5 treats a cardinal point in East Syrian theology and anthropology: did God create man mortal by nature, or did the immortal created man become mortal through sin?[26] Theodore's sixth part (*mēmrā*) of his *Commentary on Romans* is adduced,[27] in which Theodore states that there are two things that are absurd to think about God: firstly, that He in anger would do something beyond what seems good to Him; secondly, that He through regret would do any thing other than what He wanted from the beginning. 'If', Theodore says, 'God were to have wished to make us immortal, and if this were to have been destined for us as something that is good, He would never, as through regret, have changed His mind in anger.' In Chapter 8, on the question, whether God can be forced through human behaviour to do one thing instead of something else, Isaac refers to the same opinion of Theodore, as expressed in the *Commentary on Romans*.[28]

Five quotations from Theodore's works appear in the final part of the extracts in *Mingana Syr. 18*, containing (parts of) six *mēmrē* of the *Chapters of theoria*. The first quotation occurs in *mēmrā* 2.[29] This quotation is taken from the second part (*pelgūtā*) and the third treatise (*mēmrā*) of Theodore's lost work *Against those who say that sin is placed in nature*.[30] Theodore here discusses the same theme as in the

---

22 Ff. 12r–14v.

23 F. 13v. This quotation offers new evidence for Theodore's lost Commentary on Genesis. Cf. Maurice Geerard, Clavis Patrum Graecorum 2, Turnhout 1974, 345 (3827). For this topic in Theodore's theology, see U. Wickert, Studien zu den Pauluskommentaren Theodors von Mopsuestia als Beitrag zum Verständnis der antiochenischen Theologie, BZNW 27, Berlin 1962, 77–89.

24 Ff. 16v–17r.

25 F. 16v. Also this quotation offers new evidence for Theodore's Commentary on Genesis.

26 Ff. 17r–18r.

27 F. 17v.

28 F. 22v. For the preserved fragments of Theodore's lost Commentary on Romans, see Geerard, Clavis 2, p. 352 (3846). For the topic of man being created mortal in Theodore's theology, see Wickert, Studien, 101–120; S. Gerber, Theodor von Mopsuestia und das Nicänum. Studien zu den katechetischen Homilien, VigChr Suppl. 51, Leiden-Boston-Köln 2000, 176–181.

29 Ff. 35r–v.

30 For the preserved fragments of this lost work of Theodore, see Geerard, Clavis 2, 358 (3860). As far as I know, Isaac's Book of Chapters is the only known quotation from the Syriac trans-

quotation from the *Commentary on Romans* mentioned above. God never acts from anger, weakness or regret, for He knows everything from eternity. By way of scriptural testimonies Theodore adduces Jer. 1:5 and Gal. 1:15–16, which show the foreordained vocation of the prophet and the apostle. God is, Theodore says, from the beginning and from eternity perfectly acquainted with the things which are determined with Him and with how these things shall be administered in respect to all and to each one individually. But Isaac in this *mēmrā* deems it necessary to confirm this opinion of Theodore's through a second quotation. It is taken from the third *mēmrā* of Theodore's work, which he composed for his friend Mastubiya.[31] This is Theodore's work *Against the Magi*, and Isaac's quotation from this work here provides a valuable new testimony of this lost work of Theodore.[32] The import of this quotation is basically the same as that of the preceding quotation from the work *Against those who say that sin is placed in nature*. The same biblical testimonies (Jer. 1:5 and Gal. 1:15–16) are adduced to demonstrate that God does not act out of regret, but that He, from the beginning, since all things are determined in His mind (*tar'ītā*), performs according to His will the order of the things which through Him happen.

These quotations serve to illustrate the right confession of the 'orthodox' Christians, namely the unchangeableness of God's will; they are directed against 'the heretics who proclaim God to be changeable.'[33]

In *mēmrā* 5 Isaac discusses the question, whether accidents (*gedšē*) can affect men without the consent of God.[34] The negative answer to this question is exemplified by Job 2:6 and Theodore's exegesis of this verse: '[God] allowed him [i.e., Satan] to do with his [i.e., Job's] possessions what he wanted; He also allowed him to harm his [i.e., Job's] body too, but He did not allow him to touch his soul; for the free will that was bound and implanted in it [i.e., the soul] He preserved inviolable

---

lation of this work of Theodore.

31 Ff. 35v–36r.

32 For a quotation from this work in Simon's On the Union, see Reinink, A New Fragment. In the meantime, I have found another fragment of Theodore's Against the Magi, in Simon's On the Union. It is preserved in the manuscript Cambr. Or. 1317, in a part of the text of On the Union, which is lacking in Mingana Syr. 544 (see note 2). This quotation occurs in mēmrā 6 of the On the Union (Cambr. Or. 1317, 208–209). It offers highly interesting new information. Simon says that this work for Mastubiya was written against a certain Yazdat. The quotation is taken from the third *mēmrā* of the work Against the Magi. In this quotation the equality and indivisibility of the three persons of the Trinity is discussed.

33 F. 38r.

34 Ff. 38v–42v.

for the affliction of Satan.'[35] Everything, even the accidents, Isaac says a little later, is included in God's eternal thought and design.[36]

The quotation in *mēmrā* 6 presents Theodore's exegesis of Luke 22:43–44 and Christ's agony on the Mount of Olives.[37] According to Theodore these verses show that Christ was truly man, and they also teach us that it is not an amazing or embarrassing thing, if the things belonging to the weakness of human nature also happen to people who possess a strong mind.

The last quotation is found in *mēmrā* 8. Isaac here deals with the question, whether God is not some sort of artificer, while we, mankind, are no more than 'vanity', if it be that God's wisdom governs the Creation and does not leave us in every respect in the hands of our freedom. Isaac's answer is this: Would we blame a wise master of the house, if he manages his household and does not abandon his household without any order to young people?[38] In support of his words, Isaac adduces an interesting quotation from Theodore's *Commentary on Genesis*.[39] Theodore explains the whole period of this world as the age of childhood (*ṭalyūtā*). Under the guidance of the angels the divine will governs our childhood (*šabrūtā*). As children we are permanently placed under the instruction achieved through the hidden management (*mparnsānūtā*) and the care (*bṭīlūtā*) of the angels, by whom God leads us through sometimes pleasant, and sometimes harsh things to wisdom, and withholds us from things that are not expedient.[40] It is possible that this *exposé* by Theodore is connected with the exegesis of Gen. 1:24–25, since the final part of the quotation deals with the use of reptiles and beasts. With reference to Deut. 32:24 Theodore argues that birds of prey, wild beasts and snakes are neither 'quiet' nor are they

35 F. 40r. Since Isaac does not explicitly say here from which work of Theodore the quotation is taken, it remains uncertain whether it was taken from Theodore's lost Commentary on Job or perhaps from another work of Theodore, in which Theodore uses this passage from Job in his argumentation. For the preserved fragments of Theodore's Commentary on Job, see Geerard, Clavis 2, 348 (3835).

36 F. 41r.

37 F. 44r. For the preserved fragments of Theodore's Commentary on Luke, see Geerard, Clavis 2, 350 (3842); J. Reuss, Lukas-Kommentare aus der griechischen Kirche, TU 130, Berlin 1984, 12–14.

38 Ff. 46r–v.

39 Ff. 46v–47r. This quotation offers new evidence from Theodore's Commentary on Genesis.

40 For the topic of *paideia*, the instruction of mankind, in Theodore's theology, see Wickert, Studien, 89–101. For the influential role of this Theodoran theme in the East Syrian tradition, see R. Macina, L'homme à l'école de Dieu. Profil herméneutique, théologique et kérugmatique du movement scoliaste nestorien, POC 32 (1982), 87–124, 263–301; 33 (1983), 39–103; G. J. Reinink, Paideia. God's Design in World History according to the East Syrian Monk John bar Penkaye, in: Erik Kooper (ed.), The Medieval Chronicle II. Proceedings of the 2nd International Conference on the Medieval Chronicle, Driebergen/Utrecht July 1999, Amsterdam-New York 2002, 190–198 (repr. in G. J. Reinink, Syriac Christianity under Late Sasanian and Early Islamic Rule, Aldershot 2005 VII); Adam H. Becker, Fear of God and the Beginning of Wisdom. The School of Nisibis and the Development of Scholastic Culture in Late Antique Mesopotamia, Philadelphia 2006, 119–125.

'moving' to hurt us on their own accord, but that the divine will, acting through the spiritual natures (angels), providentially incites and restrains these animals.

The discourses in Isaac's *Book of Chapters*, as these are preserved in *Mingana Syr. 18*, mainly concern topics related to the definition of God's essence, His eternal and unchangeable will and foreknowledge, and His providence regarding the Creation and mankind. Isaac's arguments represent some of the most essential and distinguishing East Syrian notions concerning the nature of God (unchangeableness and impassibility), the nature of Christ (fully und truly human), and the nature of man (created mortal). In Isaac's introductory words of the *Book of Chapters* his 'household' (the East Syrian co-religionists) are incited to hold fast to the tenet – despised by the heretical 'outsiders' – of the impassibility of the divine nature. 'We shall', Isaac says, 'in many places adduce demonstrations of things concerning the impassibility of the divine essence (*ousia*) and the sublime properties of His (God's) nature against their (the Miaphysite heretics') words and we shall God set free from the absurdities they proclaim concerning Him.'[41] The ensuing explanations in the chapters, therefore, are also to be viewed in the light of this specific polemical purpose.

Further research into the possible source or sources of the collections of sayings in the Simon's *Book of Chapters* (*Mingana Syr. 18*, ff. 4r–8v) is necessary, although the fact that only a very small part of Simon's *Chapters* is included in Stephen's extracts may considerably complicate the question of the origins of Simon's sayings. However, to give an impression of the sayings in Simon's *Book of Chapters*, I conclude with one example, namely the translation of the sentence which bears the number 73 in the Mingana manuscript:[42]

> Run, in order that you will reach the Unreachable,
> that you will find the never-failing treasure in heaven
> and the purses of riches that do not waste away.
> And give Him what you have borrowed from that which belongs to Him,
> and repay Him what you have received from Him:
> the middle with the last, the first with the last and the middle,
> and raise up the last with the bar of promise of all of them.

41 F. 9v.

42 F. 4r. My translation of the final rather enigmatic words of this sentence is done under reservation.

Der ostsyrische Patriarch Timotheos in der Auseinandersetzung mit Nestorius von Bēt Nūhadrān und den Mystikern in seinem Umfeld

Martin Heimgartner

Eine allgemeine Synode des ostsyrischen Patriarchen Timotheos (im Amt 780–823), die wohl im Jahr 790 stattfand,[1] verurteilte drei Theologen mystischer Prägung[2] als Häretiker, nämlich Johannes von Apamäa aus dem 6. Jahrhundert[3] sowie Josef den Seher (Jausep Ḥazzāyā)[4] und Johannes von Dalyātā[5], die beide wohl bereits vor der

1 Zur strittigen Datierung vgl. Anm. 11.

2 Zur ostsyrischen Mystik allgemein: Georg Günther Blum, Nestorianismus und Mystik, in: ZKG 93 (1982), 273–294; Robert Beulay, La Lumière sans forme. Introduction à l'étude de la mystique chrétienne syro-orientale, Chevetogne 1987. Zu Timotheos und dem Messalianismus: Jouko Martikainen, Timotheos I. und der Messalianismus, in: Makarios-Symposium über das Gebet. Vorträge der dritten finnisch-deutschen Theologentagung in Amelungsborn 1986, hg. v. Jouko Martikainen und Hans-Olof Kvist, Åbo 1989, 47–60; Klaus Fitschen, Messalianismus und Antimessalianismus. Ein Beispiel ostkirchlicher Ketzergeschichte, FKDG 71, Göttingen 1998.

3 Zu Johannes von Apamäa: Werner Strothmann, Johannes von Apamea, PTS 11, Berlin 1972; Lars G. Rignell, Drei Traktate von Johannes dem Einsiedler, Lunds Universitets Årsskrift N.F. 1, 54.4, Lund 1960 (62: Datierung auf 2. Hälfte 5. Jh.). Peter Bruns, Johannes von Apamäa, in: Lexikon der antiken christlichen Literatur, hg. v. Siegmar Döpp und Wilhelm Geerlings, Freiburg im Breisgau ³2002, 375 (Datierung auf 1. Hälfte 6. Jh.).

4 Zu Josef dem Seher: Addai Scher, Joseph Ḥazzâyâ. Écrivain syriaque du VIIIe siècle, in: RSO 3 (1910), 45–63; Antoine Guillaumont, Sources de la doctrine de Joseph Ḥazzâyâ, in: OrSyr 3 (1958), 3–24; E. J. Sherry, The Life and Works of Joseph Ḥazzâyâ, in: The Seed of Wisdom. Essays in Honour of T. J. Meek, hg. v. William S. McCullough, Toronto 1964, 78–91; Robert Beulay, Joseph Ḥazzāyā, in: DSp 8 (1974), 1341–1349; Rabban Jausep Ḥazzaya, Briefe über das geistliche Leben und verwandte Schriften. Ostsyrische Mystik des 8. Jahrhunderts, eingeleitet und übersetzt von Gabriel Bunge, Sophia 21, Trier 1982; Peter Bruns, Joseph der Seher (Hazzaya), in: Döpp und Geerlings (s. Anm. 3), 404 (Datierung auf 2. Hälfte 7. Jh.).

5 Zu Johannes von Dalyātā: La collection des lettres de Jean de Dalyatha, édition critique du texte syriaque inédit, traduction française, introduction et notes par Robert Beulay, PO 39.3, Turnhout 1978; Jean de Dalyatha, Les homélies I–XV. Edition critique du texte syriaque inédit, traduction, introduction et notes par Nadira Khayyat, Sources syriaques 2, Paris 2007; Brian E. Colless, The biographies of John Saba, in: ParOr 3 (1972), 45–63; Robert Beulay, Jean de Dalyatha, in: DSp 8 (1974), 449–452; Robert Beulay, Précisions touchant l'identité et la biographie de Jean Saba de Dalyatha, in: ParOr 8 (1977–1978), 87–116; Robert Beulay, L'enseignement spirituel de Jean de Dalyatha. Mystique syro-oriental du VIIIe siècle, ThH 83, Paris 1990; Peter Bruns, Johannes von Dalyata, in: Döpp und Geerlings (s. Anm. 3), 386–387.

Synode verstorben sein dürften;[6] ein weiterer Theologe, Nestorius, wurde im Zusammenhang mit seiner Wahl zum Bischof von Bēt Nūhadrān des Messalianismus angeklagt und musste diesen Vorwurf in einer Verteidigungsrede vor der Synode widerlegen.

Von diesen Vorgängen ist der Fall des Nestorius von Bēt Nūhadrān am besten dokumentiert. Seine zu Protokoll genommene Apologie wurde im Corpus der Timotheosbriefe[7] an Brief 50 angefügt.[8] Die Kanones, welche die Verurteilung der drei Mystiker aussprachen, sind nicht erhalten. ʿAbdīšōʿ († 1318) zitiert in seinem

---

6 Die meisten Forscher rechnen damit, dass Josef der Seher (Jausep Ḥazzāyā) und Johannes von Dalyātā die Verurteilung nicht mehr miterlebten: Guillaumont, Sources, 6; Colless, Biographies, 54–55; Anton Baumstark, Geschichte der syrischen Literatur mit Ausschluß der syrisch–palästinensischen Texte, Bonn 1922, 226. Sherry (Life, 86) neigt vorsichtig zur Annahme, Joseph habe die Verurteilung noch miterlebt. Beulay, der zwar zur ersten Position neigt (Enseignement, 17) hält es in Précisions, 112 f. für „peu probable“, in Lumière, 215 für „possible“, dass Johannes von Dalyātā noch lebt, und weist in Précisions, 113 darauf hin, dass Johannes von Dalyātā Anfeindungen erwähnt (vgl. ep. 51,17 [PO 39.3, 321]), vgl. dazu auch Īšōʿdnaḥ von Baṣra, Buch der Keuschheit, 125 (Bedjan, 509): „Die Missgunst erhob sich aus der Bevölkerung gegen ihn [= Isaak von Ninive] wie gegen Josef den Seher, Johannes von Apamäa und Johannes von Dalyātā.“

7 Edition der Briefe 1–39: Timothei Patriarchae I Epistulae I, 2 Bde [Textus und Versio], hg. v. Oscar Braun, CSCO.S 30.2/67, Paris 1914 f. (nachgedruckt als CSCO.S 30/74, 1953; die Seitenverweise für Text und Übersetzung im Folgenden nur durch Schrägstrich getrennt, obwohl diese in verschiedenen Bänden stehen); Brief 40: Hanna P. J. Cheikho, Dialectique du langage sur dieu. Lettre de Timothée I (728–823) à Serge. Étude, traduction et edition critique, Rom 1983; Brief 41: Raphaël J. Bidawid, Les lettres du patriarche nestorien Timothée I. Étude critique avec en appendice La lettre de Timothée I aux moines du Couvent de Mār Mārōn (traduction latine et texte chaldéen), Studi e testi 187, Vatikanstadt 1956, S. ܠܗ–ܐ (syr. Text) und 91–125 (lat. Übersetzung); Brief 43: Oskar Braun, Briefe des Katholikos Timotheos I, in: OrChr 2 (1902), 1–32, ebenso Henri Pognon, Une version syriaque des Aphorismes d’Hippocrate, Leipzig 1903, XVI–XVIII/XVIII–XX; Brief 47: Oskar Braun, Ein Brief des Katholikos Timotheos I über biblische Studien des 9. Jahrhunderts, in: OrChr 1 (1901), 299–313; Brief 48: Pognon, Version, XXI–XXII/XXII–XXV; Brief 50: Oskar Braun, Zwei Synoden des Katholikos Timotheos I, in: Oriens Christianus 2 (1902), 283–311. Zu Auszügen, Referaten oder Erwähnungen anderer Briefe bei Timotheos selbst sowie bei verschiedenen späteren Autoren vgl. Bidawid, Lettres, 44–50. Brief 59 (=„Disputation“); Martin Heimgartner, Timotheos I., ostsyrischer Patriarch. Disputation mit dem Kalifen al-Mahdī. Textedition, CSCO.S 244, Leuven 2010; Einleitung, Übersetzung und Anmerkungen CSCO.S. 245, Leuven 2010. Eine Neuedition der Briefe 43, 47, 48 und 50 findet sich in meiner vom Schweizerischen Nationalfonds finanzierten Edition und Übersetzung der bis jetzt unveröffentlichten Briefe 42–58 (erscheint voraussichtlich 2011 bei CSCO).

8 Braun, Synoden, 302–310 (syr. Text) und 303–311 (dt. Übersetzung). Eine weitere Edition von Brief 50 lässt die angefügte Apologie des Nestorius beiseite: Synodicon orientale ou Recueil de Synodes nestorians. Publié, traduit et annoté par Jean-Baptiste Chabot, Paris 1902 (syr. Text 599–603, frz. Übersetzung 603–608). Brief 50 ist ein Schreiben des Timotheos im Namen einer Synode der Patriarchalhyparchie vom Jahr 782 und zitiert vier Kanones, deren einer sich gegen verschiedene Häresien wendet: Braun, Synoden, 294/295 (zur Datierung ebd. 289). Dass Brief 50 und die Apologie des Nestorius von verschiedenen Synoden stammen, zeigen die unterschiedlichen Unterschriften der beteiligten Kirchenmänner am Ende der beiden Dokumente.

Nomokanon einen Synodalbrief des Timotheos von der Synode von 790, der die traditionelle Kompetenz des Patriarchen festhält, sozusagen als „Zensurbehörde" der ostsyrischen Kirche zu prüfen, ob Bücher publiziert werden dürfen oder nicht. In diesem Zusammenhang erwähnt Timotheos etliche Fälle, die diese kirchliche Approbation nicht erlangten, darunter die „Lästerungen des Apamäers, des Josef und des Johannes von Dalyātā."[9] Eine Notiz in der „Ordo iudiciorum ecclesiasticorum" des ʿAbdīšōʿ erwähnt die Verurteilung der drei Mystiker und fügt hinzu, dass Īšōbarnūn, Timotheos' Nachfolger im Patriarchenamt, die drei genannten rehabilitiert habe.[10] Über die konkreten Vorwürfe, die den Verurteilten gemacht werden, berichten nur zwei ebenfalls spätere Quellen: Īšōʿdnaḥ von Baṣra erwähnt in seinem „Buch der Keuschheit" (um 850) in den betreffenden Kurzbiografien, Josef sei verurteilt worden, weil „vier Traktate" aus seiner Feder missbilligt worden seien,[11]

---

9 „...der Patriarch prüfte, wenn er dazu fähig war, ebendiese Schriften mit seinem eigenen Wissen. Und so wurden sie, wenn sie der Zulassung und Auszeichnung würdig waren, zugelassen und ausgezeichnet. Wenn sie aber der Zulassung nicht würdig waren, verwarf er sie als solche, die den kirchlichen Gesetzen fern waren, und verurteilte sie, wie es Katholikos Mār Sabrīšōʿ mit den Schriften des Ḥnānā aus der Adiabene tat, Īšōʿyab mit den Machwerken des Sahdōnā und dem Geschwätz des Tahaläers Jesaja [und] wir mit den Lästerungen des Apamäers, des Josef und des Johannes von Dalyātā." (ʿAbdīšōʿ, Nomokanon 9,6, vgl. SVNC X, hg. v. Angelo Mai, Rom 1838, 329b syr. Text und 167a lat. Übersetzung). Dabei bleibt völlig unklar, ob die Verurteilung von der soeben stattfindenden oder bereits an einer früheren Synode vollzogen wurde. Manche Forscher setzen daher die Verurteilung ins Jahr 170 H. (786/787), das Īšōʿdnaḥ von Baṣra nennt (s. Anm. 11).

10 „Katholikos Mār Timotheos wurde am Sonntag dem 7. Mai des Jahres 1091 der Griechen [= 780 n. Chr.] geweiht. Er hielt in seiner [Amts-]Zeit zwei Synoden ab und verurteilte den Seher, den Apamäer und den von Dalyātā und alle, die ihre Bücher lesen. Er starb am Freitag dem 9. Januar des Jahres 1134 [=823]. Īšōbarnūn wurde am Sonntag dem 18. Juni des Jahres 1134 [823] geweiht. Er hielt eine Synode ab und rehabilitierte jene drei, d. h. den Apamäer, den von Dalyātā und den Seher, und gestattete den Mönchen, deren Bücher zu lesen, da in ihnen nichts Tadelnswertes steht." (Nur lateinisch bei: Ordo Iudiciorum ecclesiasticorum, collectus, dispositus, ordinatus et compositus a Mar ʿAbdišoʿ, latine interpretatus est, notis illustravit Iacobus-M. Vosté, FCCO, ser. 2, fasc. 15, Vatikanstadt 1940, 64–65. Dabei steht auf Seite 64 für die Weihe des Timotheos irrtümlich die Jahrzahl 1901 statt 1091.)

11 „Und weil er vier Traktate [ܡܐܡܪ̈ܝܢ] in seinem Schrifttum formuliert hatte, die von den Lehrern der Kirche nicht akzeptiert wurden, hielt Mār Timotheos eine Synode ab, und exkommunizierte ihn im Jahr hundertundsiebzig Jahre [sic!] der Hāšemsöhne." (Buch der Keuschheit, 126: Liber Superiorum seu Historia monastica auctore Thoma episcopo Margensi. Liber Fundatorum monasteriorum in regno Persarum et Arabum. Homiliae Mar–Narsetis in Joseph. Documenta Patrum de quibusdam verae fidei dogmatibus, hg. v. Paul Bedjan, Paris 1901, 511.) Ob mit den vier ܡܐܡܪ̈ܝܢ vier Traktate gemeint sind oder aber vier Aussagen, die eventuell mit den Vorwürfen in der arabischen Kanonessammlung in Verbindung gebracht werden können, muss hier offen bleiben. Zur seltsamen Formulierung „im Jahr hundertundsiebzig Jahre": Scher (Joseph, 47) hält das merkwürdige überflüssige ܫܢ̈ܝܐ („Jahre") für eine Verschreibung von ܘܐܪܒܥ und datiert die Verurteilung aufs Jahr 790. Ihm folgen: Jean-Maurice Fiey, Îchōʿdnah, Métropolite de Basra et son œuvre, in: L'Orient syrien 11 (1966), 431–450, vgl. 449; Sherry, Life, 83, Anm. 19 (Sherry datiert dafür den Synodalbrief aufs Jahr 804). Bei der Datierung aufs Jahr 786/787 bleiben: Guillaumont, sources, 9, Anm. 22; Colless, Biographies, 52, Anm. 21. Marti-

und Johannes von Dalyātā sei verurteilt worden, weil er behauptete, „dass die Menschheit des Herrn seine Gottheit sehen könne.“[12] Ausführlicher ist ein Bericht über die Verurteilung von Johannes von Apamäa, Josef dem Seher und Johannes von Dalyātā, der im „Recht der Christenheit“ des Ibn aṭ-Ṭayyib in arabischer Sprache erhalten ist.[13] Neben anderen Vorwürfen wie Sabellianismus, Ablehnung der geregelten Mönchspraxis oder Lehre von der Präexistenz der Seele wird bei Johannes von Dalyātā und Josef dem Seher ausdrücklich erwähnt, sie hätten behauptet, Gott sei sichtbar.[14] Die Synode habe daraufhin jeden dem Bann unterworfen, „der behauptete, dass die Gottheit selbst von der Menschheit des Herrn oder von irgendeiner anderen Kreatur gesehen werde.“[15] Auf diesen Synodalentscheid nimmt auch Nestorius in seiner Apologie Bezug: „Ich verfluche die ganze böse Ansicht der Messalianer, die bald lästernd behaupten, dass die Gottheit des Einziggeborenen von seiner Menschheit gesehen werden könne, bald dass seine Menschheit einfach und ohne Zusammensetzung sei, entsprechend der frevelhaften und gottlosen Ansicht der Manichäer.“[16]

Der Vorwurf, „dass die Gottheit des Herrn von seiner Menschheit gesehen werden könne“, scheint also tatsächlich Inhalt des Synodalbeschlusses von 790 gewesen zu sein, denn diese Aussage findet sich, nahezu identisch formuliert, in den erwähnten Stellen bei Nestorius, bei Īšō‘dnaḥ von Baṣra (Johannes-Kurzbiografie) und in der arabischen Kanonessammlung. Sie scheint sich ausdrücklich gegen Johannes von Dalyātā zu wenden, in dessen 25. Homilie sich die genannte Vorstellung findet.[17]

Als „messalianisch“ bezeichnet wird diese Anschauung einzig bei Nestorius. Kanon 4 einer früheren Synode vom Jahr 782 spricht zwar auch von der „Häresie des Messalianismus“, ohne diese aber inhaltlich näher zu qualifizieren.[18] Guillau-

---

kainen (Timotheos, 48) datiert aufs Jahr 804, wobei er die Angaben bei ‘Abdīšō‘ mit der Synode von 782 vermengt.

12 „Die Bücher, die er machte, wurden von Katholikos Timotheos nicht akzeptiert: Dieser hielt eine Synode ab und verurteilte ihn, weil er in seinem Buch sagt, dass die Menschheit des Herrn seine Gottheit sehen könne.“ (Buch der Keuschheit, 127, Bedjan, 512)

13 Ibn aṭ-Ṭayyib, Fiqh an-Naṣrānīya. Das Recht der Christenheit 2. Teil, hg. v. Wilhelm Hoenerbach und Otto Spies, CSCO.A 167, 18, Louvain 1957, 185–187 (arab. Text); 2. Teil übers. v. Wilhelm Hoenerbach und Otto Spies, CSCO.A 168, 19, Louvain 1957, 187–188 (dt. Übersetzung). Beulay, Enseignement, 423–424, und Blum, Nestorianismus, 289, verweisen auf die Edition von Assemani in Ebedjesus, Catalogus 86, BOCV 3.1, 100, Anm. 1 (arab. Text), bzw. 101, Anm. 1 (lat. Übersetzung).

14 Ebd. zu Johannes von Dalyātā: „... er fügte hinzu, dass der Schöpfer vom Geschöpf selbst gesehen werde.“ Zu Josef dem Seher: „... er behauptete, sie [d. h. die Gottheit] sei sichtbar.“

15 Ebd.

16 Timotheos, ep. 50 (Braun, Synoden, 304–306/305–307).

17 Johannes von Dalyātā, Homilie 25,5–6 (französisch bei Beulay, Enseignement, 512), dazu Beulay, Enseignement, 441.

18 Timotheos, ep. 50 (Braun, Synoden, 294/295): „Ein jeder von den Bischöfen, Einsiedlern und Gläubigen, der der Häresie des Messalianismus oder irgendeiner anderen [Häresie] angeklagt ist, darf nicht in seinem Rang dienen oder an der Kirche und den Sakramenten teilnehmen, bevor er schriftlich vor der allgemeinen Kirche diese böse Lehre verflucht hat im Wort des Herrn.“

mont hat darauf hingewiesen, dass die Vorstellung, Gott könne mit den Augen des Körpers geschaut werden – ein traditionelles Element des „Messalianismus“[19] – in der Epoche des Timotheos neu mit der Vorstellung verbunden wird, dass die Menschheit des Christus die Gottheit schauen könne.[20]

Die Frage, ob die Vorwürfe Josef und die beiden Johannes zu Recht treffen, ist viel diskutiert worden. Bereits ‘Abdīšō‘ scheint den Entscheid des Timotheos für verfehlt zu halten, wenn er von der Rehabilitierung der drei Autoren berichtet, ihre Schriften seien wieder zur Lektüre frei gegeben worden, „da in ihnen nichts Tadelnswertes steht.“[21] Aus der Reihe der modernen Forscher, die sich dieser Frage gewidmet haben, ragt vor allem Beulays eingehende Untersuchung heraus[22]: In der Tat finden wir bei allen drei Mystikern Stellen, die undifferenziert von einer „Schau Gottes“ reden.[23] Daneben sprechen die beiden Mystiker des 8. Jahrhunderts – Johannes von Dalyātā und Josef der Seher – auch präziser von einer Schau Gottes in der Seele, im Geist, im Inneren des Mystikers[24] oder in der Menschheit des Christus.[25] Eine Besonderheit von Johannes von Dalyātā ist die Differenzierung, dass nicht Gottes Wesen, sondern dessen Glanz geschaut wird[26], womit er „mit großer Präzision die unzugängliche göttliche Natur von der mitteilbaren und erfahrbaren Herrlichkeit Gottes unterscheidet“.[27] Allerdings sind diese Präzisierungen nicht immer

19 Vgl. etwa Fitschen, Messalianismus, 131–132 und 300–301.

20 Guillaumont, Sources, 13.

21 Ordo Iudiciorum ecclesiasticorum, Vosté, 64.

22 Beulay, Enseignement, 423–464; daneben in der Knappheit treffend Blum, Nestorianismus, 284–291; Guillaumont, Sources, 8–24; ferner Marktikainen, Timotheos, 51–59; Vittorio Berti, Grazia. Visione e natura divina in Nestorio di Nuhadra, solitario e vescovo siro-orientale († 800 ca.), in: AScRel 10 (2005), 223.

23 Beulay, Enseignement, 440. Vgl. etwa Johannes von Apamäa, Traktat 1 (Rignell, Traktate, 7/28): „Das Licht des Lebens geht ihm auf, er sieht seinen Gott, erkennt seinen Schöpfer und erfreut sich an seinem Erzeuger.“

24 Beulay, Enseignement, 443–447. Vgl. ferner etwa Johannes von Dalyātā, ep 14,2 (PO 39.3, 345): „... jene, die sich selbst zu einem Spiegel machen, in dem der Unsichtbare gesehen werden kann.“

25 Beulay, Enseignement, 456–464. Vgl. etwa Josef, Buch der Fragen und Antworten: „Denn in der Person des Menschen Jesus, dem Sohn unseres Geschlechtes, werden alle Vernunftwesen in der kommenden Welt den unsichtbaren Gott schauen.“ (Bunge, Jausep, 46 sowie 71, Anm. 169.) Josef, Capita scientiae: „Für alle sichtbaren und unsichtbaren Vernunftwesen wird die Menschheit unseres Herrn ein Spiegel, in dem sie das Gott–Wort sehen, das in ihm [d. h. unserem Herrn] wohnt. [...] Außerhalb der Menschheit unseres Herrn gibt es keine Schau Gottes, weder für die Engel noch für die Menschen, weder in dieser Welt noch in der kommenden Welt.“ (Syrischer Text bei Scher, Joseph, 57, vgl. die Korrekturen zu seiner Übersetzung bei Guillaumont, Sources, 14–15; die Auslassung wird nur aus der deutschen Übersetzung bei Bunge, Jausep, 45 ersichtlich.)

26 Beulay, Enseignement, 447–456, besonders 447–449 und Beulay, Lumière, 195–196. Vgl. etwa Johannes von Dalyātā, Brief 50,5 (39.3, 464–465): „Und er zeigt das Licht seiner Natur denen, die ihn lieben in allen Welten: nicht seine Natur, sondern deren Glanz.“ Josef redet auch von Gottes „Glanz“ im Zusammenhang mit der Kontemplation, aber nicht in der begrifflichen Differenzierung zu „Natur“ (Beulay, Enseignement, 449).

27 Blum, Nestorianismus, 285.

eindeutig. Beulay räumt ein, dass manche Texte von Johannes von Dalyātā von einer unmittelbaren Gottesschau zu sprechen scheinen.[28] Vollends anstößig war für die Konzilsväter von 790, dass für Johannes von Dalyātā die mystische Schau ihre Voraussetzung darin hat, dass die menschliche Natur des Christus die Gottheit sehen kann. Damit durchbricht Johannes die klare Trennung der zwei Naturen, wie sie die ostsyrische Kirche kennt.[29]

Die Maßnahmen des Konzils waren wohl weniger gegen die drei Mystiker als Personen gerichtet, als vielmehr gegen ihre Schriften. So ist im Synodalbrief des Timotheos nur von einer Verurteilung der „Lästerungen" der drei Mystiker die Rede, und dies zudem im Zusammenhang mit der patriarchalen Zensurfunktion. Auch die arabische Kanonessammlung erwähnt das Lektüreverbot, und ʻAbdīšōʻ berichtet im Zusammenhang mit der Rehabilitation der drei Mystiker ausdrücklich, dass deren Schriften wieder zur Lektüre freigegeben worden seien.

Die Schrift „Über den Anfang der Bewegung der göttlichen Gnade" des Nestorius, von der Berti 2005 zwei bisher unpublizierte Fragmente ediert und mit italienischer Übersetzung veröffentlicht hat[30], steht ganz in der mystischen Tradition des Johannes von Dalyātā und Josef des Sehers.[31] Wie Johannes von Dalyātā differenziert Nestorius zwischen der Schau Gottes und der seines Glanzes[32]: Ausgehend vom Makarismus der Bergpredigt – „Selig, die reinen Herzens sind, denn sie werden Gott schauen" (Mt 5,8) –, nennt er den gegen ihn laut werdenden Vorwurf: „Wie soll man die göttliche Natur schauen können?" Seine Antwort ist ganz präzis: „Du Ungläubiger! Nicht seine Natur wird geschaut, sage ich, sondern der Glanz seiner Größe."[33] Anders als Johannes von Dalyātā und Josef dem Seher hält Nestorius in seiner Apologie strikt an der ostsyrischen Lehre von der grundsätzlichen Trennung der zwei Naturen des Christus und der Trennung von Göttlichem und Geschöpflichem im Allgemeinen fest, wenn er sich dort gegen eine unmittelbare Schau Gottes ausspricht:

---

28 „... certains textes de Jean de Dalyatha semblent suggérer qu'il pourrait y avoir une vision de Dieu de manière directe..." (Enseignement, 445). Beulay weist auch im Zusammenhang mit dem Vorwurf des Sabellianismus an Johannes auf eine zumindest unglücklich formulierte Stelle hin („un passage de formulation au moins malheureuse", ebd. 416).

29 Vgl. Beulay, Enseignement, 441: „... evidemment une conception de l'union des deux natures du Christ beaucoup plus étroite que celle admise par l'Église nestorienne". Blum, Nestorianismus, 286: „Damit hat Jōḥannān von Daljāṭā einen neuralgischen Punkt des nestorianischen Christusverständnisses getroffen."

30 Berti, Grazia, 219–257. Vgl. zu Timotheos ferner auch Vittorio Berti, Vita e studi di Timoteo I Patriarca cristiano di Baghdad. Ricerche sull'epistolario e sulle fonti contigue, Studia Iranica Cahier 41, Paris 2009. Eine genaue Zusammenfassung der Schrift „Über den Anfang der Bewegung der göttlichen Gnade" des Nestorius mit größeren Zitaten in französischer Übersetzung bereits bei Beulay, Lumière, 218–222.

31 Beulay, Lumière, 220 f. mit den Nachweisen 329, Anm. 90–100.

32 Beulay (Enseignement, 448–449; Lumière, 222–223) stellt fest, dass Nestorius der einzige ist, der dieses Schema „Natur Gottes – Glanz Gottes" aufgreift.

33 Paragraph 7: Berti, Grazia, 237 (syr.) bzw. 241 (ital.).

> Denn die göttliche Natur ist körperlos, unbegrenzt und für alle Geschöpfe unsichtbar, die Natur und Person der Menschheit unseres Herrn jedoch ist körperlich, begrenzt und für alle vernünftigen [Lebewesen] sichtbar, und deswegen ist sie nicht imstande, die Natur seiner Gottheit zu sehen. Denn wie die Menschheit unseres Herrn – anders als seine Gottheit – nicht unbegrenzt und ohne Anfang und ohne Ende ist und wie sie – [anders als] das Wort und der Geist – nicht unsichtbar, ungeschaffen und unkörperlich ist, so vermag die Menschheit unseres Herrn nicht seine Gottheit zu sehen, während der Logos-Sohn oder der hervorgehende Geist die göttliche Natur [durchaus] sehen. Niemand sieht den Vater, sagt unser Herr, außer derjenige, der aus Gott ewig geboren wird oder hervorgeht; der [ist es, der] den Vater sieht. [Joh 6,46][34]

Hier bezieht sich Nestorius wohl auf die 25. Homilie des Johannes von Dalyātā.[35] Anders als dieser interpretiert Nestorius das Wort Joh 6,46 strikt im Rahmen der ostsyrischen Christologie. Es ist nur die göttliche Natur des Christus, die Gott sehen kann, nicht aber die menschliche Natur. Damit ist auch ausgeschlossen, dass andere Menschen, also insbesondere die Mystiker, einer unmittelbaren Schau der Gottheit teilhaftig werden.

Vielleicht sollte man in der Apologie des Nestorius weniger einen Verrat am mystischen Gedankengut an sich sehen[36] als vielmehr den Versuch – freilich unter äußerem Druck –, die mystische theologische Grundhaltung noch stärker mit der ostsyrischen Christologie in Einklang zu bringen. In den wenigen Seiten der Schrift „Über den Anfang der Bewegung der göttlichen Gnade" lässt sich jedenfalls nicht erkennen, dass Nestorius Johannes von Dalyātā auch in der Christologie gefolgt wäre.

Aus den bisher unveröffentlichten Briefen des Timotheos, an deren Edition ich arbeite, lassen sich zwei Stellen vorbringen, an denen Timotheos selbst mystische Vorstellungen präzisiert.

Bereits Braun erwähnt, dass Timotheos in Brief 44 von einer „Bestrafung" des Nestorius von Bēt Nūhadrān berichte, aber der Text sei leider genau dort stark beschädigt.[37] Die Hoffnung, aus Brief 44 weiteren Aufschluss über die Biografie des Nestorius zu erhalten, wird jedoch enttäuscht. Es lässt sich nicht einmal bestätigen,

---

34 Timotheos, ep. 50 (Braun, Synoden, 306–307).

35 Johannes von Dalyātā, hom 25,10 (franz. bei Beulay, Enseignement, 514]): „Niemand sieht den Vater, wenn er nicht den Sohn in sich hat, denn der Vater wird nur durch seine Erkenntnis [= Christus] gesehen. Also werden der Vater und der Geist in der Einwohnung der Erkenntnis gesehen. Glücklich diejenigen, die dessen gewürdigt werden!"

36 Vgl. Beulay, Lumière, 222: „...à se désolidariser de la doctrine de Joseph Ḥazzaya (et de celle de Jean de Dalyatha)".

37 Vgl. Braun, Synoden, 284 und 285, Anm. 1: „... da Timotheos in dem nicht viel jüngeren, leider gerade an dieser Stelle lückenhaften Brief 44 an Rabban Sergius, demselben von einer Bestrafung des N. berichtet".

dass Timotheos hier „von einer Bestrafung des N. berichtet“, wie Braun behauptete.[38] Zu Beginn von Brief 44 berichtet Timotheos Sergios vom Tod des Einsiedlers Elia.[39] Timotheos gesteht seine tiefe Trauer, findet aber gleichzeitig auch Trost in Christus, der „Ursache des Lebens“, die in Elia so große „Wirkung“ gezeigt habe. Den Bericht schließt er wie folgt:

> 44,10 Soviel dazu. Denn deiner Keuschheit sind, so meine ich, die Untersuchungen bekannt, die von uns gegen unseren Bruder Nestorius, Inhaber des [Bischofs-]Sitzes von Bēt Nūhadrān, durchgeführt wurden …

Hier sind eindreiviertel Zeilen im Manuskript leer gelassen.[40] Der Textverlust muss aber größer sein, denn die Fortsetzung des Textes in 44,11 ff. bezieht sich auf einer ganze Reihe von inhaltlichen Einzelheiten, die in dem verlorenen Textstück gestanden haben müssen. Wir befinden uns in 44,11 ff. in einem Sinnzusammenhang, der nicht zu Nestorius von Bēt Nūhadrān passt; vielmehr scheint von einem Fall im Südirak die Rede zu sein, der enge Parallelen zu den Briefen 52 und 55/56 aufweist. Wahrscheinlich stammt 44,11 ff. sogar aus einem anderen Brief.[41] Der jetzige lückenhafte Zusammenhang geht wohl auf einen Blattausfall in einer Vorgängerhandschrift zurück.[42]

Dennoch kann der Anfang von Brief 44 zu unserem Thema beitragen. In der zitierten Stelle 44,10 findet sich die Formel „Soviel dazu“ (ܘܗܠܝܢ ܕܝܢ ܗܟܢ), die Timotheos in seinen Briefen so oder ähnlich verwendet, um verschiedene Themen voneinander abzutrennen. Den ersten Satz des neuen Themas setzt er danach mit ܕܝܢ („aber“, „jedoch“) ab. Hier ist dies nicht der Fall. Timotheos fügt nach der Schlussformel noch eine mit ܓܝܪ („denn“, „nämlich“) angeschlossene Erläuterung an. Also standen die verlorenen Ausführungen über Nestorius noch immer in inhaltlichem Zusammenhang mit dem vorangehenden Bericht über den Tod des Einsiedlers Elia. In der Tat lassen sich in den vorangehenden Sätzen Ausführungen des Timotheos zur Mystik finden, die mit dem Fall des Nestorius in Zusammenhang stehen:

> 44,4 Deshalb habe ich das Leiden bis zur genannten Grenze [des Todes][43] über alles Maß bis zur Erschöpfung ertragen. Denn „Tod“ ist nicht dasselbe wie „zu Tode“ und „bis zu ihm hin“. 44,5 Und dies müssen wir in allgemeiner Weise und wegen allen Menschen glauben und leiden – denn die Hoff-

38 Braun, Synoden, 28 und 285, Anm. 1. Auf diese Behauptung stützt sich auch Martikainen, Timotheos, 53.

39 Vermutlich ist Elia bar Parrūkzād gemeint, den wir aus Brief 16 (CSCO 120, 80) flüchtig kennen.

40 Bagdad, Bibliothek des Chaldäischen Klosters 509, 719a.

41 Vermutlich handelt es sich bei 44,11ff. um einen Brief aus der Zeit, als Sergios bereits Metropolit von Elam war, während Brief 44 noch an den „Priester und Lehrer“ Sergios gerichtet ist. Für die Details verweise ich auf meine im Entstehen begriffene Edition.

42 Auch die Timotheosbriefe 13 und 14 sowie 8a und 8b sind je zu einem Text zusammengewachsen.

43 Gemeint ist, dass Timotheos „zu Tode betrübt“ ist, wie er zu Beginn des Briefes schreibt (44,1).

> nung und die Erlösung der sichtbaren und unsichtbaren [Dinge] ist allgemein und von allen Menschen, wenn Gott doch allgemein und von allen [ist] und der Mensch, der in Gott aufgenommen wurde, allgemein und von allen und aus allen [ist] und der Gott-Mensch als Vereinigter (ܡܚܝܕܐ) das wurde, was der Mensch-Gott durch die Vereinigung (ܒܚܝܕܘܬܐ) [ist][44] –, besonders aber wegen jenen besonders Lobenswerten und über alles Tugendhaften, die, soweit [überhaupt] möglich, das göttliche Bild in sich tragen. 44,6 Denn aus ihnen war und ist der lobenswerte Elia.

Timotheos nimmt Bezug auf das für die Mystik zentrale Thema der Vergöttlichung: Durch die Menschwerdung des Christus ist allgemein und grundsätzlich die Möglichkeit der Vergöttlichung der Menschen gegeben. Er anerkennt auch, dass die „lobenswerten und über alles tugendhaften" Asketen „das göttliche Bild in sich tragen", verbindet diese aber mit einer typisch ostsyrischen Einschränkung: „soweit überhaupt möglich". Es muss gewahrt bleiben, dass keine *communicatio idiomatum* stattfindet. In 44,1–3 redet Timotheos davon, dass er in seiner Trauer durch eine Art geistige Schau getragen wird, für die er aber nicht das Verb ܚܙܐ („sehen"), sondern ܚܘܪ („erblicken") verwendet, und es ist nicht die göttliche Natur, die er erblickt, sondern es sind Glaubenswahrheiten: In den Glaubenden erblickt er „gleichsam das Leben der in Ewigkeit Unsterblichen" (44,1), in Christus erblickt er „die Ursache des Lebens" und im verstorbenen Elia „die Wirkung", die Christus, „der alles belebende Gott" verursacht (44,2). Es wäre spannend zu wissen, was nun Timotheos noch zu Nestorius von Bēt Nūhadrān ergänzt hat. Aber offensichtlich hat ein Blattausfall hier den Text zerstört.

Ein weiteres Textstück aus Brief 42 vermag weiter zu zeigen, wie Timotheos die Vergöttlichung der Menschen verstanden und präzisiert hat. Brief 42 richtet sich an die Scholastiker in der Schule des Mar Abraham in Ninive-Mossul, wo Timotheos selbst ausgebildet wurde, bevor er zuerst zum Bischof und dann zum Patriarchen ernannt wurde. In diesem langen Text geht es zu einem großen Teil um die Auslegung von Kernstellen von Gregor von Nazianz, die Severus von Antiochien im Sinne der westsyrischen Theologie interpretierte. Ganz offensichtlich stehen die Lehrer der Klosterschule in Mossul in der interkonfessionellen Diskussion um die richtige Auslegung des Nazianzeners. Im Abschnitt 42,6,16–28 geht es um die Auslegung eines Zitats aus Rede 29 von Gregor von Nazianz: „…damit ich so weit Gott werde, wie jener Mensch [geworden ist]."[45]

> 6,16 Und dies ist auch daraus offensichtlich, wie er [= Gregor von Nazianz] danach in ebendieser Rede über den Sohn fortfährt. Er sagt nämlich Folgendes: „…damit ich so weit Gott werde, wie jener Mensch [geworden ist]." 6,17 Denn wenn wir so weit Götter werden, wie das Wort Mensch geworden ist oder wie umgekehrt der Mensch Gott geworden ist, und [wenn zweitens]

44 Vgl. die Parallelstelle in ep. 42,6,16–19 mit den sich danach anschließenden Erläuterungen.

45 Greg.Naz.or. 29,19 (SC 250, 218,9–10): ἵνα γένωμαι τοσοῦτον θεός, ὅσον ἐκεῖνος ἄνθρωπος.

> der Gottmensch und der Menschgott eine [einzige] zusammengesetzte Natur und Hypostase wurden, dann werden also auch wir zusammen mit Gott eine [einzige] zusammengesetzte Natur und Hypostase. 6,18 Wenn wir aber nicht eine [einzige] zusammengesetzte Natur und Hypostase zusammen mit Gott werden, [und wenn] andererseits Gott und Mensch eine [einzige] zusammengesetzte Natur und Hypostase geworden sind, dann werden wir also nicht soweit Götter, wie er Mensch [geworden ist], wie der Lehrer sagt. 6,19 Wir werden aber soweit Götter, wie er Mensch [geworden ist]. Der Gottmensch und der Menschgott sind „einer" durch die Vereinigung. Also werden auch wir durch die Vereinigung Götter gemäss dem, was auch unser Herr sagte: „...dass sie einer seien, wie auch wir einer sind" (Joh 17,22). 6,20 Genauso also wie „einer" sich hier nicht auf die Natur oder die Hypostase, sondern auf den Willen und die Vereinigung bezieht, so bezieht sich auch, was der Lehrer sagte, dass „er mit Gott vermischt wurde und [mit ihm] einer wurde"[46], nicht auf die Natur und Hypostase, sondern auf die unaussprechliche Vereinigung in der Gottheit und in der Sohnschaft.

Wir finden hier in 6,19 denselben Gedanken wie in Brief 44,5, dass die Vereinigung des Logos mit dem Menschen Jesus die menschliche Wirklichkeit des Jesus vergöttlicht hat und damit die Voraussetzungen geschaffen hat, dass grundsätzlich jeder Mensch vergöttlicht werden kann. Dabei ist hier die Argumentation mit der Abwehr einer westsyrischen Interpretation verquickt, die das Gregorzitat als Beleg dafür verstehen will, dass der Mensch Jesus und der Logos „eine [einzige] zusammengesetzte Natur und Hypostase" geworden seien (6,17). „Vergöttlichung" bezeichnet nicht die Verschmelzung von Göttlichem und Menschlichem zu einer einzigen „Natur und Hypostase", sondern die „unaussprechliche Vereinigung in der Gottheit und in der Sohnschaft".

Danach differenziert Timotheos in 6,21 ff. sehr genau zwischen der Vergöttlichung des „Fleisches unseres Herrn" und derjenigen Vergöttlichung, „die dereinst den vernünftigen [Lebewesen] zuteil wird":

> 6,21 Aber es soll niemand deswegen sagen, dass folglich die Art der Gottheit und der Vereinigung ein und dieselbe sei, und [ebenso auch die] des Fleisches unseres Herrn und der unterschiedlichen Gestalt, die zwischen uns und der Menschwerdung Gottes ist. 6,22 So viel größer ist die Art der Vergöttlichung des Fleisches des Herrn als die Vergöttlichung, die dereinst den vernünftigen [Lebewesen] zuteil wird. Denn der Mensch unseres Herrn ist als Sohn des Vaters vergöttlicht worden, wir aber [werden] als Diener [vergöttlicht]. 6,23 Denn ⟨wenn⟩ das Fleisch mit dem Wort vereinigt wurde, und [wenn] das Wort der Natur nach Gottheit ist, dann wurde das Fleisch also mit der Gottheit vereinigt, die der Natur nach [so ist]. 6,24 Und das Fleisch unseres Herrn hat seine Herrlichkeit als Herrlichkeit des Einziggeborenen. Die

46 Greg.Naz.or. 29,19 (SC 250, 218,8): ἐπειδὴ συνανεκράθη θεῷ καὶ γέγονεν εἷς.

> Herrlichkeit des Einziggeborenen ist ohne Unterschied ein und dieselbe wie die des Vaters. Also ist die Herrlichkeit des Einziggeborenen auch in diesem seinem Fleisch ohne Unterschied zu [derjenigen des] Vaters. 6,25 ⟨Wir⟩ aber werden nicht dem Wort gleich – das ist nämlich nicht möglich –, sondern seinem Leib – „damit wir dem Leib seiner Herrlichkeit gleich werden" (Phil 3,21) –, und seinem Leib werden wir nicht in derselben Menge und in der Art. gleich, sondern nur in einer gewissen Weise und teilweise. 6,26 Denn wie es für uns weder der Menge noch der Art nach dasselbe ist, die Kugel der Sonne am Himmel zusammen mit ihrem Bild, das im Wasser sichtbar ist, zu sehen und zu erkennen, sondern nur eine gewisse Gleichheit, nicht aber eine völlige Gleichheit zu sehen ist, so zeigt sich auch weder die Menge noch die Art der Vergöttlichung des Leibes unseres Herrn und der unsrigen als ein und dieselbe, sondern [es ist] nur eine teilweise Gleichheit, nicht aber eine völlige Gleichheit. 6,27 Und wie nicht ein und derselbe Glanz in der Sonne und in den Sternen gesehen werden kann, weder in der Menge noch in der Art, so zeigt sich auch die Vergöttlichung des Leibes unseres Herrn und des unsrigen nicht als ein und dieselbe. Denn ihm ist der vollkommene Glanz eigen, der alles übersteigt, uns aber nur ein teilweiser, gleichsam gereinigter [Glanz]. 6,28 Wenn aber die Vergöttlichung des Leibes unseres Herrn und die unsrige wie zum Vergleich nebeneinandergestellt werden, so sind die vernünftigen [Lebewesen] im Vergleich mit ihm wie die Sterne im Vergleich mit der Sonne.

Durch sprachliche Einschränkungen, Relativierungen und Differenzierungen betont Timotheos, dass es sich bei der Vergöttlichung der menschlichen Natur des Christus und der Vergöttlichung der Menschen nicht um eine „völlige Gleichheit", sondern nur um eine „gewisse Gleichheit", eine „teilweise Gleichheit" (6,26) – auf Deutsch würden wir „Ähnlichkeit" sagen – handelt: Die menschliche Natur des Christus wird „als Sohn des Vaters" vergöttlicht, die Menschen „als Diener" (6,22). Zudem werden die Menschen gemäß Phil 3,21 nicht „dem Wort gleich", sondern [nur] „seinem Leib", und auch dies „nur in einer gewissen Weise und teilweise" (6,25). Dem „vollkommenen" Glanz des Christus steht ein „teilweiser, gleichsam gereinigter" Glanz der Menschen gegenüber (6,27). Als bildliche Vergleiche dienen Timotheos „die Sterne im Vergleich mit der Sonne" (6,28) und die „Sonne am Himmel und ihr Spiegelbild im Wasser" (6,26).

Bei Timotheos und Nestorius wird ein Instrumentarium greifbar, das bei mystischen Vorstellungen wie der „Schau Gottes" oder der „Vergöttlichung" Differenzierungen vornimmt, um diese in die ostsyrische Theologie und Christologie mit ihrer klaren Unterscheidung von geschöpflicher und göttlicher Sphäre einzuordnen. Nestorius tut dies, indem er zum einen die Differenzierung von Johannes von Dalyātā übernimmt, dass nur Gottes „Glanz" und nicht Gott selbst geschaut werde, und indem er zum anderen sich in seiner Apologie klar zur ostsyrischen Christologie bekennt und eine direkte Gottesschau ebenso ablehnt wie die Lehre, die menschliche Natur des Christus könne die göttliche Natur sehen.[47]

Timotheos selbst ist der Mystik gegenüber nicht grundsätzlich abgeneigt. Für ihn ist aber entscheidend, dass die christologischen Grundlinien der ostsyrischen Kirche eingehalten werden, und er selbst entwickelt dazu Differenzierungen: „Vergöttlichung“ darf nicht in dem Sinne verstanden werden, dass dadurch eine „einzige Natur und Hypostase“ entstünde. Zudem ist zwischen der Vergöttlichung der menschlichen Natur des Christus und derjenigen der Menschen zu differenzieren. Die Asketen wiederum tragen das göttliche Bild in sich, nur „soweit überhaupt möglich“. Offenbar war es also nicht die „Dynamik mystischen Erlebens“ (Blum)[48] an sich, die zur Exkommunikation der Mystiker führte, sondern das Überschreiten des klar begrenzten Rahmens der ostsyrischen Christologie, wie wir es im Fall von Johannes von Dalyātā deutlich fassen können. In den Augen des Timotheos drohte die Mystik dadurch zu einer chalkedonischen oder westsyrischen Position abzudriften – für Timotheos das theologische Schreckgespenst ersten Ranges![49] Timotheos selbst ist weniger ein Mystiker, als vielmehr ein Grundlagentheoretiker der Mystik.

47 Es wäre interessant, in einer eingehenden Analyse zu untersuchen, ob sich in der Apologie nicht gar Spuren der Hand des Timotheos nachweisen lassen. Es fällt immerhin auf, dass sich zu etlichen Passagen der Apologie enge Parallelen bei Timotheos finden. Auch das für die präzise argumentative Sprache des Timotheos typische Partikelpaar ܡܢ ... ܕܝܢ findet sich in der Apologie des Nestorius, nicht aber in seiner Schrift „Über den Anfang der Bewegung der göttlichen Gnade“.

48 Blum, Nestorianismus, 288.

49 Vgl. Timotheos, Disputation 15, 14 und 20,1–9; ep. 42,5–7 passim.

Der Mönch als Turteltaube: Ein mystisches Symbol und sein theologischer Gehalt bei Sabrišō' I. (596–604)

Martin Tamcke

Der Katholikos-Patriarch Sabrišō' I. (596–604) vergleicht die Existenz eines Mönchs mit der einer Taube. Die Taube liebe die Wüste. Diese Aussage zur Taube hat ihren Sitz im Vergleich zum Mönch, dessen geistige Heimat ebenfalls die Wüste ist.

I.

Sabrišō' verortet diesen Vergleich im Kontext der Schilderung der Ereignisse um die versuchte Plünderung des Tempels in 2 Makk 3: Da der antiochenische König Seleukos IV. die Tributzahlungen an Rom nicht leisten konnte, sandte dieser Heliodor nach Jerusalem, um die im Tempel befindlichen Schätze zu beschlagnahmen. Aufgrund der Weigerung der Priester, den Schatz auszuliefern, stürmte Heliodor mit einer Truppe in den Tempel, während der Hohepriester Onias am Altar betete. Daraufhin hatte Heliodor eine gewaltige Erscheinung, in der er von Männern und einem Reiter angegriffen wurde, und daraufhin zu Boden stürzte, so dass er schwer verletzt aus dem Tempel getragen werden musste und nur durch das Gebet des Onias überlebte.

Auf den Ausgang der biblischen Geschichte geht Sabrišō' nicht ein. Ihn interessiert nur das Vergehen des Heliodor am Tempel, die Entweihung des Heiligtums. Diese Situation lässt den betenden Onias Gott bitten: „Wer gibt mir leichte Flügel, wie die der jungen, vollkommenen Taube, dass ich mich im Fluge erhebe aus Jerusalem, der Herrin der Streitigkeiten und Händel, welche die Propheten tötet und die Gerechten steinigt, und wohne in der Wüste wie eine die Wüste liebende Turteltaube.“[1]

---

1 Synodicon orientale ou recueil de synodes nestoriens, hrsg. von J. B. Chabot, Paris 1902, 205 (468), und O. Braun, Das Buch der Synhados oder Synodicon orientale, Stuttgart/Wien 1900 (Neudruck Amsterdam 1975), 294. Mit diesem Bild klingt Ps 55,7f an, wie Braun mit einem Fragezeichen versehen bemerkt: „O hätte ich Flügel wie Tauben, dass ich wegflöge und Ruhe fände! Siehe, so wollte ich in die Ferne fliehen und in der Wüste bleiben.“ Vgl. hierzu und zum

Freilich hat Sab̲rīšōʿ mit seiner Schilderung weniger das alte Israel als vielmehr die Kirche als das neue Israel im Blick. Wie Heliodor in den Tempel zu Jerusalem eindrang, so wütete der Widersacher von Anfang an in der Kirche.[2] Wie in Jerusalem unter den Juden seinerzeit Bestürzung angesichts des Ansinnens des Heliodor herrschte, so auch unter den Christen angesichts des Widersachers, der in der Kirche, der „großen, prophetischen und apostolischen Schatzkammer"[3], wütet und Zwietracht sät und so die Freude verdunkelt, die über die kirchliche Eintracht bestehen sollte. So ist die Lage der Kirche mit der Situation der Juden in der Zeit Heliodors darin vergleichbar, dass damals wie heute das Heiligste entweiht worden sei: Damals sei es der Tempel gewesen, heute, zur Zeit des Katholikos-Patriarchen, die Einmütigkeit in der theologischen Lehre.

In dieser Situation sieht sich mit dem Propheten Jeremia verbunden: Wie dieser Trauer und Schmerz empfand und ihm die Augen zu Tränenquellen wurden angesichts der Zerstörungen und Entweihungen unter seinem Volk durch die babylonische Eroberung, so weint Sab̲rīšōʿ über diejenigen, die den Gläubigen ein Vorbild sein sollten, die zwar von Anfang an mit Verstand begabt waren, das Wort Gottes hörten und Taufe und Eucharistie empfingen, und trotzdem den Gläubigen zum Ärgernis wurden.[4] So bietet sich dort, wo Erlösung erfahrbar sein sollte, ein Bild des Jammers dar.

Sab̲rīšōʿ erfasst also seine gegenwärtige Situation mittels biblischen Vokabulars. Auch die Taube wandert über diese biblische Sprache in den gegenwärtigen Diskurs ein.

II.

In Anbetracht dieser Lage, die Sab̲rīšōʿ anhand der biblischen Vergleichssituationen als traurig und schmerzhaft versteht, weist er darauf hin, was denn den Mönch im Blick der Menschen positiv zu charakterisieren habe. Angesichts aller Verfehlung gelte es, vorsichtig zu sein, das Böse zu fliehen, dem Guten zu nahen und „ein reines, heiliges Gefäß zu sein, geeignet zum Gebrauch für Gott zu jedem vollkommenen Werk."[5] Damit ist deutlich: Ein ethisch korrektes Verhalten ist eine notwendige Voraussetzung. Das Bild des Gefäßes kennzeichnet derartige äußerliche Vorbereitung als eine notwendige Voraussetzung. Als eine solche kann etwa die Askese weder Selbstzweck sein noch den eigentlichen Gehalt darstellen. Denn der Gehalt, mit dem das Gefäß gefüllt wird und dadurch erst seine Verwendung findet, ist Gott und

Folgenden: M. Tamcke, Der Mönch als die die Wüste liebende Turteltaube. Vom inneren Wesen monastischen Daseins nach Sab̲rīšōʿ I. (596–604), in: FS Rev. Fr. Emmanuel Thelly, The Harp XXI, Kottayam 2006, 55-60.

2 Synodicon, Chabot, 203 (465f); Braun, Synhados, 291.

3 Braun, ebd.

4 Synodicon, Chabot, 204 (466); Braun, Synhados, 292.

5 Synodicon, Chabot, 205 (467); Braun, Synhados, 292f.

sein Wille selbst, welcher den Menschen sozusagen instrumentalisiert und dabei den menschlichen Eigenwillen, der bei der Askese und dem ethischen Verhalten durchaus noch wirksam ist, hinter sich lässt und durch den göttlichen Willen ersetzt.

Wie aber ist das anzustellen? Deutlich weist Sabrišōʿ darauf hin, dass es allein mit äußeren Vollzügen gerade nicht getan ist.[6] Wer meint, er müsse nur in die Wüste fliehen, um die Welt hinter sich zu lassen, dem hält er entgegen: „Die Wüste bewirkt keine Heiligkeit, ihr Menschen Gottes.“ Wer die Einöde aufsucht, um der Verwirrung des Vielerlei zu entgehen, und meint, damit das Entscheidende dafür getan zu haben, dass Gott sich ihm zeige, dem widerspricht er: „Nicht die Einöde erfreut mit Offenbarungen Gottes.“ Und wer schließlich meint, die Freiheit von materiellem Besitz sei die Bedingung für wirkliche Freiheit, dem stellt er entgegen: „Nicht die Entäußerung an Besitz macht den Menschen des Geistigen teilhaft.“

Statt auf das äußere Tun richtet Sabrišōʿ sein Augenmerk also ganz auf die innere Haltung, das innere Ziel. Alle Äußerlichkeiten, alle äußeren Mittel und Maßnahmen führen nicht automatisch und von selbst zu dem, was das Ziel aller asketisch-monastischen Bemühungen ist. So heiligt die Wüste nur, „wenn die Seele mit dem Leib im Umgang mit Gott übereinstimmt“[7], wenn der Umgang mit Gott sowohl körperlich als auch spirituell geschieht, also der Religiosität eine entsprechende Ethik folgt, und so der ganze Mensch geprägt und aufgrund seiner Beziehung zu Gott zwingend zu einem korrekten ethischen Verhalten sich verpflichtet weiß. So kann die Einöde nur dann herrliche Offenbarungen zeitigen und derer würdig machen, „wenn der Verstand sich trunken vermischt mit dem göttlichen Tun“[8]. Selbst der Verstand ist kein Beobachter, der außerhalb bleibt, sondern wird hineingenommen in das Handeln Gottes. Entsprechend bereichert die Entäußerung jeglichen Besitzes nur diejenigen, die sich nicht nur äußerlich, sondern wahrhaftig und wirklich von allem frei gemacht haben und erst dann dem Apostel Paulus ehrlich beipflichten können: „Da wir nichts besitzen, haben wir alles.“[9]

III.

Mag die „Lossagung von den Plagen der verwirrten, erregten Welt“[10] auch Bewunderung erzeugen, mag Demut erhaben sein, Askese als ein Ausdruck von erstrebenswerter Freiheit gelten und das Einsiedlerleben geradezu als schön angesehen werden – sie ist jedenfalls nichts, worauf man vor der Welt stolz sein könne. Mönchisches Dasein ist zwar „Fremdlingschaft“, aber doch eben „Fremdlingschaft Got-

6 Zum Folgenden: Synodicon, Chabot, 204f (467); Braun, Synhados, 293.
7 Braun, ebd.
8 Ebd.
9 2 Kor 6,10.
10 Braun, Synhados, 293.

tes".[11] Die Fremdlingschaft Gottes ist nicht durch ihre Außenwirkung zu verstehen, sondern durch ihre innere Haltung: ein Bemühen um das Gute, ein Geprägtsein durch Demut sowie ein Wissen um die Notwendigkeit ordnender und das Leben ermöglichender Gesetze. Als Fremdlingschaft aufgrund ihrer Bindung an Gott stellt sie auch den Menschen hinein in die Schöpfung Gottes, in der Tiere wie Naturerscheinungen ihre Gesetze haben.[12] Überall in der Schöpfung entdeckt Sabrīšōʿ das von Gott gegebene Gesetz, wie etwa bei Ochse und Esel, bei Turteltaube, Kranich, Schwalbe und Ameise, aber auch bei Sonne und Mond, Luft und Wind, Erde und Pflanzen, selbst bei den Fischen. Entsprechend steht auch der Mönch unter lebensdienlichen Gesetzen, denn nur von Gott kann ausgesagt werden, dass er an kein Gesetz gebunden ist.[13]

Das Bild der Turteltaube als Symbol für den monastischen Asketen dürfte Sabrīšōʿ aus dem „Physiologus", einem Kompendium frühchristlicher Tiersymbolik, übernommen haben.[14] Dort wurde die Taube vor allem hinsichtlich ihrer Charakteristika für die Verkündigung gedeutet: Sie lasse ihre Stimme hören im Lande, sie meide die Menge und lebe lieber zurückgezogen in der Wüste. Schon der „Physiologus" parallelisiert den Lebensstil der Taube in der Wüste mit dem Aufstieg Jesu zusammen mit Petrus, Jakobus und Johannes auf den Berg Tabor. Die Erscheinung des Mose und des Elia und das Bekenntnis der himmlischen Stimme Gottes zu Jesus als seinem Sohn dokumentieren eine kaum vorstellbare Nähe zu Gott. Wie die Turteltaube die Einsamkeit liebt, so sollen auch die Mönche die Einsamkeit lieben. Jedoch achtet die Turteltaube auf ihre Zeit und weiß, wann sie wiederkommen muss. So wird ausgerechnet die scheinbar nur Freiheit symbolisierende Turteltaube zum Ausdruck der Bindung ans Gesetz.

Sabrīšōʿ, mit dem erstmals wieder ein Mönch an der Spitze der Kirche des Ostens stand, setzt hier nun mit konkreten Anweisungen für ein ethisches Verhalten ein, das seiner Auffassung des Mönchtums entspricht und dessen Ziele Gottgefallen, Freude, Frieden, Eintracht und Ruhe sind.[15] Von dieser Grundlage her geht er in seinem Brief, der an die Mönche der Bruderschaft von Barqita gerichtet ist, auf deren Haltung und Selbstverständnis ein. Dort war man stolz darauf gewesen, sich schon rein äußerlich in seiner Erwähltheit von der Welt abzuheben und ebenso

---

11 Braun, Synhados, 291. Chabot erschien dieser Passus als Bestandteil des Briefes wenig glaubwürdig und nahm dessen Bearbeitung durch einen Kopisten an, vgl. Synodicon, 465 Anm. 2.

12 Synodicon, Chabot, 205 (468); Braun, Synhados, 294.

13 Braun ließ dieses vermeintliche Prophetenzitat ebenso ohne Nachweis (Synhados, 294), wie Chabot ausdrücklich anmerkte, dass er dies Zitat nicht habe finden können (Synodicon, 468 Anm. 6).

14 Einen Überblick zu den Übersetzungen und der Überlieferung des „Physiologus" bietet in knapper Form Ursula Treu in ihrem Nachwort zu ihrer Übersetzung aus dem Griechischen, in: U. Treu, Physiologus, Naturkunde in frühchristlicher Deutung, Hanau [3]1998, 111–132. Dort führt sie als den ursprünglichen Text zur Turteltaube Nr. 28 an (mit Nachweis der Schriftzitate), 52 (spätere Ausdeutungen folgen 53f; zu der sehr anders gearteten Überlieferung zu Taube allgemein vgl. 68–72 „Von der Taube" unter Nr. 35).

15 Synodicon, Chabot, 206f (469f); Braun, Synhados, 295f.

äußerlich durch Erscheinungsbild und Verhalten bereits als religiöse Elite auf der Erde erkennbar zu sein. Das Argument der Brüder, schon der mit Vernunft begabte Mensch wisse Gott Folge zu leisten, erscheint nur noch am Rand und wird seiner fundamentalen Bedeutung, die es im Bundesvertrag von Barqita gehabt hatte, entkleidet. Da sich für Sabrišōʿ alles Geschaffene dadurch auszeichnet, dass es dem Gesetz unterworfen sei, müssen auch die, die den Glauben der Kirche annehmen, das entsprechende Leben spendende Gesetz einhalten. Für ihn geht es darum, dass die Bejahung des christlichen Glaubens nicht im Abstrakten verbleibt, sondern zu Leben in Konkretheit auf den Anruf Gottes hin wird. Und diese Konkretheit macht er zunächst an der konfessionellen und kirchlichen Zugehörigkeit fest. Nur auf der Grundlage der Regeln für das mönchische Leben werde sich der Mönch inne, dass er von der Forderung Gottes überfordert und der Unmöglichkeit überführt werde, gerecht zu sein. Rühmen könne man sich nur im Herrn, der darum wisse, dass Gott als der Schöpfer in der Form des Gesetzes in das Leben der Menschen, der Kreatur und aller Natur schon immer als dessen letzte Tiefe und dessen „Leben spendendes Haupt" eingestiftet sei.

Deshalb griff Sabrišōʿ in das scheinbar beliebige monastische Leben der Brüder von Barqita zugunsten einer strafferen Unterstellung unter die Oberen ein. Denn wie schon Menschen in der Welt nicht ohne Obrigkeit leben können, so könne kein Leib sein Leben ohne belebendes Haupt fristen. Deutlicher konnte der Abt in seiner Funktion im Kloster nicht mehr in Parallele zu Gott gebracht werden.

IV.

Sabrišōʿs Mystik hat einerseits einer zu rationalen Interpretation des Glaubens durch Mönche seiner Kirche zu wehren gehabt, andererseits unternahm er mit ihr den Versuch, sie in ein weltumspannendes Dasein in Harmonie mit der Natur und allem Geschaffenen einzubinden. Die Erfahrung der Einigung ist letztlich unsagbar. Der Ausdruck von der trunkenen Vermischung[16] menschlichen und göttlichen Willens deutet in seiner Verschwommenheit dabei eben nur gerade dies an: Was sich da vollzieht, liegt außerhalb menschlich-intellektueller Klarheit, die sich zwar im Zustand der Trunkenheit noch ihrer selbst gewahr ist, aber eben wie mitgenommen durch etwas, was anders ist, und den Geist des Menschen aus der Selbststeuerung herausholt. Der Charakter dessen, was dem Mönch hier als etwas Überwältigendes widerfährt, ist unverkennbar, auch wenn damit das Selbstsein nicht einfach ausgelöscht, sondern mit hinein genommen wird in ein verändertes Sein. Was das Bild schon nicht mehr zu sagen vermag, ist der Gefäßcharakter des Menschen für Gott,[17] den der ethisch und asketisch vorbereitete Mönch erhält. Fülle und Inhalt sind allein Gottes.

16 Braun, Synhados, 293.
17 Braun, Synhados, 292.

Hilfreich für die Einübung in dieses sich selbst übersteigende Bewusstsein hin zu einem Bewusstsein, das sich und die Menschen und die Welt aus ursprünglicher und zugleich erhöhter Perspektive sieht, ist das Gesetz, die Bindung an Obere und Lehrer spirituellen Lebens, aber natürlich auch an die Führer und Leiter der Kirche. An ihnen kann gelernt werden, wie der Mensch in das der Taube eigene Wissen um die Stimme ihres Herrn und die rechte Zeit zurückfinden kann. Wie die Taube an die Erscheinung Gottes auf dem Tabor erinnert, so wird auch der in rechter Weise ringende Mönch zum Wegzeichen hin zum Göttlichen, dessen er selbst nie habhaft wird, das ihn aber im Prozess der Vermischung mit zu bestimmen beginnt.

In der Turteltaube drückte sich für Sa<u>b</u>rišōʿ bereits all dies aus, seitdem sie im „Physiologus" zum Träger der Verkündigung, zum Sinnbild des Lebens der Einsiedler und zum Zeichen mystischer Nähe zu Gott wurde. Was der Taube als Wissen unterstellt wird, wird Ziel monastischen Daseins, das auf den Akt mystischer Einigung zielt.

Damit aber gelang Sa<u>b</u>rišōʿ die Öffnung des mönchischen Lebensvollzuges über die ethische Dimension hinaus, ohne die Ethik zu vernachlässigen. Gehorsamsethik und die Vermischung von Göttlichem und Menschlichem kennzeichnen den unabschließbaren Weg und den ständig zu erneuernden Charakter des Menschen als Gefäß des göttlichen Tuns. Der Weg des Mönchs und Einsiedlers ist dann der Weg zu Gott und zugleich von Gott her. So kündet auch der Mönch um sein Herkommen und Hingehen, wie die Taube.

Mystische Schau und Gestalt Christi bei Johannes von Dalyatha

Karl Pinggéra

1. Einleitung: Mystik und Trinität

Nadira Khayyat stellte ihrer 2007 erschienenen Edition der ersten 15 Homilien des Johannes von Dalyatha eine gehaltvolle Einleitung in das Werk dieses syrischen Mystikers aus dem 8. Jahrhundert voran. Um die Besonderheit seiner Theologie zu erfassen, erwähnt Khayyat auch eine Charakterisierung christlicher Mystik von Karl Rahner.[1] Im Blick auf die vielfältigen Zeugnisse mystischer Erfahrung hatte Rahner konstatiert, dass die Trinität in der Geschichte der Mystik nicht jene Rolle gespielt habe, die man vom Standpunkt der christlichen Glaubenslehre aus eigentlich erwarten sollte. Bis in die Moderne hinein sei das grundlegende Schema der Mystik die Vereinigung mit Gott gewesen, und zwar mit einem Gott, der als absolut transzendent und als absolut einfach vorgestellt worden sei. Mystische Einung habe sich „in der stillen Wüste der Gottheit" vollzogen. Die Mystik habe es nicht verstanden, die genuin christliche Einsicht fruchtbar zu machen, wonach Gottes Wesen zuerst und zuinnerst als Beziehung zu denken ist.

Damit war eine Anfrage an die klassischen Entwürfe christlicher Mystik formuliert worden, die auch evangelischer Theologie nicht fremd ist. Vor allem die kritische Studie von Dorothea Wendebourg zu Gregor Palamas (1296–1359) hat hier für einiges Aufsehen, gelegentlich auch für Irritationen gesorgt.[2] Die Arbeit kam zu dem Ergebnis, dass die Trinität als Bestandteil der traditionellen Dogmatik bei Palamas zwar beibehalten wurde, die Unterscheidung der drei göttlichen Personen für die spirituelle Erfahrung und ihre konzeptionelle Entfaltung aber ganz funktionslos geworden sei. Weil Palamas an der Unerreichbarkeit des göttlichen Wesens unbedingt festhielt, kamen die innergöttlichen Relationen auf der Seite jenes Bereiches

1 Jean de Dalyatha, Les Homélies I–XV. Édition critique du texte syriaque inédit. Traduction, introduction et notes par Nadira Khayyat, Sources Syriaques 2, Antelias-Hadath 2007, 71. Khayyat zitiert hier Karl Rahner, Artikel Trinitaire (mystique), in: Ders./Herbert Vorgrimler, Petit dictionnaire de Théologie catholique, Livre de vie 99, Paris 1970, 491.

2 Dorothea Wendebourg, Geist oder Energie. Zur Frage der innergöttlichen Verankerung des christlichen Lebens in der byzantinischen Theologie, MMHST 4, München 1980. Zur kritischen Diskussion um diese Arbeit innerhalb der evangelischen Theologie vgl. besonders die Rezension von Fairy von Lilienfeld in: KO 25 (1982), 193–206.

zu stehen, der der menschlichen Erfahrung *a limine* vorenthalten bleibt. Der Mystiker hat es demnach nicht mit der Erfahrung Gottes, des Vaters, des Sohnes und des Geistes, zu tun – wie es einem heilsgeschichtlichen Verständnis des Glaubens besser entsprechen würde –, sondern mit den göttlichen Energien, den Abstrahlungen des *einen* göttlichen Wesens. Wendebourgs Kritik führte über Palamas selbst insofern hinaus, als sie schon für einige griechische Theologen des 4. Jahrhunderts eine tendenzielle Funktionslosigkeit der Trinitätslehre im Weltbezug Gottes konstatierte.

Schon länger wird in der dogmengeschichtlichen Forschung ein Funktionsverlust der immanenten Trinität im Laufe der Theologiegeschichte beobachtet. Die immanente Trinität habe sich gegenüber der ökonomischen verselbständigt und sei für das Verständnis des Heilshandelns Gottes zunehmend irrelevant geworden. Es sei nicht länger erkennbar gewesen, wie Gottes Handeln nach außen in seinem inneren Leben gründe.[3]

Das hier aufgeworfene theologische Problem ließe sich etwa auch an Evagrius Ponticus (4. Jh.) verdeutlichen, von dem die Mystik des syrischen Christentums tief beeinflusst wurde.[4] Die Erfüllung der menschlichen Sehnsucht nach Vereinigung mit dem Göttlichen kann Evagrius als Schau des göttlichen Lichtes beschreiben, und zwar als Schau des „Lichtes der Trinität". Damit wird die Dreifaltigkeit Gottes zwar genannt, doch kann man bezweifeln, ob oder inwiefern eine in Gott sich vollziehende Relationalität für diese höchste Schau irgendwie bedeutsam wäre. Zugespitzt drängt sich der Eindruck auf, dass der Begriff der „Trinität" letztlich mit dem „Einen" der neuplatonischen Philosophie austauschbar ist. Namentlich die Gestalt Christi, des menschgewordenen Logos, scheint auf dem Gipfel mystischer Einung ganz funktionslos geworden zu sein.[5]

Nun hat Nadira Khayyat die kritischen Bemerkungen Karl Rahners aufgegriffen, um zu zeigen, dass sie auf Johannes von Dalyatha gerade *nicht* zutreffen. Für Khayyat stellt Johannes eine bemerkenswerte Ausnahme dar in der Geschichte der ostkirchlichen Mystik. Bei ihm begegne uns eine Form wahrhaft trinitarischer Erfahrungstheologie, die es verdienen würde, im theologischen Gespräch der Gegenwart Gehör zu finden. Im Folgenden greifen wir diese Spur auf und fragen danach, wie Johannes von Dalyatha die mystische Erfahrung mit den innergöttlichen Relationen in Zusammenhang bringt. Dabei gilt unsere Aufmerksamkeit insbesondere der Gestalt Christi, der zweiten trinitarischen Person. Als Zugang wählen wir eine Hermeneutik mystischer Aussagen, die von der Unterscheidung verschiedener Textsorten ausgeht.

---

3 Vgl. etwa Walter Kasper, Der Gott Jesu Christi (Das Glaubensbekenntnis der Kirche, 1), Mainz 1982, 318.

4 Vgl. Antoine Guillaumont, Les ‚Kephalaia Gnostica' d'Évagre le Pontique et l'histoire de l'origénisme chez les Grecs et chez les Syriens, PatSor 5, Paris 1962.

5 So die klassische Kritik an Evagrius bei Irénée Hausherr, Le Traité de l'Oraison d'Évagre le Pontique (Pseudo-Nil), in: RAM 15 (1934), 34–93 und 113–70, hier 117. Eine abweichende Interpretation hat vor allem Gabriel Bunge vorgelegt; zur Diskussion siehe Bernard McGinn, Die Mystik im Abendland, Bd. 1: Die Ursprünge, Freiburg/Breisgau 1994, 225–228.

2. Zu Leben und Werk des Johannes von Dalyatha

Zahlreiche syrische, arabische und äthiopische Handschriften enthalten Texte eines gewissen „Saba“ („der Alte“) oder „Johannes Saba“.[6] Die ältesten Handschriften gehen bis in das 9. Jahrhundert zurück. Auf der Suche nach der Identifizierung dieses Johannes führt die Synode des Katholikos Timotheos I. 786/87 weiter. Dort wurden die Schriften einiger Angehöriger der ostsyrischen („nestorianischen“) Kirche verurteilt. Unter den Verurteilten findet sich ein Johannes von Dalyatha.[7] Einige Vorwürfe findet sich nahezu wörtlich in den Schriften des „Johannes Saba“ wieder. Der 786/87 verurteilte Johannes von Dalyatha wird sodann von zwei späteren syrischen Schriftstellern mit „Johannes Saba“ identifiziert: von Gregor Bar Hebraeus († 1286) und Abdischo von Nisibis († 1318).

Anhaltspunkte zur Biographie des Johannes von Dalyatha liefert neben einigen verstreuten anonymen Notizen besonders der *Liber castitatis* des Ischodenah von Basra (8. Jh.).[8] Johannes wurde demnach Ende des 7. Jahrhunderts in einem Dorf im Nordirak geboren, verließ als junger Mann seine Heimat und trat in das Kloster von Mar Yozadaq im Gebirge Qardu (in der heutigen Südosttürkei) ein. Dort wurde er von Stefan, einem Schüler des Klostergründers Afnimaran, in das monastische Leben eingeführt. Nach rund sieben Jahren zog sich Johannes in die Einsamkeit der nördlich des Klosters gelegenen Bergwelt von Dalyatha zurück. In den letzten Lebensjahren kehrte er in die Nähe seines Klosters zurück, wo er einen Schülerkreis um sich versammelte. Mit hoher Wahrscheinlichkeit verstarb Johannes, ehe die Synode von 786/87 seine Werke unter dem Vorwurf des Messalianismus und des Sabellianismus verurteilt hat.

Der Nachfolger des Timotheos, Ischo Bar Nun, der das Amt des Katholikos 823 antrat, hat Johannes rehabilitiert.[9] Das bedeutet aber, dass die Schriften des Johannes bis dahin nur im Verborgenen gelesen und weitergereicht werden konnten. Wohl auf Grund der Verurteilung auf der Synode des Timotheos sind sie der Nachwelt nur unter dem unverfänglichen Namen eines „Johannes Saba“ erhalten geblieben. Das

---

6 Vgl. zum Folgenden Robert Beulay, Jean de Dalyatha et sa Lettre XV, in: ParOr 2 (1971), 261–279; Ders., Des centuries de Joseph Hazzāyā retrouvées?, in: ParOr 3 (1972), 5–44; Ders., Artikel Jean de Dalyatha, in: DSp 8 (1974), 449–452; Ders., Précisions touchant l'identité et la biographie de Jean Saba de Dalyatha, in: ParOr 8 (1977/78), 87–116; Ders., L'enseignement spirituel de Jean de Dalyatha mystique syro-oriental du VIIIe siècle, ThH 83, Paris 1990, 13–25. Siehe auch zusammenfassend: Giovanni di Dalyatha, Mostrami la tua Bellezza, Preghiere e lodi. Introduzione, traduzione dal siriaco e note a cura di Sabino Chialà, Testi dei Padri della Chiesa 25, Magnano 1996, 3–12.

7 Eine französische Übersetzung des arabisch erhaltenen Textes findet sich bei Robert Beulay, La lumière sans forme. Introduction à l'étude de la mystique chrétienne syro-orientale, Chevetogne [1987], 229–231.

8 In Paul Bedjan, Liber Superiorum seu historia monasteriorum a Thoma episcopo Margensi, Paris und Leipzig 1901, 512.

9 Das berichtet Abdischo von Nisibis in seinem Ordo judiciorum ecclesiasticorum; vgl. Beulay, Précisions (wie Anm. 6), 89f.

Werk besteht aus 29 Homilien und mindestens 48 echten Briefen. Ferner werden ihm acht Centurien zugeschrieben, von denen er allerdings nur für die erste Centurie und die erste Hälfte der zweiten Centurie als Verfasser in Anspruch genommen werden kann.

3. Mystische Erfahrung

Wenn wir uns der geistlichen Lehre des Johannes nähern, so können wir von folgenden zentralen Gedanken ausgehen: Der Ort der Gottesschau liegt im Inneren, im innersten Wesen des Menschen. Für sich genommen beinhaltet diese Vorstellung natürlich nichts Typisches. Einen eigenen Charakter tragen die Aussagen des Johannes, weil sie die Vereinigung mit Gott oftmals in einer sehr individuell geprägten Sprache beschreiben. In den Schriften des Johannes begegnen immer wieder Passagen, die das eigene Erleben in Bildern zu erfassen suchen und die in hohem Maße unabhängig erscheinen von vorgegebenen theologischen Reflexionsmustern und Deutungen.

Georg Günther Blum hat für seine Interpretation solcher Abschnitte sorgsam zwischen mystologischen, mystographischen und mystagogischen Textstücken unterschieden.[10] Über weite Strecken wären die Homilien und Centurien, teils auch die Briefe, demnach als mystologische oder mystagogische Texte zu klassifizieren: Es handelt sich um lehrhafte (*mystologische*) Aussagen, die den mystischen Weg in theologischen Schemata erklären. Oder es werden (*mystagogische*) Anweisungen gegeben, wie dieser Weg im Einzelnen zu beschreiten ist. In beiden Fällen lassen sich die Traditionen mystischer Theologie, die Johannes aufgreift, deutlich erkennen.[11] Grundlegend ist die Gliederung des mystischen Aufstieges nach Pseudo-Dionysius Areopagita mit der Abfolge von Reinigung, Erleuchtung und Einigung. Hinzu tritt die evagrianische Unterscheidung verschiedener Kontemplationen, die von der Schau der geschaffenen Wesen emporsteigen, alle Formen bildhafter Vorstellungen sowie des diskursiven Denkens hinter sich lassen, um so mit einem gänzlich „nackt“ gewordenen Geist zur Schau des göttlichen Lichtes vorzudringen. Dort

---

10 Georg Günther Blum, Die enstatischen Konfessionen des Johannes von Dālyāthā, in: Martin Tamcke/Wolfgang Schwaigert/Egbert Schlarb (Hg.), Syrisches Christentum weltweit. Studien zur syrischen Kirchengeschichte. Festschrift Wolfgang Hage, Studien zur Orientalischen Kirchengeschichte 1, Münster 1995, 202–219 (auch in: Günter Georg Blum, „In der Wolke des Lichtes“. Gesammelte Aufsätze zu Spiritualität und Mystik des Christlichen Ostens, hg. v. Karl Pinggéra [Oikonomia 40], Erlangen 2001, 181–196). Diese Differenzierung verschiedener Textsorten in der mystischen Literatur geht zurück auf Carl Albrecht, Psychologie des mystischen Bewußtseins, Bremen 1951, Mainz ²1976; Ders., Das mystische Erkennen, Bremen 1958, Mainz ²1982.

11 Vgl. dazu zusammenfassend Beulay, Lumière sans forme (wie Anm. 6), 112–116 und 214f. sowie Ilaria Ramelli, Note per un'indagine della mistica siro-orientale dell'VIII secolo: Giovanni di Dalyatha e la tradizione evagriana, in: Ilu. Revista de Ciencias de las Religiones 12 (2007), 147–179.

erst vollzieht sich dann die Vereinigung mit Gott. Es sind vor allem die Briefe, die auch *mystographische* Selbstzeugnisse überliefern, also Stellen, an denen Johannes bewusst eigene Erfahrungen schildert.

In *ep.* 16,1 wird ein solcher Bericht eingeleitet mit der Aufforderung: „Höre, mein Bruder, was mir ein glaubwürdiger Mann berichtet hat …“[12] Im Folgenden wird beschrieben, wie der Mensch durch die Begegnung mit dem „Geliebten“ in einen Zustand der Vernichtung geführt wird, in dem alle welthaften Bezüge ausgelöscht sind, wie eine Phase der Kraftlosigkeit und der Verlassenheit folgt, die in die Erfahrung des „Staunens“ einmündet. Dieses „Staunen“ (syr. *temhā*) bezeichnet eine absolute Stille ohne alle sinnliche Wahrnehmung. Es folgt die Lösung aus diesem Zustand; die Verborgenheit des Geliebten wird dabei schmerzlich erfahren. Das Ende des mystographischen Berichts ist mit der Beteuerung gegeben, das eben Geschehene sei in menschlicher Sprache nicht adäquat wiederzugeben: „Ist es überhaupt möglich, dies mit Feder und Tinte mitzuteilen? Nein! Aber wer dich gekostet hat, o Süßer, o Kostbarer, er wird verstehen!“[13]

In anderen Berichten finden sich weitere bildhafte Beschreibungen der mystischen Erfahrung. Da begegnet die Vorstellung, über den „Abgrund der Gottheit“ zu fliegen: „Ich beginne über den Abgrund der Gottheit zu fliegen und das Pneuma des Lebens zu atmen.“[14] Oder es wird geschildert, wie der menschliche Geist in das Meer des göttlichen Lichtes eintaucht:

> „Er badet sich in den Wellen des Lichtes, er taucht ein und er taucht auf, er atmet den Duft des Lebens, er befindet sich im Staunen, er schwingt sich auf, er lässt sich nieder, er strahlt auf, er tummelt sich in den Wassermassen seiner (des Meeres) Größe …. Dann entrückt ihn (das Meer) und lässt ihn auf eine höhere Weise das heilige Licht durchdringen, und er wird in ihm eingeschlossen wie in einen Berg aus Licht von vielfältigen Strahlen, er wird ergriffen von Bewunderung beim Anblick des Schönen, der in Licht gehüllt ist; er wird gefangen von der Herrlichkeit des Allerhöchsten. Alle Dinge sind für ihn wie nichtseiend, und er selbst erkennt sich nicht mehr. Siehe, die Seele ist allen Dingen gestorben, damit der Vater aller Dinge sie auferweckt durch seine Schau.“[15]

---

12 PO 39/3, 352,24 Beulay.

13 PO 39/3, 354,12 f. Beulay.

14 Ep. 46,1: PO 39/3, 454,5 Beulay; Übersetzung bei Blum, Enstatische Konfessionen (wie Anm. 10), 210.

15 Hom. 8,7f.: Jean de Dalyatha, Les Homélies, ed. Khayyat (wie Anm. 1), 204–206; Übersetzung nach Blum, Enstatische Konfessionen (wie Anm. 10), 217f.

4. Theologische Deutung

Unter den Anschuldigungen, die von der Synode des Timotheos 786/87 erhoben wurden, befindet sich unter andere der Vorwurf des Sabellianismus.[16] Johannes folge dem Sabellius und glaube, der Sohn und der Geist seien nur „Kräfte" Gottes (arab. *quwan*), aber keine eigenständigen Hypostasen (arab. *aqānīm*). In *hom.* 25 könnte ein Ansatzpunkt für diesen Vorwurf liegen. Johannes schreibt dort die göttliche Natur dem Vater zu; Sohn und Geist seien „Kräfte" (syr. *ḥaylē*) innerhalb dieser göttlichen Natur.[17] Es steht außer Frage, dass diese Sätze zumindest „unglücklich" formuliert sind.[18] Zu beachten ist aber der Kontext, in dem sie stehen. Johannes will zeigen, warum der Logos „Sohn Gottes" genannt wird: Weil Gott, der Vater, sich in ihm erkennt und durch ihn die Welt erschaffen hat. Zu beachten und Ernst zu nehmen ist ferner, dass Johannes ansonsten die rechtgläubigen Termini verwendet und die drei trinitarischen Personen im Einklang mit der kirchlichen Tradition *qnōmē* („Hypostasen") nennt. Freilich bleibt er an machen Stellen begrifflich unpräzise.

In *ep.* 50,8–11 findet sich eine Erklärung der Trinität, die das Bild des Meeres aufgreift, dem wir in den mystographischen Selbstzeugnissen begegnet sind. Nun wird das Bild trinitarisch gewendet:

> „Betrachte das sinnlich wahrnehmbare Meer ... Betrachte den Vater von Allem sozusagen als die Natur dieses mit den Sinnen wahrnehmbaren Meeres, den Sohn, der verehrungswürdiger als Alles ist, als die Feuchtigkeit des Wassers, und den Geist, der herrlicher als alles ist, als die Bewegung des Wassers im Meer. Wer könnte die Kräfte des Meeres von seiner Natur trennen, so dass das Wasser des Meeres ohne Feuchtigkeit und ohne dauernde Bewegung wäre? ... Die Kräfte sind nicht getrennt von der Natur und die Natur nicht von ihren Kräften. Betrachte in gleicher Weise die herrliche Natur des geistigen Meeres mit seinen überflutenden und vielstrahlenden Wassern ... Wer könnte eine von diesen [sc. Natur/Kräfte] für sich allein sehen ohne die drei, die doch eins sind? Wer die drei sieht, der sieht eins. Und wer das Eine sieht, der sieht die drei zusammen mit den Kräften des Einen. Man kann die Kräfte nicht trennen von der Natur, und die Natur nicht trennen von ihren Kräften. ... Betrachte den Vater als die Natur, den Sohn als sein Erkennen, und den Geist als das Leben, das mit der Natur, die das Leben selbst ist, verbunden ist.

16 Vgl. zum Folgenden Beulay, L'enseignement (wie Anm. 6), 415–422 („Jean de Dalyatha et le dogme trinitaire").

17 Siehe die Übersetzung von hom. 25,4 (in der Zählung Beulays) bei Beulay, L'enseignement (wie Anm. 6), 512. Die Edition des syrischen Textes mit englischer Übersetzung gibt (in anderer Zählung als Discourse 16) Brian E. Colless, The Mysticism of John Saba. I. The Mystical Discourses of John Saba, II. John Saba and the Legacy of Syrian Mysticism, Melbourne 1969, 61 (syr.); 192 (engl.).

18 So Beulay, L'enseignement (wie Anm. 6), 416 („un passage de formulation pour le moins malheureuse").

Wenn die Kräfte des sinnlich wahrnehmbaren Meeres nicht von ihm getrennt werden können, und keine von ihnen für sich allein genannt werden kann, wer könnte dies behaupten von der herrlichen Natur der heiligen, dreifach gepriesenen Dreiheit? Wer könnte von den angebeteten Hypostasen sprechen, und dabei die eine von den anderen trennen? Denn wenn sie drei genannt werden, sind sie doch eines. Und insofern sie eines sind, werden sie dreifach gepriesen. Das Eine sieht man nicht ohne die drei, und die drei sieht man nicht ohne zugleich das Eine – so wie man das sinnlich wahrnehmbare Meer nicht als eines sehen kann ohne die drei, oder wie man von ihm ohne die drei nicht sagen kann, es sei eines."[19]

Das Bild des Meeres als Licht tritt bei Johannes also in zweifacher Weise auf. Einmal zur Beschreibung der mystischen Versenkung: Der menschliche Geist badet in den Wellen des Lichtes. Dann aber begegnet das lichthafte Meer auch in theologischer Deutung: als Bild der Trinität. Beides greift ineinander, insofern die ständige Bewegtheit des Meeres auf die Trinität hin durchsichtig gemacht wird: Der unentwegte Wellengang des Meeres wird zur Metapher für die Kräfte innerhalb der göttlichen Natur. – Man könnte versucht sein, dem Synodaltext (und mit ihm den modernen Kritikern der Mystik) an dieser Stelle Recht zu geben. Reduziert Johannes die Unterschiedenheit der göttlichen Personen nicht tatsächlich so weit, dass Sohn und Geist als bloße Modi des Vaters erscheinen? Im Bild gesprochen: Kann zwischen dem Meer und seinen Wellen im Sinne distinkter Hypostasen unterschieden werden?

Es ist das Privileg des Mystikers, dass seine theologischen Aussagen nicht die Präzision des dogmatischen Lehrbuches erreichen müssen. So dürfen bestimmte Einzelaussagen bei Johannes von Dalyatha nicht verallgemeinert werden. Im Zusammenhang betrachtet, unterscheidet er sehr wohl zwischen den göttlichen Personen. Das geschieht vornehmlich, wenn Johannes darüber nachdenkt, wie das unendliche Licht der Gottheit vom Menschen überhaupt wahrgenommen werden könne. Johannes steht dabei das grundsätzliche Problem vor Augen, das die antiochenische Tradition ostsyrischer Theologie umgetrieben hat: Göttliches und menschliches, ewiges und endliches, ungeschaffenes und geschaffenes Sein können sich niemals miteinander vermischen und müssen in der theologischen Reflexion strikt getrennt bleiben.[20] Johannes von Dalyatha hat dieser Maxime dadurch Rechnung getragen, dass er zwischen der Natur der Gottheit und ihrer „Herrlichkeit" (syr. *tešboḥtā*) unterschied.[21] Die fundamentale Unterscheidung von Natur und Herrlichkeit Gottes

19 PO 39/3, 464,24–466,16 Beulay.

20 Vgl. dazu Peter Bruns, Finitum non capax infiniti. Ein antiochenisches Axiom in der Inkarnationslehre Babais des Großen († nach 628), in: OrCh 83 (1999), 46–71.

21 Vgl. Beulay, L'enseignement (wie Anm. 6), 447–456, sowie Ders., Le Visage Divin: Connaissance et Inconnaissance de Dieu chez les Pères Syriaques, in: Le Visage de Dieu dans le Patrimoine Oriental, Patrimoine Syriaque. Actes du colloque VII, Bd. 1, Antélias/Liban 2001, 7–20, hier 15f. Siehe auch Nadira Khayyat in der Einleitung zu: Jean de Dalyatha, Les homélies (wie Anm. 1), 57.

betrifft bei Johannes die Trinität: Die göttliche Natur wird mit dem Vater als der Quelle der Gottheit in eins gesetzt. In einer Reihe von Aussagen betont Johannes, dass der Vater für uns stets transzendent bleibt. Sein Angesicht bleibt für immer unsichtbar. Was wir sehen bzw. erfahren können, ist sein Abglanz, seine Herrlichkeit. In diesem Rahmen gewinnt 2 Kor 3,18 in der Fassung der Peschitta eine entscheidende Bedeutung: „Wir alle sehen mit enthülltem Angesicht die Herrlichkeit des Herrn wie in einem Spiegel, und im Bild werden wir verwandelt von Herrlichkeit zu Herrlichkeit, nach dem Herrn, dem Geist." Als weiterer Schlüsseltext dient Johannes ferner 2 Kor 4,6, wo vom Licht, das in unseren Herzen scheint, die Rede ist, „durch das wir erleuchtet werden durch die Erkenntnis der Herrlichkeit Gottes, die auf dem Angesicht Christi ist."[22]

Für Johannes von Dalyatha ist es die *conditio sine qua non* mystischer Erfahrung, dass die Herrlichkeit Gottes auf dem Angesicht Christi aufleuchtet.[23] Nur so kann uns der Heilige Geist umgestalten in jenes Licht hinein, das auf dem Spiegel im Inneren des Menschen aufleuchtet. Das bringt es mit sich, dass der Mensch allein durch den Sohn, durch die Schau seines Antlitzes, Zugang zu den Strahlen des göttlichen Lichtes erhalten kann. Ein bekenntnishafter Text in *ep.* 27,1 ordnet die trinitarischen Personen einander in folgender Weise zu: „Ich *erkenne* den Vater in seinem Christus; den Sohn aber *sehe* ich durch den Geist."[24] Hier wird deutlich unterschieden zwischen dem geistigen Akt des Erkennens und dem Akt des Schauens. Der Sohn ist es, der im Heiligen Geist „gesehen" werden kann. Darin wird ein theologischer Grundsatz formuliert, der auch von den Aussagen wenige Zeilen später nicht aufgegeben wird: „Wenn ich ins Staunen fortgeführt bin, dann sehe ich die drei als eine Lampe und ich erglänze wie sie. Dann gerate ich in Verwunderung über mich und jauchze auf in geistlicher Weise, weil sich die Quelle des Lebens in mir befindet ..."[25]

Johannes ist davon überzeugt, dass sich Christus in den Tiefen des menschlichen Wesens finden lässt. In der Tradition des Pseudo-Macarius bildet das Herz das Zentrum des inneren Menschen. Dort zeigt Gott denen, die ihn lieben, seine Schönheit. Neben der Lichtmetapher ist die Schönheit Gottes eines der zentralen Motive bei Johannes. Voraussetzung solcher Erfahrung ist freilich der Weg asketischer Reinigung. Der innere Spiegel auf dem Grund der Seele muss von allem Sünderschmutz gereinigt werden.[26] Auch die Trennung von allen weltlichen Bindungen, auch von

22 Zur Bedeutung dieser beiden Schriftstellen im Werk des Johannes siehe Nadira Khayyat, Le Visage du Christ resplendissant dans le miroir du cœur, in: Le Visage de Dieu dans le Patrimoine Oriental (wie Anm. 21), 77–87.

23 Vgl. Beulay, L'enseignement (wie Anm. 6), 443–447, sowie Ders., La Beauté de Dieu et le Visage du Père chez Jean de Dalyatha, in: Le Visage de Dieu dans le Patrimoine Oriental (wie Anm. 21), 67–74.

24 PO 39/3, 386,24 f. Beulay.

25 PO 39/3, 388,1–3 Beulay.

26 Vgl. beispielsweise ep. 28,2: „Reinige deinen Spiegel, und ungeteilt wird dir das eine Licht dreifach erstrahlen. Nimm dir dies zu Herzen, und du wirst erfahren, dass dein Gott lebt." (PO

zwischenmenschlichen Beziehungen, wird gefordert. Man darf nicht vergessen, dass Johannes von Dalyatha ausschließlich von der geistlichen Erfahrung von Einsiedlern handelt. Ihnen allein kann es gelingen, alle Gedanken zum Schweigen zu bringen und offen zu werden für die Schau der göttlichen Schönheit. Ob und wann diese Schau eintritt, bleibt Gott selbst vorbehalten. Doch ist Johannes davon überzeugt, dass Gott seine Schönheit den Menschen zeigen will. Gott will sich von den Menschen finden lassen.[27] In immer neuen Wendungen versucht Johannes den Zustand zu beschreiben, der eintritt, wo sich Gottes Schönheit offenbart. In *ep.* 2,6 finden wir als charakteristische Aussage: „Die Seele sieht nun sich selbst (wörtl: ‚ihre eigene Hypostase') und Christus, der in ihr erscheint, und sie jubelt über seine Schau. Hier sieht sie die staunenswerten Schönheiten der Engel, die im Staunen vor der Herrlichkeit des Einen stehen, der ewig lebt. Auf geheimnisvolle Weise zeigt sich hier die heilige Trinität, und ihre Hypostasen erscheinen dem nackten Geist. Groß ist dieses Geheimnis, das nur von einem reinen Geist geschaut wird."[28]

Johannes spricht hier wie an anderen Stellen von der Schau der glorreichen Hypostasen. Das scheint sich mit der Betonung der absoluten Transzendenz der göttlichen Natur zunächst nur schwer vereinbaren zu lassen. Doch finden die verschiedenen Aussagen des Johannes durch den Gedanken der Schönheit Gottes ihre innere Zuordnung. Denn in der Erfahrung der unauslotbaren Schönheit Gottes scheint die Transzendenz Gottes des Vaters hindurch auf das Angesicht des Sohnes.

Die Schau der göttlichen Schönheit wird also zurückgebunden an die Gestalt Christi. Wenn Johannes von dem Angesicht („Prosopon", syr. *parṣōpā*) spricht, so muss mitgehört werden, dass „Prosopon" in der antiochenisch-ostsyrischen Glaubenslehre göttliche und menschliche Naturen und Hypostasen Christi zugleich umfasst. Es ist also der *inkarnierte* Gottessohn, der uns den Zugang zum göttlichen Licht vermittelt. An einigen Stellen weist Johannes der Menschheit Christi eine besondere Funktion für die mystische Schau zu. In *cent.* 1,2 heißt es, dass die „göttliche Natur" von unserem geistigen Auge nicht geschaut werden könne ohne den „angebeteten Tempel der Menschheit unseres Herrn".[29] Christus ist Abbild, in dem und durch das die heilige Trinität gesehen wird. Denn aus der Menschheit Christi gehen jene Lichtstrahlen hervor, von denen der Geist der vernunftbegabten Wesen erleuchtet wird.[30]

Nicht recht deutlich wird auf den ersten Blick, wie die Leiblichkeit des inkarnierten Gottessohnes Bedeutung für ein inneres, rein geistig vorgestelltes Erleben gewinnen kann. Johannes hat die Beschaffenheit der Menschheit Christi nicht ausführlicher beschrieben; das spezifisch inkarnationstheologische Vokabular der kon-

39/3, 388,16–18 Beulay). Siehe dazu Beulay, L'enseignement (wie Anm. 6), 327f.

27 Vgl. besonders ep. 26,3 (PO 39/3, 386,15–21 Beulay).

28 PO 39/3, 310,25–312,2 Beulay.

29 Vgl. Beulay, L'enseignement (wie Anm. 6), 457.

30 Cent. 1,2; ebenda.

fessionell fixierten Christologie verwendet er kaum.[31] Hier erweisen sich verwandte Gedankengänge bei Joseph Ḥazzaya und Nestorius von Nuhadra, zwei Zeitgenossen des Johannes, als hilfreich.[32] Bei ihnen wird die Beschaffenheit der Menschheit Christi präziser erfasst, und zwar als die *verherrlichte* Menschheit des Erlösers. Das wird man nun auch bei Johannes von Dalyatha voraussetzen dürfen. Offensichtlich stellten sich die ostsyrischen Mystiker die Menschheit des Herrn nach seiner Auferstehung so vergeistigt („einfach" bzw. „unzusammengesetzt") vor, dass sie im Inneren des Menschen Wohnung zu nehmen vermag.

Irritierend bleibt bei Johannes die unstete Ausdrucksweise. In der eben genannten Passage aus *cent.* 1,2 spricht er unbedacht nun doch von der Schau „der göttlichen Natur"[33] – auch wenn man den Text in seinem weiteren Verlauf so verstehen kann, dass tatsächlich nur die Abstrahlungen vom Angesicht Christi als Herrlichkeit Gottes geschaut werden. Solche Inkonsistenzen haben dazu geführt, dass Johannes von der Synode 786/87 nicht nur des Sabellianismus, sondern auch des Messalianismus beschuldigt wurde.[34] Der abgetragene Ketzerhut diente dabei zur Bezeichnung der Lehre, dass die göttliche Natur von körperlichen Augen geschaut werden könne. Das galt es zurückzuweisen als häretische Verwischung des Unterschieds von göttlicher und menschlicher Natur.[35]

5. Ausblick: Mystik als Herausforderung für die Trinitätslehre

Man wird sagen können, dass die Synode von 786/87 der Intention des Johannes von Dalyatha nicht gerecht geworden ist, obgleich seine unscharfe Diktion durchaus Anlass zur Kritik bot. Sein Anliegen bestand darin, die mystische Bewegung, die in den Klausen und Klöstern der ostsyrischen Christenheit blühte, an die gott-menschliche Gestalt Christi und an die Eigentümlichkeiten der trinitarischen Personen zurückzubinden. Die Traditionen mystischer Theologie wie auch die Praxis mystischer Erfahrung betonten eine *unio mystica* mit dem *einen* Gott. Johannes von Dalyatha scheint es bewusst gewesen zu sein, dass solche Auffassungen mit den Grundaxiomen der antiochenischen Theologie in Widerspruch treten konnten. Er selbst suchte

---

31 Deswegen konnten seine Werke, wie die handschriftliche Tradition zeigt, auch in miaphysitischen („jakobitischen") Kreisen mit nur geringen Interpolationen überliefert werden; vgl. Nadira Khayyat in der Einleitung zu: Jean de Dalyatha, Les homélies (wie Anm. 1), 22f.

32 Vgl. Beulay, L'enseignement (wie Anm. 6), 460 f.

33 Dazu die Bemerkung bei Beulay, L'enseignement (wie Anm. 6), 457 Anm. 163: „Cette expression semble avoir échappé à Jean du fait de la complexité de la comparaison qu'il propose."

34 Vgl. dazu Beulay, L'enseignement (wie Anm. 6), 423–428, sowie Klaus Fitschen, Messalianismus und Antimessalianismus. Ein Beispiel ostkirchlicher Ketzergeschichte, FKDG 71, Göttingen 1998, 300.

35 Nachdrücklich wurde diese Möglichkeit auch für Jesus, den vom ewigen Logos angenommenen Menschen, verneint. Das geht v.a. aus dem Bericht über die Synode bei Elias von Nisibis (11. Jh.) hervor; vgl. dazu Emmanuel-Karim Delly, La Théologie d'Élie bar Šénaya. Étude et traduction de ses entretiens, SU 1, Rom 1957, 77f.

die hier herrschende Spannung so zu lösen, dass er Gottes Transzendenz und Immanenz nicht statisch erfasst hat. Das Ineinander von bleibender Entzogenheit und Offenbarwerden des göttlichen Wesens wird bei Johannes vielmehr in das trinitarische Leben Gottes selbst hinein verlegt.

Weil Gott als dreifaltiger Gott existiert, ist eine mystische Vereinigung mit ihm überhaupt erst möglich. Es ist eine berechtigte Frage, ob es Johannes gelungen ist, diesen Grundgedanken immer durchzuhalten. In anderer Weise wird man aber auch danach fragen können, ob sein theologisches Wollen heute noch Denkanstöße vermitteln kann. Johannes von Dalyatha sollte allerdings nicht zu rasch in die Nähe von theologischen Entwürfen gerückt werden, die das Ineinander von Gottes ökonomischer und immanenter Trinität neu und entschieden zur Geltung gebracht haben.[36] Zwar traten die göttlichen Hypostasen in der theologischen Reflexion des Johannes auseinander und er entdeckte die unverzichtbare Funktion des menschgewordenen Christus für die mystische Erfahrung. Doch spielt das Handeln Gottes in der Geschichte bei ihm keine zentrale Rolle für die innere Erfahrung. Bei Johannes ist es der *erhöhte* Christus, dem der Mensch in seinem Inneren begegnet. Die Befürchtung scheint nicht unberechtigt, dass der historische, der leidende und gekreuzigte Christus dadurch leicht aus dem Blick gerät.[37] Umgekehrt ließe sich fragen, ob es nicht auch eine Schwäche mancher trinitarischen Theologien ausmacht, dass sie das Wirken des dreifaltigen Gottes zu einseitig in die Immanenz der Geschichte verlegen. Kontemplatives Innewerden der göttlichen Wirklichkeit kann aber nur Begegnung mit dem gegenwärtigen Gott sein, der sich von dem Suchenden *hier und jetzt* finden lässt. Das Zueinander von geschichtlicher und mystischer Selbstbezeugung des trinitarischen Gottes bleibt der Theologie aufgegeben. Johannes von Dalyatha zu lesen regt dazu an, das trinitarische Dogma für die Sehnsucht des menschlichen Herzens nach der Erfahrung Gottes neu aufzuschlüsseln.

36 Besonders der von Nadira Khayyat zitierte Karl Rahner (siehe Anm. 1) hat sich für eine solche Identifizierung programmatisch ausgesprochen. Vgl. etwa Karl Rahner, Der dreifaltige Gott als transzendenter Urgrund der Heilsgeschichte, in: Mysterium Salutis II, Einsiedeln 1967, 317–401; 328: „Die ökonomische Trinität ist die immanente Trinität und umgekehrt." Aufschlussreich ist zu solchen trinitätstheologischen Entwürfen der problemorientierte Überblick bei Wolfhart Pannenberg, Systematische Theologie I, Göttingen 1988, 355–364.

37 Dies ist eine Anfrage, die man heute etwa an eine trinitarische Grundlegung mystischer Erfahrung zu richten hätte, wie sie bei Henri Le Saux (1910–1973) begegnet. Vgl. zur Rolle der Trinität bei Le Saux: Thomas Friedrich, Henri Le Saux' Gott der Saccidananda-Trinität. Eine Hindu-Christliche Integration, in: ZMWRW (2003), 181–199.

„Einige hilfreiche Ratschläge zum asketischen Leben“: Ein Werk Babais des Großen?

Till Engelmann

In diesem Beitrag soll geprüft werden, ob „Einige hilfreiche Ratschläge zum asketischen Leben“[1] authentisch waren, die dem ostsyrischen mystischen Theologen Babai dem Großen zugesprochen werden. Auf eine Skizze von Babais Stellung innerhalb der Tradition der syrischen Asketen (1) folgt eine Darstellung der Lehre der „Ratschläge“ (2). Inwiefern die „Ratschläge“ als ein Werk Babais anzusehen sind, soll dann abschließend zu beantworten versucht werden (3).

1. Babai der Große und seine Stellung im ostsyrischen Mönchtum

Als Babai der Große von der Mitte des 6. Jahrhunderts bis etwa 628 lebte, blickten asketische Bewegungen in der „Kirche des Ostens“ auf eine lange Geschichte zurück. Schon in den ersten syrischen Bibelübersetzungen zeigte sich ein prägendes Ideal: Nur der sexuell enthaltsam lebende Mensch konnte ein vollwertiger, der Taufe würdiger Christ werden.[2] Dies änderte sich im Laufe der Zeiten. Im frühen vierten Jahrhundert wurde die asketische Lebensweise eine hoch geschätzte Ausnahme christlichen Lebens. Noch immer nämlich wurden die Asketen im Sinne einer Zwei-Stufen-Ethik als „Vollkommene“ den nur „Gerechten“, in Ehe lebenden Christen übergeordnet.[3]

Im späten fünften Jahrhundert kam es zu Konflikten zwischen den Asketen und der Kirchenleitung. Dass die früher so hoch geschätzte Gruppe starken Widerstand erfuhr, hing mit einem ausgeprägten Individualismus und zum Teil mit messalianischen Lehren, also dem Verzicht auf die Sakramente und ihre Abwertung zugunsten des inneren Gebets zusammen.[4] Als weiterer Vorwurf gegen die „falschen Asketen“ war im Umlauf, dass diese ihre Heiligkeit nur vorgaben, tatsächlich aber sexuell aktiv waren und somit das Bild der Kirche befleckten. Gerade im persischen Reich

---

1 Geevarghese Chediath (Hg.), Mar Babai the Great. Some Useful Counsels on the Ascetical Life, Moran Etho 15, Kottayam 2001 (engl. Übersetzung).

2 Vgl. Wolfgang Hage, Das orientalische Christentum, Die Religionen der Menschheit 29.2, Stuttgart 2007, 29f. und 272.

3 Vgl. das Liber Graduum als einen deutlichen Beleg dafür; Michael Kmosko (Hg.), Liber Graduum, PS 3, Paris 1926.

4 Vgl. Klaus Fitschen, Messalianismus und Antimessalianismus. Ein Beispiel ostkirchlicher Ketzergeschichte, FKDG 71, Göttingen 1998.

wurde die Ehe für Zoroastrier als religiöse Pflicht angesehen. Die Kirchenleitung beendete den Konflikt damit, dass sie auf zwei Synoden 484/6 die Asketen strikt aus dem Umfeld der Stadtgemeinden verbannte und zudem Geistlichen nachdrücklich die Eheschließung empfahl.[5]

Zu Babais Lebzeiten kehrte das Mönchtum nach und nach in das Zentrum der Kirchenleitung zurück. Von zentraler Bedeutung für diese Entwicklung war Abraham von Kaschkar, der sowohl durch die Schule von Nisibis als auch durch das ägyptische Anachoretentum geprägt war und 570 mit dem „Großen Kloster" auf dem Izla einen Ort schuf, wo Asketen im Einklang mit den Idealen der Kirchenleitung lebten.[6]

Babai wirkte von 604–628 als dritter Abt dieses Großen Klosters auf dem Izla und ab 609 als Klostervisitator der „Apostolischen Kirche des Ostens".[7] Zu dieser Zeit war die Lage der „Kirche des Ostens" durch Druck an mehreren Fronten sehr angespannt, und Babai trat äußerst entschlossen gegen jegliche Form von dogmatischer Abweichung und ethischer Aufweichung an. Seine Klosterregeln[8] geben auch heute noch ein Bild von dieser Strenge wieder, und zeitgenössische Quellen berichten von mancherlei Konflikten, die Babai auszufechten hatte. Neben der Klosterregel sind aber noch weitere Texte Babais überliefert, die als asketisch-mystische Schriften einzuordnen sind: Kommentare zum geistlichen Gesetz des Vaters Markus[9] und der „Kleine Kommentar" zu den *Kephalaia Gnostika*[10] des Euagrios Pontikos. Die Klosterordnung mit einem asketischen Schwerpunkt und der Euagrioskommentar mit seiner mystischen Intention ermöglichen es, die monastische Theologie Babais nachzuvollziehen. Inwiefern diese Konzeption mit „einigen hilfreichen Ratschlägen zum asketischen Leben" übereinstimmt, die ebenfalls unter Babais Namen überliefert sind, soll nun überprüft werden.

---

5 Vgl. Hage, Christentum, 276.

6 Zu Abraham dem Großen vgl. Martin Tamcke, Abraham von Kaschkar, in: Syrische Kirchenväter, hg. v. Wassilios Klein, Stuttgart 2004, 124–132.

7 Vgl. zur Biographie Babais und für weitere Literatur knapp meinen Beitrag im Biographisch-Bibliographischen Kirchenlexikon 28, Nordhausen 2007, 64–67 und als ausführliche, aus den Quellen erarbeitete Darstellung Geevarghese Chediath, The Christology of Mar Babai the Great, Oriental Institute of Religious Studies 49, Kottayam und Paderborn 1982.

8 Arthur Vööbus, The rules of Babai, in: Arthur Vööbus (Hg.), Syriac and Arabic documents relative to Syrian Ascetism. Papers of the Estonian Theological Society in Exile 11, Stockholm 1960, 176–184 (arab. Text, engl. Übersetzung).

9 Dieses Werk ist noch nicht ediert worden und bisher nur in der Handschrift Br.Mus.Add. 17270 belegt.

10 Wilhelm Frankenberg (Hg.), Euagrius Ponticus, AGWG.PH, Neue Folge, 13.2, Berlin 1912, 8–471 (syr. Text und gr.-dt. Übersetzung).

2. Die Ratschläge im Kontext der monastischen Schriften Babais

2.1 Die Form der „Ratschläge“

In der zur Edition herangezogenen Handschrift finden sich neben dem zu besprechenden Text auch noch Werke von Isaak von Ninive, Babai von Nisibis, Joseph Hazzaja, Johannes Penkaje und zwei anonyme Schriften, wobei Babais Text von denen anderer Asketen gerahmt ist.[11] Er gliedert sich in vier Memre, von denen die ersten beiden deutlich länger als die dritte und vierte sind. Die gleich noch näher zu erläuternden Hauptthemen begegnen in allen Teilen der Schrift, ohne dass man eine Entwicklung oder Struktur der Aussagen erkennt. Ihr Charakter ist apodiktisch und durch eine Vielzahl von sprachlichen Bildern geprägt.

Anders als bei den anderen Werken Babais des Großen wird hier dessen Name erwähnt, ohne auf seine Würde als Abt des Großen Klosters hinzuweisen. Stattdessen begegnen die Titel „der Heilige“, „der Große“ und „der Gesegnete“,[12] die sonst erst *post mortem* belegt sind. So ist es sehr wahrscheinlich, dass zumindest in dieser Handschrift erst der Kopist die Verbindung zwischen dem Text und Babai als Autor herstellte. Aus diesem formalen Grund ist die Verfasserschaft Babais zumindest fraglich. Ob dazu noch inhaltliche Diskrepanzen hinzutreten, soll im Folgenden geprüft werden.

2.2 Der Inhalt der „Ratschläge“

In den Ratschlägen begegnen eine Vielzahl von Themen: Ihr Herausgeber Chediath erwähnt die Christologie, das Verhältnis der Mönche zu Frauen, die Attitüde gegenüber Häretikern, die Eigenschaften eines guten Lehrers, die Kontrolle von Körper und Seele, das Gebet und die bilderreiche Sprache als Charakteristika.[13] All diesen Aspekten soll im Detail nicht nachgegangen werden, sondern das Thema „Gebet“ und die Polaritäten „Asket – Welt“ und „Seele – Körper“ sollen exemplarisch behandelt werden.

2.2.1 Das Gebet

Der Beginn des Werks legt dar, dass die Grundlage allen asketischen Handelns das Gebet ist, und am Ende der ersten, dritten und vierten Memra steht jeweils ein Lobpreis Gottes. Diese Rahmung einer Schrift durch Gebete ist nun gewiss im Kontext des syrischen christlichen Schrifttums nichts Ungewöhnliches, sondern weit verbreitet.[14] Welche Funktion aber hat nun die Rede vom Gebet in dieser Schrift? Zu-

---

11 Ich verdanke Grigory Kessel den Hinweis, dass in den drei anderen Handschriften die „Ratschläge“ zusammen mit teilweise abweichenden Schriftstellern wiedergegeben sind. Neben dem von Chediath herangezogenen Manuskript Vat.Syr. 562 von 1918 sind dies Seert 109 (1609), Notre Dame des Semences/Sher 116 aus dem 19. Jh. und Sharfeh Rahmani 80 aus dem frühen 20. Jh.

12 Der erste und zweite Titel jeweils bei Chediath, Counsels, 12.27; der dritte Titel ebd., 59.

13 Ebd., 7–11.

14 Die meisten Kapitel von Babais christologischem Hauptwerk Liber de Unione enden mit

nächst einmal fällt auf, dass keine Theorie der betenden Person präsentiert wird, eher begegnet so etwas wie eine Ratgeberspalte zur rechten Art des Betens. Das Gebet ist gewissermaßen die Grundbefindlichkeit des Asketen, der alle seine Handlungen als Betender vollzieht.[15] Dies ist zwar im Gefolge von 1 Thess 5,17 ein weit verbreiteter Gedanke im Mönchtum, aber erinnert in der Konfliktsituation mit den Messalianern auch an deren Lehre vom ständigen inneren Gebet. Das aber bedeutet nicht, dass das Gebet beiläufig geschehen soll: Ohne vorherige Sammlung[16], ohne Lernen[17] und ohne Glauben kann auch das Gebet nicht gelingen, ohne das Gebet wiederum sind alle asketischen Mühen vergeblich.[18] Gerade die Nacht ist eine Zeit des Gebets, es soll so gebetet werden, als ob am nächsten Tag das Jüngste Gericht stattfinden werde.[19]

Wenn man nun diese Aussagen mit der Theorie des Gebets bzw. des Beters aus dem Kommentar zu den „Gnostischen Kapiteln" vergleicht, so fällt deutlich das Fehlen eines für den Kommentar zentralen Gedankens auf: Nach der Euagriosauslegung Babais folgt auf ein asketisches Leben die Schau zuerst der körperlichen, dann der unkörperlichen Schöpfung. Als dritte und letzte Stufe folgt dann eine Schau der Trinität. Um nun aber einer Vergottung des Menschen nicht das Wort reden zu müssen, zitiert Babai eindrücklich und immer wieder den paulinischen Gedanken, dass alle Schau Gottes in dieser Welt wie in einem Spiegel, also vorläufig-fragmentarisch, sei.[20] Weder diese höchst charakteristische Relativierung, die das bleibende Verbundensein des Asketen mit der Welt aussagt, begegnet aber bei den Aussagen über das Gebet, noch kann man überhaupt die Rede vom Gebet als einem mystischen Erlebnis finden.

2.2.2 Die Weltbeziehung des Asketen

Die Welt bzw. andere Menschen sind nach den Ratschlägen generell so bedrohlich, dass sich Asketen möglichst von ihnen fernhalten sollten. Die Gefahr, die die Welt mit sich bringt, kann einerseits allgemein ausgesagt werden, andererseits aber auch in Bezug auf konkrete Gruppen. Hier sind es vor allem die Frauen und Lehrer, die als Beispiele der Gefährlichkeit der Welt dienen. Diese Konstellation erinnert zunächst durchaus an die Zeit Babais, der sich mit verheirateten Mönchen ebenso wie

---

hymnischen Lobpreisungen. Vgl. Luise Abramowski, Die Christologie Babais des Grossen, in: OrChrA 197 (1974), 219–245, hier 228.

15 Vgl. Chediath, Counsels, 23.

16 Vgl. ebd., 12.

17 Vgl. ebd., 23.

18 „If you do not believe, do not pray. If you do not pray, do not work." Chediath, Counsels, 23.

19 „Be vigilant during the night, and pray and beseech as if you will enter the next day the place of judgement and you will be demanded of every thing you are in debt." Chediath, Counsels, 57.

20 Vgl. z. B. Logion I.45 aus Frankenberg, Euagrius Ponticus, 87. Nachdem die Rede vom Aufstieg der reinen Vernunft zur Gottesschau war, schränkt Babai dies durch den paulinischen Verweis auf 2 Kor 3,18 ein, dass die Vernunft nur in die Ähnlichkeit des Spiegelbildes verwandelt werde.

mit Henana von Adiabene, dem Leiter der Hochschule von Nisibis, auseinandersetzte.

Die „Ratschläge“ sind von Polaritäten geprägt, dem guten, aber verführbaren Adressaten wird die verlockende und böse Welt entgegengesetzt. Der Welt und insbesondere den Frauen muss der Asket unbedingt entfliehen. Mit Frauen soll nicht gesprochen werden,[21] und wenn ein Freund mit Frauen zu tun hat, so soll man diesem die Freundschaft kündigen.[22] Nicht nur aufgrund ihrer sexuellen Reize gelten Frauen als gefährlich,[23] sondern aus den Mahnungen lässt sich auch auf lehrende Frauen schließen.[24]

Die Lehrer jedoch waren zu Babais Lebzeiten natürlich in der Regel Männer. Dass es hier als so riskant gilt, falsch unterwiesen zu werden, ist mit der Situation zu Babais Lebzeiten nicht unmittelbar in Einklang zu bringen. Denn im Großen Kloster diente das gemeinsame Wohnhaus der Unterweisung der Novizen, so dass ein Unterricht im Sinne des Abtes Babai gewährleistet sein sollte. Wichtige Vorbehalte des Verfassers gegen falsche Lehrer sind, dass diese nicht aus der Stadt kommen[25], keinen Ruhm haben und nicht jung sein sollten[26]. Die ersten Einwände ließen sich durchaus als Spitze Babais gegen Henana plausibel machen, der der renommiertesten ostsyrischen Hochschule in der Metropolitenstadt Nisibis vorstand, letzteres aber nicht, da Babai jünger als Henana war. Die Funktion dieser Abgrenzung liegt mithin wohl nicht in einer konkreten Warnung, sondern in einer diffamierenden Aussage gegen andere asketische Gruppen und der impliziten Selbstversicherung, weder ruhmsüchtig zu sein noch den Komfort der Städte zu suchen.

Dass es den Ratschlägen weniger um inhaltliche Kriterien geht, wie man sich in der Welt orientieren soll, sondern um die rechte Hochschätzung der eigenen Gruppe, zeigt sich daran, dass die Gruppenzugehörigkeit als entscheidendes (und in dieser Zuspitzung einziges!) Kriterium für Gottesliebe gilt.

---

21 Vgl. Chediath, Counsels, 13.

22 Vgl. ebd., 20.

23 Vgl. ebd., 15f. und 17f.

24 „Do not teach a woman, lest you should become her disciple. Do not learn from a woman, lest she should make you a disciple of Satan.“ Chediath, Counsels, 17. Dass auch hier ein sexueller Unterton mitschwingt, verdeutlich die Fortsetzung der Aussage: „Flee from an old and honest woman, lest you should find her as a lascivious child unto your perdition.“ Da es aber merkwürdig wäre, die Gefährdung des Keuschheitsgelübdes anhand alter Frauen zu exemplifizieren, scheint der Verfasser davon auszugehen, dass es bei der negativ konnotierten Gruppe tatsächlich lehrende Frauen gab, was er wiederum durch die polemische Sexualisierung dieses (unterstellten?) Sachverhaltes angreift.

25 „He who learns from city dwellers about spiritual behavior and takes counsel from them, resembles him who asks the adulteress about morality and sanctity.“ Chediath, Counsels, 19.

26 „Do not ask anything of any body, except of the one who is wise in your way. Do not ask him because you have heard of him. But because you have tested him that he is a believer in God. Keep away from the young man who thinks he is holy. Adhere to an old man who has hidden his perfections.“ Chediath, Counsels, 14.

> Er, der Gott liebt, wird daran erkannt: Er ehrt und respektiert die Heiligen Gottes.
> Der Schüler Satans wird daran erkannt: Er ist weit entfernt von der Gemeinschaft der Heiligen und schmäht sie sehr zu jeder Stunde vor allen.[27]

Dass nun die asketische Abgrenzung gegen die Welt auch die Abgrenzung gegen andere asketische bzw. theologische Gruppen einschloss, ist den Ratschlägen und anderen Schriften Babais gemeinsam. Allerdings werden im Euagrioskommentar eine Vielzahl von Gruppen und ihre jeweilige Irrlehre namentlich genannt, dies fehlt in den Ratschlägen fast völlig. Auch Hinweise auf zeitgenössische Widersacher Babais sucht man (fast) vergeblich: Henana und die Messalianer werden nie namentlich genannt, auf die Theopaschiten gibt es nur einen Hinweis, aber ohne Verbindung mit dem charakteristischen Ausdruck „Severianer“.[28]

2.2.3 Das Leib-Seele-Verhältnis des Asketen

Der Asket, der stets den Verlockungen der Welt absagt, ist zugleich auch derjenige, der stets gegen die Forderungen des Körpers kämpft, bis er sich als gleichsam reine Seele dem Gebet widmen kann. Der Dualismus zwischen dem christlichen Leben und der Welt findet sich im Individuum ebenfalls als Spannung zwischen Körper und Seele. Der Körper kann zum Kampfplatz gegen die Dämonen werden:

> Es gibt zwei mächtige Kräfte gegen dich: Fleisch und Blut und böse Geister; körperliche Mühen unterdrücken die eine, körperliche und seelische Mühen die andere.[29]

Bei diesen Mühen, den Körper zu unterdrücken, um die Seele rein zu halten, ist wieder der einzelne Asket im Blick. Sicher mussten die frommen Männer letztendlich alleine die der Askese zuwiderlaufenden Regungen unterdrücken, aber dennoch ist es auffällig, dass in keiner Weise vom Kloster als einem Ort der Gemeinschaft und Hilfestellung beim inneren Ringen die Rede ist. Dieses innere Ringen findet den Ratschlägen zufolge lokal in der Wildnis und sozial in der Einsamkeit statt,[30] ohne dass auf ein gemeinschaftliches Noviziat oder gemeinsame Gottesdienste Bezug genommen wird, wie es der Realität des Großen Klosters entsprochen hätte. Wenn nun aber das innere Ringen von Erfolg gekrönt war und die dämonischen Einflüsse zurückgewiesen wurden, dann ist das Ziel nicht mit dem des Kephalaiakommentars identisch: Auf die innere Ruhe folgt nicht die aufsteigende Schau über die körperliche und unkörperliche Schöpfung hin zur vereinigenden Schau der Trinität wie in

27 Vgl. Chediath, Counsels, 19 f.

28 Vgl. ebd., 51.

29 Vgl. ebd., 25 (vgl. auch 24).

30 Nachdem Mose, Elia und Jesus als Beispiele für Personen benannt wurden, die sich in der Einsamkeit bewährten, heißt es: „It is not in the midst of women and in the streets of town that the earthly soldiers exhibit their glorious deeds, but in the wilderness and in the array of battle. So do all the saints who are the soldiers of Christ. Being armed for battle, they went out to the wilderness and upset Satan and all his strength.“ Chediath, Counsels, 52.

einem Spiegel, sondern der Asket erlebt einen Zustand des Friedens mit der Schöpfung.[31] Dies könnte natürlich als ein begrifflicher Platzhalter für die Asketen gemeint gewesen sein, die zwar schon mystische Erlebnisse hatten, aber noch nicht zur Deutung mittels der euagrianischen Systematik fähig waren, die Babai den Fortgeschrittenen ermöglichte, aber m. E. ist dies doch eine recht gezwungene Deutung. Stattdessen ist hier eine inhaltliche Inkongruenz anzunehmen.

3. Die „Ratschläge“ als ein pseudepigraphisches Werk

Sind die „Ratschläge“ also ein Werk, das von Babai stammt? Diese Frage ist m. E. zu negieren, denn es gibt eine Fülle von außergewöhnlichen Positionen und Widersprüchen zu anderen Aussagen Babais, die dies unwahrscheinlich machen.

Hier ist zunächst an die formale Besonderheit zu erinnern, dass einerseits die Verfasserangabe Titel Babais nennt, die sonst erst nach seinem Tod begegnen, andererseits aber die typische Aussage „Babai, Abt des Großen Klosters auf dem Berge Izla“ fehlt. Als eine zweite Besonderheit ist festzuhalten, dass die Aussagen offenkundig an ungebundene Asketen gerichtet sind und die soziale Ordnung eines Klosters mit seiner Form der christlichen Gemeinschaft dem Verfasser und seinen Adressaten nicht bekannt zu sein scheint. Das „Große Kloster“ stand zwar auch unter Babai deutlich in der eher eremitischen Tradition des Antonius, aber dennoch gab es ein Koinobion und gemeinsame Gottesdienste. Neben dieser formalen und sozialen Diskrepanz ist auch auf inhaltliche Unterschiede hinzuweisen: Die „Ratschläge“ sind im Vergleich zu der Auslegung der „Gnostischen Kapitel“ kaum mystisch geprägt. Hier könnte man noch erwägen, es handele sich bei ihnen um Prolegomena zur vertiefenden Schrift, aber am Beispiel des Gebets zeigte sich, dass die Schriften an wichtigen Nahtstellen nicht übereinstimmen würden.

Die Auseinandersetzung mit Gegnern beschränkt sich in der Regel auf den Hinweis, dass die eigene Gruppe rein und die andere verworfen sei. Die Namen der Gegner begegnen nicht, ihre theologischen Konzepte lassen sich allenfalls erahnen, und auch dies nur gelegentlich. In anderen Schriften Babais wird diese Auseinandersetzung geführt, auch in der volkstümlichen Märtyrerbiographie des Giwargis. Hierzu passt dann auch, dass die Christologie Babais Lehre zwar nicht widerspricht, ihr aber auch nicht in der Spätform des *Liber de Unione* entspricht, da das Konzept zweier *Qnume*/Hypostasen nicht begegnet.

Diese Beobachtungen schließen es nun alles in allem aus, dass Babai die „Ratschläge“ verfasst hatte.

---

31 „Keep the tranquillity of the body and mind that you can subdue your emotions. Then the creatures will be at peace with you, and the wicked devils and the wicked men will tremble you.“ Chediath, Counsels, 23.

A Fragment from the Lost "Book of Admonition(s)" by Abraham bar Dašandad in *Risāla fī faḍīlat al-ʿafāf* ("Letter on the Priority of Abstinence") of Elias of Nisibis

Grigory Kessel

I. Introduction

In 1968 a Lebanese scholar, Georges Rahmé, edited for the first time *Risāla fī faḍīlat al-ʿafāf* ("Letter on the priority of abstinence")[1] in the periodical "Al-Machriq"[2]. The text was written by an East Syriac author, Elias of Nisibis (A.D. 975–1046) – one of the most prominent Arabic Christian theologians,[3] who is regarded by modern scholarship as "le figure de proue" who stood at the beginning of the period of the Syriac Renaissance.[4] Since then the publication has been considered as the only available edition, which later received the criticism of Khalil Samir, who evaluated the edition as "très incorrecte"[5] and envisaged a new edition of the text.

However there is one more edition of the *Risāla*, supplemented by German translation (thus making it the only available European translation of the text), which seems to have almost completely escaped the attention of scholars.[6] In 1969 Andreas Hau (unaware of Rahmé's edition) submitted a thesis entitled "Brief über den Vorzug der Enthaltsamkeit gegenüber dem Geschlechtsverkehr von Elias von Nisibis" at

---

I would like to thank Prof. Allan Turner who kindly helped me to correct the English of the paper and Dmitry Morozov for providing me with helpful suggestions.

1 Heafter *Risāla*.

2 Georges Rahmé, رسالة في فضيلة العفاف لايليّا النصّيبيني, in: Al-Machriq 62 (1968), 3–74.

3 On Elias and his works see articles of Khalil Samir collected in the volume Samir Khalil Samir, Foi et culture en Irak au XIe siècle. Elie de Nisibe et l'Islam, CStS 544, Aldershot and Bookfield/VT 1996.

4 Herman Teule, La renaissance syriaque (1026–1318), in: Irénikon 75 (2002), 176.

5 Robert Caspar, Abdelmajid Charfi and Samir Khalil Samir, Bibliographie du dialogue islamochrétien, in: Islamochristiana 3 (1977), 278. Samir mentions a further manuscript containing the text of the *Risāla*: Alep, Archevêché Maronite 1314. It is worth noting in passing that one more apograph of the same text is preserved in München, Bayerische Staatsbibliothek arab. 948 (see forthcoming paper of Samir Khalil Samir, Remembrement de cinq manuscrits arabes des Coptes entremêlés, presented at the VIIIth Conference on Arab Christian Studies, Granada 2008) and in Balamand 181 (Rachied Haddad, Manuscrits du couvent de Belmont [Balamand], Beyrouth 1970, ١٢٨; I due the last reference to Dmitry Morozov).

6 I am aware of only one reference to that edition in Ralf Lange-Sonntag, Elias von Nisibis, in: BBKL 28 (2007), 369–374.

the Faculty of Philosophy of the University of Bonn.[7] The edition is preceded by a succinct introduction which contains information on the background and the contents of the text, as well as a description of the orthography of the manuscripts. As is indicated by the author, the edition was prepared using the standards of the series "Corpus Scriptorum Christianorum Orientalium" and is based on exactly the same manuscript which was proposed by Khalil Samir as the most reliable one (viz. Vat. ar. 126).

II. Contents of the *Risāla*[8]

The *Risāla* is a refutation of the opinion of the well-known Muslim Muʿtazilite theologian of the 9th c. al-Ǧāḥiẓ,[9] who stated in *Kitāb al-Ḥayawān* that chastity is not attainable for a human being: "It is neither possible nor conceivable for anyone to shut up the desire for women, because such desires and cravings are extant abundantly in a human being"[10].

The text of the *Risāla* can be divided into two parts. The first one contains the refutation of al-Ǧāḥiẓ's statement, while the second has a more independent character and aims to demonstrate that chastity is preferable to marriage and sexual intercourse.

Elias set as an object to refute systematically the view of al-Ǧāḥiẓ following the list of reasons that can help abolish the desire for sexual intercourse. Here they are:

1. Mind and the love of sciences.
2. Piety and the fear of God.
3. Admonitions of learned and wise men.
4. Poverty, extreme privation and the pursuit of rest for soul and body.
5. Zeal and wrath.
6. Sad melodies and unfortunate news.
7. Self-abasement and discipline.
8. Firm determination and strong will.
9. Generosity, dignity and the pursuit of heavens.

Having set forth the list, Elias proceeds to narrate stories or cite quotations for confirmation of each issue. And what deserves special remark is that Elias provides an explicit reference to the original source for almost every citation,[11] thus facilitat-

---

7 Andreas Hau, Brief über den Vorzug der Enthaltsamkeit gegenüber dem Geschlechtsverkehr von Elias von Nisibis. Einführung, Übersetzung, Text, Bonn 1969 [unpublished PhD thesis].

8 For detailed exposition of the contents of the *Risāla* and of its *Sitz im Leben* see the article of Sidney Griffith in the present volume.

9 On him see: Charles Pellat, al-ʿDjāḥiẓ, in: EI 2, Leiden ²1965, 385–387.

10 Hau, Brief über den Vorzug der Enthaltsamkeit, 14.

11 This particular feature of Elias' approach was also revealed in his "Chronicle", see Witold Witakowski, Elias Bar Shenaya's Chronicle, in: Syriac Polemics. Studies in Honour of Gerrit Jan Reinink, ed. by Wout Jac. van Bekkum, Jan Willem Drijvers and Alex C. Klugkist, OLA

ing their investigation and verification for a modern reader. And if the first part of the *Risāla* contains stories which are to a certain extent paraphrases based on the original sources, then in the second part Elias provides citations *sensu stricto*.

III. Sources

Here is the list of the citations in the order of their appearance in the text of the *Risāla*.[12]

First part of the *Risāla*:

- The story about Hippocrates and Polemon (ca. A.D. 88–144) – who was an author of a treatise on physiognomy influential in the Arabic tradition – which is in fact a recast version of the account concerning the meeting of Socrates and Zopyros.[13]
- Story of the monk Martinianos borrowed from the third part of the "Paradise of the Fathers".[14]

170, Leuven 2007, 233: "... Elias's Chronicle is exceptional among other Syriac works of the kind, from the fact that it regularly states its sources, with some exceptions though".

12 A few short quotations from Sirach and Matthew are given at the beginning of the treatise. Hau identified most of the citations. Since it is not necessary to repeat it, I confine myself to providing a reference to the edition of Rahmé and Hau [following the pattern: Rahmé's article / Hau's thesis] and adding – when lacking in Hau's thesis – data on editions, translations and studies.

13 20–23/١١–١٥ [Arabic], 46–48 [German tr.]. On him and his work see Jan Just Witkam, Aflīmūn, Fulaymūn, Iflīmūn, in: EI 12, Leiden ^{2}2004, 44–45. The same story features in many sources. For instance, in Pseudo-Aristotelean "Secretum secretorum" (see Regula Forster, Das Geheimnis der Geheimnisse. Die arabischen und deutschen Fassungen des pseudo-aristotelischen Sirr al-asrār/Secretum secretorum, Wissensliteratur im Mittelalter 43, Wiesbaden 2006, 93–94).

14 24–28/١٦–٢٣ [Arabic], 48–51 [German tr.]. Edition: Acta Martyrum et Sanctorum Syriace. Vol. 7, Paradisus Patrum, ed. by Paul Bedjan, Paris and Leipzig 1897, 923–924; English translation: The Book of Paradise. Being the Histories and Sayings of the Monks and Ascetics of the Egyptian Desert by Palladius, Hieronymus and others. The Syriac Texts, according to the Recension of ʿAnân-Îshôʿ of Bêth ʿÂbhê. Vol. 2, English Translation, Continued Index and Syriac Text, ed. and transl. by E.A. Wallis Budge (Lady Meux Manuscript 6), London 1904, 1026–1027. It is notable that Elias while citing a story of Martinian refers to the "third part" of the "Paradises of Fathers", for according to the authoritative table of contents of the "Paradise of the Fathers" preserved in the ms dated A.D. 794 it features in the "second part" (the "Paradise of the Fathers" is normally divided into four parts in the manuscript tradition). Moreover, another aspect of the significance of Elias' citation for the study of the "Paradise of the Fathers" is that the text he gives is different from that published by Bedjan (an earlier and fuller recension was edited by Michel van Esbroeck, La vie de saint Martinianus en version syriaque, in: ParOr 20 (1995), 237–269. On different recensions of the Syriac version of the history of Martinian see René Draguet, Les formes syriaques de la matière de l'histoire lausiaque. Vol. I: Textus. Les manuscrits. Édition des pièces liminaires et des ch. 1–19, CSCO.S 169, Louvain 1978, 81f*.

- Story about Plato[15] and his disciple, who fell in love – from Muḥammad Abū Bakr b. Zakariyyā' al-Rāzī "The Book of the Spiritual Physics".[16]
- Story about an Egyptian monk who was tempted to become married from the fourth part of the "Paradise of the Fathers".[17]
- Story about Anton and Paul from the first part of the "Paradise of the Fathers"[18].
- Story about the Greek king Agamemnon borrowed from Denḥā's the Logician's "Commentary on the Eisagoge of Porphyrios", but whose ultimate source is Homer's "Odyssey".[19]
- Story about a certain Abū l-Ḥasan b. Uḫt ibn ʿAmr ibn Šabaklā, who refused to get married – the story was told to Elias by a doorkeeper of Catholicos Mar Ibrahim.[20]
- The story circulated among the people about Buyid Emir ʿAḍud al-Daula (A.D. 936–983)[21] and his slave[22].
- Story heard from a preacher about the leader of *fityān*[23] who fell in love with a youth[24].

Second part of the *Risāla*:

- Quotation from 1 Cor 7,9[25]
- A saying of the "founder of the Muslim religion"[26]

---

15 Richard Walzer, Aflāṭūn, in: EI 1, 234–237.

16 29–30/٢٣–٢٦ [Arabic], 52–53 [German tr.]. On the author and the book see: Lenn E. Goodman, al-Rāzī, Abū Bakr Muḥammad b. Zakariyyā, in: EI 8, Leiden ^{2}1995, 474–477; Mehdi Mohaghegh, Notes on the "Spiritual Physic" of Al-Rāzī, in: Studia Islamica 26 (1967), 5–22. Ar-Rāzī is quoted also in the *Kitāb al-Maǧālis* of Elias of Nisibis: Samir Khalil Samir, Langue arabe, logique et théologie chez Élie de Nisibe, in: MUSJ 52 (1991–1992), 294–295.

17 31–32/٢٧–٢٩ [Arabic], 54–55 [German tr.]. Edition: Bedjan, Paradisus Patrum, 657–658 [no. 560], Budge, Book of Paradise. Vol. 2, 588 [no. 553] (cf. footnote 14); English translation: The Book of Paradise. Being the Histories and Sayings of the Monks and Ascetics of the Egyptian Desert by Palladius, Hieronymus and others. The Syriac Texts, according to the Recension of ʿAnân-Îshôʿ of Bêth ʿÂbhê. Vol. 1: English Translation, ed. and transl. by E.A. Wallis Budge, (Lady Meux Manuscript 6), London 1904, 772 [no. 553]. The passage in Elias' *Risāla* is considerably more extensive.

18 33–36/٣٠–٣٤ [Arabic], 55–57 [German tr.]. Edition: Bedjan, Paradisus Patrum, 81–87, Budge, Book of Paradise. Vol. 2, 154–159; English translation: Budge, Book of Paradise, Vol. 1, 183–189. The passage in Elias' *Risāla* diverges from the published text and seems to an abridged version of the latter.

19 37–39/٣٥–٣٨ [Arabic], 58–59 [German tr.].

20 40–42/٣٩–٤٢ [Arabic], 60–62 [German tr.]. The Catholicos in question is likely to be Abraham III Abraza (A.D. 906–937) and not Metropolitan Abraham of Baṣra († A.D. 999/1000) as suggested by Hau.

21 On him see: Harold Bowen, ʿAḍud al-Dawla, in: EI 1, Leiden ^{2}1960, 211–212.

22 43–44/٤٣–٤٤ [Arabic], 62–63 [German tr.].

23 Most probably, of eunuchs, see Ed(s)., Fatā, in: EI 2, 837.

24 45–47/٤٥–٤٨ [Arabic], 64–66 [German tr.]. In addition to the listed reasons Elias also mentions the assistance that one can find in ruses (as is done by monks and ascetics) and advice for chastity from the medical books.

25 57/٦٥ [Arabic], 76 [German tr.].

26 58/٦٥–٦٦ [Arabic], 76 [German tr.]. Hau refers to the twelfth book of al-Ġazālī's "Iḥya ʿulūm

- Quotation from the 15th Book of Muḥammad abū Bakr b. Zakariyyā' ar-Rāzī's "Book of the Spiritual Physic"[27]
- Quotation from the monastic canons[28]
- Quotation from the work of a learned monk[29]
- Quotation from the work of the Monk Abraham ibn Dašidad[30]
- Quotation from an unnamed Book of a monk, who encountered with three Ṣufis[31]
- Two storied heard from the learned scholars[32]
- Quotations from Ecclesiastes 7,26[33]
- Sayings of Socrates[34].

---

al-dīn". However it should be mentioned that in the text of al-Ġazālī the saying is attributed to the famous early Ṣufi Abū Sulaymān al-Dārānī, on whom see Richard Gramlich, Abū Sulaymān ad-Dārānī, in: Oriens 33 (1992), 22–85 [the author provides a list of the sayings attributed to al-Dārānī, and the saying in question is lacking].

27 On him see Goodman, al-Rāzī, 474–477 (cf. footnote 16). 65–67/٧٩–٨٢ [Arabic], 83–85 [German tr.].

28 67/٨٣–٨٤ [Arabic], 85 [German tr.]. Hau does not suggest any possible source of the quotation; it might have been borrowed from a certain East Syriac collection of canons for the monks, however it does not feature among canons published in Syriac and Arabic documents. Regarding legislation relative to Syrian asceticism, ed., transl. and furnished with literary historical data by Arthur Vööbus, Papers of the Estonian Theological Society in Exile 11, Stockholm 1960.

29 67–68/٨٤–٨٥ [Arabic], 86 [German tr.].

30 68–69/٨٥–٨٦ [Arabic], 86 [German tr.].

31 69–72/٨٦–٩٢ [Arabic], 87–89 [German tr.]. The work was not identified by Hau. It is evidently different from the melkite "Dispute" of George the Monk (Georg Graf, Geschichte der christlichen arabischen Literatur. Bd. 2: Die Schriftsteller bis zur Mitte des 15. Jahrhunderts, Studi e testi 133, Città del Vaticano 1947, 79–81), which is called in some manuscripts "A disputation between a Christian monk and three learned Muslims" (Moritz Steinschneider, Polemische und apologetische Literatur in arabischer Sprache zwischen Muslimen, Christen und Juden, nebst Anhängen verwandten Inhalts, AKM 6,3, Leipzig 1877, 87–88).

32 72–73/٩٢–٩٤ [Arabic], 89–90 [German tr.].

33 73/٩٤–٩٥ [Arabic], 90 [German tr.].

34 73–74/٩٥ [Arabic], 90–91 [German tr.]. The saying as it is given by Elias is lacking in the collection of Socrates' saying excerpted from Muslim and Christian Arabic sources by I. Alon, Socrates Arabus. Life and Teachings. Sources, Translations, Notes, Apparatus, and Indexes, The Max Schloessinger Memorial Series. Texts 8, Jerusalem 1995. Nevertheless one can easily detect affinities with other saying which deal with topos "women-deadly poison":

Elias' *Risāla*.	The wise Socrates said: "Women are a deadly poison. Who abstains from it, is safe from it. And who takes it, it kills him."

As one can see Elias makes use of different kinds of sources of both Christian and Muslim origin: the Bible, oral communications, sermons, "Paradise of the Fathers", ascetic, apologetic, medical, logical and physiognomic treatises. In case of some quotations from Christian sources it is not quite clear in which language they were written and in what language they were accessible to Elias. He certainly uses the original Syriac text of the "Paradise of the Fathers"[35] and, most probably, of the monastic canons.[36] The language of the quotations from the text of the "learned scholars" and "learned monk", as well as of the "Book of a monk, who encountered with three Sufis" might have been either Syriac or Arabic.[37] The sayings of Socrates must have been borrowed from Arabic tradition, for such sayings attributed to Soc-

No. 276:61 [transl.], ٧١ [Arabic]. It features in the works of Ḥunain b. Isḥāq, Al-Mubaššir b. Fātik, Ibn Abī Uṣaibiʿa and Ibn ʿAqnīn.	… He said to a disciple of him: "My son, if [you] cannot avoid women, then deal with them as if you had to eat dead [animal's] flesh, which you should only do when in great need, and only as much as to sustain life. For if one takes [from that meat] more than one needs, it will sicken him and kill him. Women are likewise: He who only associates with them when in need will escape unharmed. He, on the other hand, who befriends them while in no such need will regret it and will be subject to hateful [consequences]."
No. 278:61 [transl.], ٧١ [Arabic]. It features in anonymous "Bustān al-ḥukamā'".	…"She is a fatal adder that drinks poison with which she can kill."

Thus it is not clear whether Elias cites a so far unknown saying verbatim, or whether he paraphrases the available texts. Evidently, he was aware of such sayings attributed to Socrates, for in his "Maxims" one reads: "The women are like the oleander tree, which is beautiful and glorious, but when an inexperienced person tastes it, it kills him" [No. 159: 51 [transl.], ٦٤ [Arabic]. And it precisely corresponds to the saying that features in the works of Ḥunain b. Isḥāq, Ibn Abī Uṣaibiʿah, Šams al-Dīn Šahrazūrī and in "ʿUnwān al-Saʿādah" [no. 274, 61 [transl.], ٧١ [Arabic].

35 On that see in more details below.

36 I could not find any collection of monastic canons originally written in Arabic (and not translated from Syriac). On the East-Syriac monastic canons see: Walter Selb, Orientalisches Kirchenrecht, Bd. 1: Die Geschichte des Kirchenrechts der Nestorianer (von den Anfängen bis zur Mongolenzeit), SAWW.PH 388, Veröffentlichungen der Kommission für Antike Rechtsgeschichte 3, Wien 1981, 145–147.

37 There are apologetic works of the similar kind both in Syriac and in Arabic, see an overview in Sidney H. Griffith, Disputes with Muslims in Syriac Christian Texts. From Patriarch John († 648) to Bar Hebraeus († 1286), in: Religionsgespräche im Mittelalter, ed. by Bernard Lewis and Friedrich Niewöhner, Wolfenbütteler Mittelalter-Studien 4, Wiesbaden 1992, 251–273 (repr. in Sidney H. Griffith, The Beginnings of Christian Theology in Arabic. Muslim-Christian Encounters in the Early Islamic Period, CStS 746, Aldershot 2002, ch. V); Louis Sako, Bibliographie du dialogue islamo-chrétien. Auteurs chrétiens de langue syriaque, in: Islamochristiana 10 (1984), 273–292; Michael Philip Penn, Syriac Sources for Early Christian/Muslim Relations, in: Islamochristiana 29 (2003), 59–78.

rates are not known in Syriac.[38] The case of Denḥā the Logician is not quite clear. He was identified by Hau with a disciple of Catholicos Īšōʿ bar Nūn († A.D. 828)[39] who according to the "Catalogus auctorum" of ʿAbdīšōʿ of Nisibis[40] wrote commentaries on the Psalms, on the "second part" of Gregory of Nazianzus, on the "Dialectics"[41] of Aristotle and some other treatises. No authentic works of that Denḥā are known.[42] Thus if we follow the identification of Hau, the quotation of Elias turns out to be an important witness both for the "Odyssey" and for the history of the commentaries of Aristotle in the Syriac tradition and hence deserves a proper investigation on ist own right.[43]

---

38 There is a dialogue of a philosophical content entitled "Socrates" in British Library Add. 14658 (on it see William Romaine Newbold, The Syriac Dialogue "Socrates". A Study in Syrian Philosophy, in: PAPS 57.2 (1918), 99–111). According to the available studies, in the numerous gnomic collections the sayings of Socrates are absent (Nicole Zeegers-Vander Vorst, Une gnomologie d'auteurs grecs en traduction syriaque, in: Symposium Syriacum 1976. célebré du 13 au 17 septembre 1976 au Centre Culturel "Les Fontaines" de Chantilly (France). Communications, OCA 205, Roma 1978, 163–177; Sebastian Brock, Syriac Translations of Greek Popular Philosophy, in: Von Athen nach Bagdad. Zur Rezeption griechischer Philosophie von der Spätantike bis zum Islam, ed. by Peter Bruns, Hereditas 22, Bonn 2003, 9–28).

39 Hau, Brief über den Vorzug der Enthaltsamkeit, 59.

40 In the edition of Assemani one reads as the name of the author "Iba" (Josephus Simonius Assemanus, BOCV 3.1: De scriptoribus Syris Nestorianis, Romae 1725, Reprint Hildesheim 1975, 175–176); the reading "Denḥa" is provided by the edition of Ecchelensis (Abraham Ecchellensis, Tractatum Continentem Catalogum Librorum Chaldaeorum, tam Ecclesiasticorum, quam Profanorum. Auctore Hebediesu Metropolita Sobensi, Romae 1653, 82).

41 ʿAbdīšōʿ uses the same title *pūššāqā/nūhhārā da-mlīllūtā* at few other occurrences: Sergios of Rešʿaynā wrote "Commentaries on Dialectics" (Assemani, BOCV, 87), Abraham of Kaškar – "Elucidation of the Dialectics" (154), and Īšōʿdnaḥ of Baṣra – "Commentary on Dialectics" (Assemani, BOCV, 195), – and normally it is considered to refer to the corpus of Aristotle's "Organon", although the original contribution of either of the Syriac commentators is disputed by modern scholarship (Sebastian Brock, The Syriac Commentary Tradition, in: Glosses and commentaries on Aristotelian logical texts. The Syriac, Arabic and medieval Latin traditions, ed. by Charles Burnett, Warburg Institute Surveys and Texts 23, London 1993, 3–18 [repr. in Sebastian Brock, From Ephrem to Romanos. Interactions between Syriac and Greek in Late Antiquity, CStS 664, Aldershot 1999, chapter 13]; Hans Daiber, Die Aristotelesrezeption in der syrischen Literatur, in: Die Gegenwart des Altertums. Formen und Funktionen des Altertumsbezugs in den Hochkulturen der Alten Welt, ed. by Dieter Kuhn and Helga Stahl, Heidelberg 2001, 327–345).

42 The problem of the authorship of the extant "Commentary on the Psalms" attributed to Rabban Denḥa and Rabban Grigor, the monk of Gamre is not yet clear. Anton Baumstark, Geschichte der syrischen Literatur mit Ausschluß der christlich-palästinensischen Texte, Bonn 1922, 220; see also Lucas Van Rompay, Development of Biblical Interpretation in the Syrian Churches of the Middle Ages, in: Hebrew Bible, Old Testament. The History of Its Interpretation. Vol. I/2: The Middle Ages, ed. by Magne Sæbø, Göttingen 2000, 572.

43 The complete text of the Syriac version neither of the "Iliad" nor of the "Odyssey" is extant. And while available fragments, citations and paraphrases from the "Iliad" suggest that the Syriac translation (at least partial) of it once existed, the knowledge of the "Odyssey" in the Syriac sources is so far limited to a single reference in the "Chronicle" of Michael the Great (A.D. 1126–1199), which in turn was borrowed from the Syriac translation of Eusebius of Caesarea

Nevertheless one must not exclude the possibility that Denḥā's "Commentary on the Eisagoge" was written not in Syriac, but in Arabic. In that case it should also be considered as a valuable record of the textual transmission of the "Odyssey" in Arabic tradition, for since there were no complete Arabic translation of either the "Iliad" or the "Odyssey" until the 19th c. each relevant piece of evidence cannot be disregarded.[44]

Approaching two biblical quotations (1 Cor 7,9 and Eccl 7,26) one faces two possible options. Elias could either quote from the Syriac Bible (and then translated a passage into Arabic) or he could make use of the available Arabic translation of the texts in question. What do we know about Arabic versions of 1 Cor and Ecclesiastes? Regrettably, the comprehensive history of the Arabic Bible is not yet written and its research is extremely complicated due to the presence of various Arabic versions (some were made – often more then once[45] – from Syriac, other from Greek, Hebrew, Coptic and Latin) of one particular text.[46]

As for the Arabic versions of Ecclesiastes, one can say, following the study of Georg Graf, that the text present in the majority of the manuscripts derives from the Septuagint.[47] However apart from the manuscripts with uncertain *Vorlage*[48], there is

---

"Chronicle" (Lawrence I. Conrad, Varietas Syriaca. Secular and Scientific Culture in the Christian Communities of Syria after the Arab Conquest, in: After Bardaisan. Studies on Continuity and Change in Honour of Professor Han J.W. Drijvers, ed. by G.J. Reinink and A.C. Klugkist, OLA 89, Leuven 1999, 91–94 with further references in the notes).

44 The statement of Gotthard Strohmaier is still valid: "Der echte Homer ist der islamischen Welt fremd geblieben". Among the reasons for that one should mention the fact that the Arabs were convinced of the superior value of their own poetry and the difficulty of the Greek text. On the knowledge of Homer's epics by the Arabs and their translations see Gotthard Strohmaier, Homer in Bagdad, in: Byzantinoslavica 41 (1980), 196–200; Michael Kreutz, Sulaymān al-Bustānīs Arabische Ilias. Ein Beispiel für arabischen Philhellenismus im ausgehenden Osmanischen Reich, in: Die Welt des Islam 44.2 (2004), 155–157; Bo Holmberg, Transculturating the Epic. The Arab Awakening and the Translation of the Iliad, in: Literary History: Towards a Global Perspective. Vol. 3: Literary Interactions in the Modern World 1, ed. by Margareta Petersson, Berlin 2006, 141–165.

45 For instance, K. Samaan in his recent study on the Arabic translations of Ben Sira (Kamil W. Samaan, Sept traductions arabes de Ben Sira, EHS.T 23, 492, Frankfurt am Main 1994, managed to distinguish seven different version deriving from Greek, Syriac, Coptic and Latin. It is worth noting that the study is not a satisfactory one, for the analytical approach of the author impeded him from generalizing about the procured data. He does not give a personal opinion on the question of the date of translation of any of the versions and in concluding his research he merely refers to the opinions of other scholars (ibid., 401). Moreover apart from a description of the manuscripts used there is no investigation of the manuscript tradition of any version.

46 Georg Graf, Geschichte der christlichen arabischen Literatur. Bd. 1: Die Übersetzungen, Studi e testi 118, Città del Vaticano 1944, 85–195; Ignazio Guidi, Le traduzioni degli Evangelii in arabo e in etiopico, in: AAL.M (1888) Serie 4, Vol. 4, 4–37; Henri Hyvernat, Arabes (versions) des écritures, in DB(V) 1 (1895), 845–856.

47 Graf, Geschichte der christlichen arabischen Literatur, 127–128. The Ecclesiastes edited in both the Paris and London Polyglots is based on Paris ar. 1 that dates back to the 16th c. and depends on the Septuagint as well.

48 Graf, Geschichte, 130–131.

a number of witnesses to the Arabic version of Ecclesiastes which is a translation from Syriac carried out by al-Ḥāriṯ ibn Sinān ibn Sinbāṭ who most likely lived in 9 th–10th c.[49] Furthermore there is an indication that it was not the only translation of Ecclesiastes made on the basis of the Syriac Bible. The vague subtitle of the Codex Biblioteca Ambrosiana X 200 sup. (11th–12th c.) containing Ecclesiastes mentions the name of Fiṯyaun (Pethion) that was interpreted by Oscar Löfgren as indication of its translator's name who supposedly lived in the 9th c.[50] According to Graf, Pethion is known to be translator of Job, Sirach and of the three Great Prophets.[51] Thus the relation between translations of Ecclesiastes attributed to al-Ḥāriṯ ibn Sinān ibn Sinbāṭ and Pethion is still to be revealed.[52]

Any further Investigation of Elias' quotation from Ecclesiastes will undoubtedly from the edition of any Arabic translation of the text as soon as any of them becomes available. Whereas a comparison of quotation from Ecclesiastes with the London Polyglot[53] edition used for the present study reveals considerable differences which are sufficient to infer that Elias did not use the Arabic version deriving from the Septuagint, the wording of the quotation found in the *Risāla*, in contrast, has some apparent affinities in vocabulary[54] with the Pšīṭtā[55]. Although there is not enough evidence for drawing a definitive conclusion concerning the language of the version that was used by Elias, the available material clearly demonstrates that the Biblical text he used represents either the Syriac (Pšīṭtā) or the Syro-Arabic (Arabic tanslation of Pšīṭtā) Biblical tradition.[56]

---

49 Graf, Geschichte, 129–130. On translator see also Joseph Nasrallah, Deux versions Melchites partielles de la Bible du IXe et du Xe siècles, in: Oriens Christianus 64 (1980), 206–210; Joseph Nasrallah, Histoire du mouvement littéraire dans l'Église melchite du Ve au XXe siècle. Contribution à l'étude de la littérature arabe chrétienne. Vol. II. Tome 2: 750–Xe siècle, Louvain 1988, 187–188.

50 Oscar Löfgren and Renato Traini, Catalogue of the Arabic Manuscripts in the Biblioteca Ambrosiana. Vol. 1: Antico fondo and medio fondo, Fontes ambrosiani 51,5–6.

51 Graf, Geschichte, 126.130.134.

52 It is worth noting that there is evidence that their translations were mixed. Thus Nasrallah argued that translation of the Sirach transmitted in some manuscripts together with other Biblical texts that were translated by al-Ḥāriṯ ibn Sinān ibn Sinbāṭ is to be attributed to Phetion (Nasrallah, Deux versions Melchites partielles de la Bible, 209 (cf. footnote 49) [the author was unaware of the ms. Biblioteca Ambrosiana X 200 sup.]).

53 Brian Walton (ed.), Biblia sacra polyglotta. Vol. III, London 1655 (Reprint: Graz 1964), 415. The wording is quite close to that in the Van Dyck's Bible. The London Polyglot depends on the Paris Polyglot, whereas in the letter the text of Ecclesiastes was taken from the Paris ar. 1 and is considered to be translated from the Septuagint.

54 E.g. فخّ – ܦܚܐ, مصيدة – ܡܨܝܕܬܐ against featuring in London Polyglot synonymous أشراك and شباك respectively.

55 The Old Testament in Syriac. According to the Peshiṭta version. Part 2, fascicle 5: Proverbs. Wisdom of Solomon. Ecclesiastes. Song of Songs [Qoheleth ed. by David J. Lane], Leiden 1979, 13.

56 There are however some disagreements with the Pšīṭtā as well. But that is most probably due to Elias' adjustment of the Biblical wording to the narrative.

Regarding the quotation from 1 Cor we are again facing numerous options concerning its provenance: the Syriac Bible, an Arabic translation made from one of the Syriac versions or an Arabic translation made from the Greek New Testament.[57] Fortunately, there are editions of the Arabic versions of Epistles of Paul as they are preserved in Sinai Ar. 151 (A.D. 867) made from the Syriac Bible (Pšīṭtā) and in Sinai Ar. 155 (9th–10th c.) made from the Greek New Testament enable us to discern on which Biblical tradition depends the quotation of Elias. Let me compare a quotation in Elias' *Risāla* with readings of the Pšīṭtā, Sinai Ar. 151 and that of Sinai Ar. 155.

Elias' *Risāla*[58]	Pšīṭtā[59]	Sinai Ar. 151[60]	Sinai Ar. 155[61]
فإن لم يصبروا، فليتزوجوا، فإن الزواج خير من الاحتراق بالشّهوة	ܐܠܐ ܐܢ ܡܣܝܒܪܝܢ ܢܣܒܘܢ. ܦܩܚ ܓܝܪ ܠܡܣܒ ܐܢܬܬܐ ܛܒ ܡܢ ܕܠܡܐܬܘܢ ܒܪܓܬܐ	ولكنهم ان لم يقدروا على ذلك فليتزوجوا، فانه اخير ان يتزوج الانسان من ان يحترق بالشهوة	فان لم يصبروا فليتزوجوا فانه اخير له تزوج من ان يحترق

Although at first sight Elias' reading seems to be remarkably closer among the two Arabic versions to that of Sinai Ar. 155 (the text of Sinai Ar. 151 is more expositive) at the same time there are clear hints witnessing that in all likelihood Elias did not use an Arabic version deriving from the Greek New Testament. One of the most significant hints is that the latter faithfully renders the infinitive form of the

57 For an overview of the Arabic translations of the New Testament see Bruce M. Metzger, The Early Versions of the New Testament. Their Origin, Transmission and Limitations, Oxford 1977, 257–268 and for the Epistles in particular see Graf, Geschichte, 170–181.

58 Hau, Brief über den Vorzug der Enthaltsamkeit, 57.

59 Das Neue Testament in syrischer Überlieferung. II. Die paulinischen Briefe. Teil 1: Römer- und 1. Korintherbrief, ed. by Barbara Aland and Andreas Juckel, ANTT 14, Berlin-New York 1991, 351.

60 Harvey Staal, Mt. Sinai Arabic Codex 151. I Pauline Epistles, CSCO 452. Scriptores arabici 40, Louvain 1983, 58 [edition]; Harvey Staal, Mt. Sinai Arabic Codex 151. I Pauline Epistles, CSCO.A 41, Louvain 1983, 62 [transl.]. On this version see Paul Feghali, Les épitres de Saint Paul dans une des premières traductions en arabe, in: ParOr 39 (2005), 103–130. The relevant passage is unfortunately lacking in the ms The National Library of Russia, Arabic New Series 327 dated A.D. 892 (see edition Sten Edvard Stenij, Die altarabische Übersetzung der Briefe an die Hebräer, an die Römer und an die Corinther aus einem in St. Petersburg befindlichen Codex Tischendorfs vom Jahre 892 n. Chr., Helsingfors 1901 [I would like to thank Rev. Professor Serafim Seppälä who kindly helped me to get a photocopy of this extremely rare book]) whose text is considered to depend on East Syriac Biblical tradition (Graf, Geschichte, 173).

61 Margaret Dunlop Gibson, An Arabic Version of the Epistles of St. Paul to the Romans, Corinthians, Galatians, with part of the Epistle to the Ephesians, from a ninth century MS. in the convent of St. Catharine on Mount Sinai, Studia Sinaitica 2, London 1894, ٤٩. On this versions, see Robert Henry Boyd, The Arabic text of I Corinthians in Studia Sinaitica no. II. A comparative, linguistic, and critical study, Princeton University 1942 [unpublished PhD thesis].

Greek πυροῦσθαι with ان يحترق as introducing a verbal clause, whereas the Syriac Pšīṭtā gives a more descriptive expression, "to burn in desire" (ܠܡܬܚܡܡܘ ܒܪܓܬܐ)[62], which was taken over in Sinai Ar. 151. However, there is not enough evidence to distinguish with certainty which version – either the Syriac or an Arabic translation from Syriac – was used by Elias and the issue is further complicated by the possible quoting from memory and adjustment of the Biblical text to Elias' exposition.

It goes without saying that with regard to the Syriac sources used by Elias, the detailed study of the quotations and paraphrases may shed a new light on the history of the textual tradition of the extant Syriac texts (such as that of the "Paradise of the Fathers"), and on the history of the Arabic translations of the Syriac texts (Bible) but it is even more important as the source of borrowings from lost works (for example Denḥā's commentary on the "Eisagoge", and the unnamed Book of a monk who had a conversation with three Sufis).

IV. Abraham

Elias attributed the quotation in question to the monk Ibrāhīm b. Dāšīdād, who was identified with Abraham bar Dašandad, an East Syriac ascetic author of the 8th c., by both Rahmé and Hau. None of them, however, tried to verify such a pretty possibility.

When in 1922 the "Geschichte der syrischen Literatur" of Anton Baumstark was published, the paragraph on the life of Abraham was compiled using the short accounts of Thomas of Marga, *Kitāb al-Mağdal* and the Letters of Catholicos Timothy I – thus identifying Abraham bar Dašandad with Abraham the teacher at the school of Bašoš.[63] Concerning the literary heritage of Abraham, Baumstark could not say more than one can read in "Catalogum auctorum" of ʿAbdīšōʿ of Nisibis, namely: "Abraham bar Dašandad composed the the Book of Admonition, Commentary on Abba Marcos, Disputation with Jews, Book of the King's way, mēmrē on repentance, different letters written on various matters".[64] The learned German scholar

62 The literal rendering of the Greek can be found in the Harklean version: ܠܡܬܝܩܕܘ.

63 It is worth noting that the identification of different Abrahams is not so evident as it might seem, and a thorough examination of the available accounts has not yet been undertaken (the problem arises from the fact that one can find in the Syriac sources two rather different portrayals of Abraham: the first provides an image of the author of the ascetic works (ʿAbdīšōʿ of Nisibis), while the other depicts a learned scholar capable of teaching Aristotelian philosophy (letters of Timothy I); two conflicting images were taken for granted by scholarship as telling about one and the same person, although occasionaly some scholars were reluctant to agree with standard identification: Oskar Braun, Der Katholikos Timotheos I und seine Briefe, in: OrChr 1 (1901), 138; Raphaël J. Bidawid, Les lettres du patriarche nestorien Timothée I. Étude critique avec, en appendice, la lettre de Timothée I aux moines du couvent de Mār Mārōn (traduction latine et texte chaldéen), StT 187, Città del Vaticano 1956, 1, note 2.

64 Assemani, BOCV, 194 (cf. footnote 40). Baumstark, Geschichte der syrischen Literatur, 214 (cf. footnote 42). It should be mentioned that in some sources the name of Abraham is vocal-

could not help but regret that none of the ascetic works from the list had survived,[65] furthermore he lamented the loss of Abraham's philological work, which was considered by Bar Bahlūl, an East Syrian lexicographer of the 10th c., as one of the main sources of his "Lexicon".[66]

And it was not until 1934, when Alphonse Mingana edited some texts preserved in the East Syriac monastic anthology Mingana Syr. 601,[67] that the first authentic works – "Letter to the brother" and "Advices that follow the Letter" – of Abraham bar Dašandad appeared.[68] Because of their general ascetic contents little attention has been paid to them and the article of Ludin Jansen seems to give an exhaustive analysis of the contents.[69]

Since the publication of Mingana no new texts or copies of already edited ones have been found, which inevitably suggests an image of a completely forgotten 8th c. author, whose works ceased to be copied. However, it seems to be not quite true, and the real evaluation of the author and his literary heritage should be postponed for the future while awaiting new data. By way of example it can be said that both texts edited by Mingana feature anonymously in two other manuscripts: Metropolitan Library of the Church of the East in Baghdad 145 (A.D. 1742), fol. 424–445[70] and Jerusalem, Greek Orthodox Patriarchate 21, (A.D. 1593), fol. 156r–168r.[71] What is especially remarkable, is that the text entitled "Advices that follow the Letter" presents in both manuscripts a different (longer) recension in comparison with the edited text. That longer recension appears further (also anonymously) with certain

ized differently, viz. Abraham bar Dašnādad.

65 Baumstark hesitated concerning the "Anonymous commentary on abba Markos", preserved in British Library Add. 17270. Modern scholarship is inclined to attribute it to Babai the Great (Paul Krüger, Überlieferung und Verfasser der beiden Memre über das "geistige Gesetz" des Mönches Markus, in: OstKSt 6 [1957], 297–299).

66 Baumstark, Geschichte der syrischen Literatur, 214, note 3.

67 Mingana Syr. 601 (A.D. 1932) on a par with Baghdad Chaldean Monastery syr. 681 (A.D. 1901; *olim* Notre Dame des Semences/Vosté 238) and Vat. Syr. 509 (A.D. 1928) were copied from the unique East Syriac monastic anthology Baghdad Chaldean Monastery syr. 680 (A.D. 1289; *olim* Notre Dame des Semences /Vosté 237).

68 Alphonse Mingana, Woodbrooke Studies. Christian Documents in Syriac, Arabic and Garshūni. Vol. 7: Early Christian Mystics, Cambridge 1934, 248–255 (facsimile edition of Mingana Syr. 601, fol. 60v–67v), 185–197 [ET].

69 H. Ludin Jansen, The mysticism of Abraham bar Dashandad, in: Numen 4 (1957), 114–126. The doctrine of Abraham was also treated in Vittorio Berti, Abramo bar Dashandad. Custodisci te stesso. Lettera a Giovanni. Ammonizioni, Testi dei padri della chiesa 84, Monastero di Bose 2006, 11–17.

70 Al-Muṭrān Kīwarkīs Ṣlīwā, Fihrist maḫṭūṭāt maktabat murṭāniyyat kanīsat al-mašriq fī Baġdād, Baghdad 2005, 145. See also my forthcoming study on that manuscript.

71 Jean-Baptiste Chabot, Notice sur les manuscrits syriaques conservés dans la bibliothèque du patriarcat grec orthodoxe de Jérusalem, in: Journal Asiatique 3 (1894), 114–115 [Chabot does not distinguish and identify the pieces by Abraham; my examination is based on the microfilm provided by the Library of Congress].

regularity in some East Syriac manuscripts containing a corpus of 24 *mēmrē* of Isaac of Antioch attributed to Isaac of Nineveh.[72]

V. Text[73]

Index siglorum[74]:
A – Vat. ar. 144, Egypt, 14th c. (?) [Kh. Samir]
B – Vat. ar. 181, Tripoli, AD 1584
C – Vat. ar. 126, Egypt, AD 1688
D – Vat. ar. 115, Egypt, AD 1250 [epitome]

وقال إبراهيم ابن داشيداد[75] الرّاهب في كتاب المواعظ[76]: إنّي لأعجب ممّن تعرض[77] له هذه الشهوة الدنيّة[78] كيف لا[79] يهجرها ويدفعها عنه ليكون عند الله كبعض الملائكة وعند الناس كبعض الأنبياء وتفتخر به[80] أصدقاؤه ، وتحسده أعداؤه من حيث لا يدخل في هجرها[81] غرامة مال ولا بذل جاه ولا تعب جسم ولا ألم نفس[82] ولا شغل قلب.

And Ibrāhīm b. Dāšīdād the Monk says in his "Book of Admonition" [ms. **C** – "Corpus of Admonitions"]: Indeed, I wonder at the one, who, when that inferior lust appears in him, neither tries to forsake it nor to get rid of it in order to become as an angel for God and as a prophet for the people. His friends would be then proud of him while his foes would be envy on him because the heavy fine is not imposed on him for he had forsaken [the desires]. He does not lose his face, his body is not overburden, his soul does not suffer, and his heart does not succumb.

72 E.g. British Library Or. 9358, fol. 103r–105r (A.D. 1896; not yet catalogued), Cambridge University Library Add. 2017, fol. 108r–110r (A.D. 1883).

73 I reproduce the fragment following the edition of Rahmé (Georges Rahmé, رسالة في فضيلة العفاف لايليًّا النصّيبيني, in: Al-Machriq 62 (1968), 68–69) and not that of Hau mainly for the following reason. In my view the readings of the name of Abraham bar Dašandad (see footnote 75) as well as of the title of his work (see footnote 76) as it can be found in the ms **C** are to be considered if not corrupted then at least staying further in comparison to other witnesses from the supposed Syriac wording and its literal Arabic translation.

74 On manuscripts of the *Risāla* see note 5.

75 **BC**: إبراهيم بن شداد

76 **C**: في جملة مواعيظه

77 **C**: يعر

78 **B**: البدنية

79 **C**: ولا

80 **B**: ويفتخر

81 **B**: تحسده أعداؤه من حيث ليس يدخل عليه في هجرها ; **C**: وتحسده اعدايه وحيث ليس يدخل عليه في هجرانها

82 **B**: ولم ألم نفس

وإنّني[83] لأعجب ممّن تعرض له هذه الشهوة فيتبعها فيكون[84] عند الله آثمًا وعند الناس فاجرًا ويحزن أصدقاءه[85] وتشمت به أعداءه، ومع ذلك يضيق نفسه ويضيع ماله ويوكس جاهه ويؤلم جسمه ويؤذي نفسه ويتعب قلبه ويفسد عقله[86]

Indeed I wonder at the one, who, when that inferior lust appears in him, gives in to it and thus becomes a sinner for God and an adulterer for the people. His friends grieve over him while his foes feel malicious joy about him. And thereby he harasses himself, forfeits his wealth, loses his face, causes pain to his body, damages his soul, tortures his heart and corrupts his reason.

VI. Commentary

1. Comparison of the fragment with the published works of Abraham bar Dašandad

Approaching the issue of the source text of the given quotation it is first of all necessary to examine if it comes from any of the already known texts of Abraham. The passage as it can be found in the *Risāla* is absent in the "Letter to John" as well as in the "Advices that follow the Letter"[87]. However the comparison of both pieces with the quotation reveals some similarities between them. First of all one should mention ascetic and exhortative contents as a distinctive feature of both texts. The "Letter" stresses the necessity of acquiring and refining of the virtues[88] in order not to be abandoned by God in the afterlife.[89] Such a practical attitude (in which the mystical concern is moved aside) agrees with the kernel of the quotation. Although the "Letter" treats predominantly the abandonment of the world[90] the issue of

83 **BC**: واني

84 **C**: وهو عالمًا انه يكون

85 **C**: وتحزن أصدقاه

86 **B**: وتشمت به أعدايه، ومع ذلك يضيع ماله ويوكس جاهه ويؤلم جسمه ويؤذي نفسه ويتعب قلبه ونفسه وعقله; **C**: وتشمت به أعداه، ومع ذلك يضيع ماله ويوكس جاهه ويؤلم جسمه ويؤذي نفسه ويتعب قلبه ويفسد عقله.

87 Hereafter I refer to the two texts of Abraham – "Letter to John" and to the "Advices that follow the Letter" – as "Letter".

88 Abraham mentions prayer, fasting, reading, watchfulness, love for Christ, solitude, prudence, vigil, upright conduct, penitence and others.

89 Fol. 61^{r}, lines 4–6 [edition], 187, lines 16–20 [transl.]; fol. 62^{r}, lines 10–12 [edition], 188, last line – 189, lines 1–3 [transl.]; fol. 63^{v}, lines 4–6 [edition], 191, lines 1–3 [transl.]; fol. 63^{v}, lines 15–17 [edition], 191, lines 12–14 [transl.]; fol. 65^{v}, lines 12–15 [edition], 194, lines 8–10 [transl.]; fol. 66^{r}, lines 11–12 [edition], 194, lines 34–35 [transl.].

90 "As to you, O my beloved, disentangle yourself from the harmful bonds of this temporary sojourn, which is full of injuries and wretchedness, and bind yourself with all your soul, with all your power and with all your mind, to the love of Christ" (fol. 62^{v}, lines 10–13 [edition], 189, lines 27–31 [transl.]).

maintaining chastity finds its proper place in the framework of the text.[91] In particular, Abraham speaks about silencing the "natural passions"[92] and about "prevailing over the desires", considering it as one of the aims to be achieved[93]. The clue term of the Arabic fragment – شهوة – can be rendered as "desire, ardent wish, longing, lust"[94] and normally corresponds to Syriac ܪܓܬܐ[95]. Thus the call contained in the fragment matches well to the ascetic doctrine that can be found in the "Letter".

Apart from similarities on the conceptual level there are points which bring together two texts from the stylistic and formal point of view. The Arabic fragment is organized using the method of contraposition of arguments: if one withstands the attack of passions, then he/she gains God's goodwill and deliverance from torments; while if one tolerates that there is no other end for him/her than disgrace and suffering. The same arrangement can be found in the "Letter" on a few occasions. While arguing for the necessity of abandoning the temporary world, Abraham makes a distinction between the fate of the one who is a subject of the world, his wealth and habits, and the model of an attitude to the world which is founded upon the comprehension of the difference between God and the world.[96] On another occasion Abraham contrasts one who is preparing for Doomsday already in this world by means of acquiring virtues with another who will have to pay off his debts with sorrow.[97]

Another stylistic feature of the Arabic fragment is a chain of parallel constructions. We may read, in the fragment, two different effects each attitude towards passions produces. Those two sequences are intended to cover in general terms all the aspects of human existence: body, soul, heart, mind, wealth, esteem. Such chains are used frequently in the text of the "Letter" as well. Here is just one example: "Guard your eyes from sight, your ears from hearing and your tongue from speech, so that your heart may rejoice in the truth".[98]

---

91 Fol. 61^{r}, lines 18–20 [edition], 187, lines 32–34 [transl.]; fol. 61^{v}, lines 17–20 [edition], 188, lines 19–22 [transl.]; fol. 62^{r}, lines 5–6 [edition], 188, 31–33 [transl.].

92 ܚ̈ܫܐ ܟܝܢ̈ܝܐ (fol. 63^{r}, line 10 [edition], 190, line 18 [transl.]).

93 ܙܟܘܐ ܠܪ̈ܓܝܓܬܐ (fol. 64^{v}, lines 12–13 [edition], 192, lines 27–28 [transl.])

94 Hans Wehr, A Dictionary of Modern Written Arabic (Arabic-English), ed. by J. Milton Cowan, Wiesbaden ^{4}1979, 574.

95 Richard James Horatio Gottheil (ed.), Bar ʿAlī (Īshōʿ). The Syriac-Arabic Glosses, Reale accademia nazionale dei lincei. ser. V. vol. XIII. parte II, Roma 1910–1928, 380; Rubens Duval (ed.), Lexicon syriacum auctore Hassano bar Bahlule. Tomus secundus, Parisiis 1901, col. 1874–1874. One can find a correspondence of cognate words also in Elias' *Kitāb al-targumān* (editions: Paul Anton de Lagarde, Praetermissorum libri duo, Gottingae 1879, 34, line 79; Binyāmīn Ḥaddād (ed.), Targmānā, Dohūq 2007, 107). Cf. also the following verses in Syriac and Arabic translation: Rom 7:8, Gal 5:16, 1 Th 4:5, 2 Pet 2:10, 1 Joh 2:16, Rev 18:14.

96 Fol. 62^{v}, lines 7–15 [edition], 189, lines 23–32 [transl.].

97 Fol. 63^{v}, lines 17–23 [edition], 191, lines 15–22 [transl.].

98 Fol. 61^{v}, lines 1–2 [edition], 188, lines, 2–4 [transl.]. Other occasions: fol. 60^{r}, penultimate line – 61r, line 3 [edition], 187, lines 13–16 [transl.]; fol. 61^{v}, lines 14–17 [edition], 188, lines 17–19 [transl.]; fol. 63^{r}, line 20 – fol. 63^{v}, line 1 [edition], 190, lines 29–32 [transl.]; fol. 67^{r}, last line – fol. 67^{v}, line 7 [edition], 196, line 28 – 197, line 2 [transl.].

In conclusion, the comparison of Arabic fragment with the "Letter" reveals clear similarities both on a conceptual and a formal level: prevalence of ascetic and instructive approach, emphasis on acquiring virtues and upright conduct, usage of contrapositions and chains. These similarities are by no means sufficient to confirm with accuracy the Abraham's authorship of the fragment, because each of the mentioned features can be found in the texts of other Syriac monastic authors. However, on the grounds of the revealed traits of the quotation, one may maintain that the close affinities between two texts are due, with high degree of probability, to the authorship of one writer.[99]

Last but not least, the authenticity of the fragment is confirmed by Elias himself who, as it can be seen in other works of his – for instance in his "Chronicle" – when giving a quotation from a particular text, almost never fails to provide a reference to the source from which the quotation was borrowed.[100]

2. Language of Abraham's text as consulted by Elias

Elias knew perfectly both Syriac and Arabic, and that enabled him to use different kinds of sources. Thus in the case of the present quotation from Abraham bar Dašandad two options are ready at hand: Elias could either use the original Syriac text and translate it into Arabic or he could make use of the Arabic version of Abraham's treatise. The determination of the language of the original text used by Elias may be helped by investigation of other quotations from the source that had been originally written in Syriac in the *Risāla*, namely three quotations from the "Paradise of the Fathers".

When introducing those three quotations Elias indicates that one comes from the first and the two others from the fourth part (جزء) of the "Paradise of the Fathers". It seems to be clear that in either case he is certainly referring to the well-known com-

99 In already mentioned monastic anthology Baghdad Chaldean Monastery syr. 680 as well as in its copies one can read two unpublished texts attributed simply to "Mar Abraham" without any further specifications (No. XV and XVI in the description of Vosté (Jacques-Marie Vosté, Recueil d'auteurs ascétiques nestoriens du VIIe et VIIIe siècle, in: Ang. 6 (1929), 152–153; cf. Mingana Syr. 601, fol. 93^r^, 93^v^–96^r^). Both of them were tentatively considered by Mingana as written by Abraham bar Dašandad (Alphonse Mingana, The Catalogue of the Mingana Collection of Manuscripts now in the Possession of the Woodbrooke Settlement, Selly Oak, Birmingham. Vol. 1: Syriac and Garshūni manuscripts, Cambridge 1933, col. 1149) whereas Vosté not quite reasonably argued in favor of Abraham's of Nathpar authorship (Vosté, Recueil d'auteurs ascétiques nestoriens, 197) and Chahine considered both pieces as dubious (Charbel C. Chahine, Abraham de Bēṯ-Neṯprā: Discours (Mēmrē). Introduction, texte critique et traduction. Roma 2004 [unpublished PhD thesis], 45); no further investigation has yet been undertaken though. My preliminary comparison of those two texts with authentic ones reveals abundantly the same characteristic traits: practical concern, chains of parallel constructions and contraposition. Although not containing the quotation given by Elias, the evident similarities to authentic works of Abraham bar Dašandad show those two texts as indeed worthy of detailed examination with regard to the possible authorship of Abraham.

100 See footnote 11.

pilation by the East Syrian monk ʿEnanišoʿ (7th c.) "Paradise of the Fathers".[101] Leaving aside the significance of those quotations for the study of the textual history of the compilation,[102] what is important for the present study is to establish whether Elias excerpted the passages from the original Syriac text of the "Paradise of the Fathers" (and then translated them into Arabic), or whether he used the available Arabic version.

It would be much easier to approach that problem if there were critical editions and thorough studies of both the original Syriac text and its Arabic version, but neither has been done so far. What makes the analysis even more complicated is that the original Syriac text of the "Paradise of the Fathers" is preserved in different recensions which vary in size;[103] while in the case of the Arabic version it is not even clear if there ever existed a complete Arabic translation of the "Paradise of the Fathers", as those manuscripts which were considered by Graf as containing the Arabic translation are rather copies of an abridged Arabic version of the "Commentary on the Paradise of Fathers" written by Dadīšōʿ Qaṭrāyā.[104] Nevertheless it is known that

---

101 For an overview of available editions, translations and studies see Grigory Kessel and Karl Pinggéra, Bibliography of Syriac Mystical Literature, Eastern Christian Studies 10, Leuven (forthcoming).

102 See footnotes 14, 17, 18.

103 Cuthbert Butler, The Lausiac History of Palladius. A critical discussion together with notes on early Egyptian monachism, Texts and Studies 6,1, Cambridge 1898, 77–96,266–267; René Draguet, Les formes syriaques de la matière de l'histoire lausiaque, 44*–113* (cf. footnote 14).

104 Sachau and later Baumstark identified Berlin syr. 244, fol. 1v–112v as containing the Arabic translation of Dadīšōʿ's "Commentary on the Paradise of the Fathers" attributed to Philoxenos of Mabbug on the basis of comparison with original Syriac text which is preserved partially in British Library Add. 17175, Add. 17264, Add. 17263, Or. 2311 and Add. 14589 (Eduard Sachau, Verzeichniss der Syrischen Handschriften der Königlichen Bibliothek zu Berlin. Vol. II, Berlin 1899, 742; Baumstark, Geschichte der syrischen Literatur, 226, notes 7. 8 (cf. footnote 42); see also André de Halleux, Philoxène de Mabbog. Sa vie, ses écrits, sa theologie, Louvain 1963, 291–292). That the Arabic version of Dadīšōʿ's "Commentary" features also in Vat. ar. 85, fol. 2v–250v was demonstrated later by Tisserant, who moreover managed to identify the same text in Ethiopic translation (Eugène Tisserant, Philoxène de Mabboug, in: DThC 12 (1935), 1521–1522). The fact that the Vat. ar. 85 presents the texts in the form of four parts attributed to Philoxenos, Barsanuphius, Hieronimus and Palladius respectively accounts for its identification with "Paradise of the Fathers" (normally divided into four parts) by Graf, who found two more manuscripts of the same text (Petersburg, Institute for Oriental Studies, Arabic 8 [the present shelf number is A 340] and Jerusalem, Greek Orthodox Patriarchate 24, see Graf, Geschichte, 384–385). And most recently Sims-Williams argued that the "Commentary on the Paradise of the Fathers" was translated into Arabic in an abridged form (so-called epitome); furthermore he added some other copies of the Arabic translation on the list (Mingana Syr. 174, 370, 403 and 457, Cairo, Coptic Museum, Theol. 294, see Nicholas Sims-Williams, Dādišoʿ Qaṭrāyā's Commentary on the Paradise of the Fathers, in: AnBoll 112 [1994], 33–64, esp. 38). On Ethiopic version, made by the metropolitan of Ethiopia Abba Sälama around the year A.D. 1365 see Witold Witakowski, Filekseyus, the Ethiopic Version of the Syriac Dadisho Qatraya's Commentary on the Paradise of the Fathers, in: Rocznik orientalistyczny 59 (2006), 281–296. The Arabic translation, according to the colo-

at least a part of the "Paradise of the Fathers" was translated into Arabic, as demonstrated by Joseph-Marie Sauget in his study of Arabic manuscript Paris ar. 253 containing the "Apophthegmata patrum".[105] Although the collection of apophtegmata preserved in Paris ar. 253 has a highly complicated history of provenance, after the examination by Sauget one can safely maintain that one of its constituent parts is a remoulded Arabic version of the "Apophthegmata patrum" as preserved in the Syriac "Paradise of the Fathers".[106]

The absence of a complete[107] Arabic translation of the "Paradise of the Fathers" certainly does not rule out the possibility that it might have existed and perhaps it will be eventually identified in one of the numerous Arabic manuscripts that contain the texts of with similar contents.[108] However, regarding the problem of the *Vorlage* of Elias' quotation from the "Paradise of the Fathers", one should take into account two facts. First, Elias was a Christian belonging to a Syriac ecclesiastical tradition and Syriac must have been his mother tongue, so it seems to be quite difficult to imagine that he read the "Paradise of the Fathers" not in its original language, but in the Arabic translation. And secondly, the first half of the 11th c., when Elias flourished, is a very early date for Arabic translations of East Syriac ascetic works.[109]

---

phon, found in some Ethiopic manuscripts, was made in A.D. 1305 (Tisserant, Philoxène de Mabboug, 1522). A critical edition of Dadīšōʿ's "Commentray on the Paradise of the Fathers" is being prepared by D. Philipps and R. Kitchen based on the recently discovered complete text in the Metropolitan Library of the Church of the East in Baghdad (see Robert A. Kitchen, Dadisho Qatraya's Commentary on Abba Isaiah. The Apophtegmata Patrum Connection, in: StPatr 41 [2006], 35–50).

105 Graf considered the manuscript as containing the Arabic version of a Greek alphabetical collection of the "Apophthegmata patrum", Geschichte, 382.

106 Joseph-Marie Sauget, Une traduction arabe de la collection d'Apophthegmata Patrum de ʿEnānīšōʿ. Étude de ms. Paris arabe 253 et de témoins parallèles, CSCO.Sub 78, Louvain 1987.

107 It is worth stressing that no purposeful search for the Arabic version of the "Paradise of the Fathers" has been undertaken so far.

108 On different types of Arabic collections of monastic histories and apophtegmata see Graf, Geschichte, 380–389 and also general remarks in Sauget, Une traduction arabe, 198–199; some particular collections were studied by Joseph-Marie Sauget, Le Paterikon du Ms. Mingana Christian Arabic 120a, in: Orientalia Christiana Periodica 28 (1962), 402–417; La Collection d'apophtegmes du manuscrit 4225 de la Bibliothèque de Strasbourg, in: OrChrP 30 (1964), 485–509; Le Paterikon du manuscrit arabe 276 de la Bibliothèque Nationale de Paris, in: Muséon 82 (1969), 363–404; Un nouveau témoin de la collection d'apophtegmata patrum: le Paterikon du Sinaï arabe 547, in: Muséon 86 (1973), 5–35; Le Paterikon arabe de la Bibliothèque Ambrosienne de Milan: L 120 Sup. (Sp II, 161), in: AAL.M Serie VIII 29 (1989), 473–516.

109 The history of the Arabic translations of the Syriac ascetic and mystical texts in particular and of Syriac texts in general still remains an important desideratum and the field still awaits its explorer (as a starting point one can use the research of Graf (see Graf, Geschichte, 421–456). However what one can learn from the available data is that, for instance, the corpus of John of Dalyatha was translated by the deacon Yūḥannā and the priest Ibrāhīm around the middle of the 13th c. (ibid., 434–436; Robert Beulay, La collection des lettres de Jean de Dalyatha, PO 39,3, Turnhout 1978, 23–25); roughly the same date is valid for the Arabic ver-

Therefore, if the "Paradise of the Fathers" was ever translated into Arabic, it probably happened considerably later than Elias wrote the *Risāla.*[110] Thus, with good reason, one can safely maintain that Elias used not the Arabic translation but the original version of the "Paradise of the Fathers".

The same reasoning seems to be valid for the case of Elias' quotation from Abraham bar Dašandad. The additional argument for the assertion that the text of Abraham used by Elias was Syriac comes from the fact that so far no Arabic text with an attribution to Abraham bar Dašandad has been discovered.

3. Title

According to the majority of the manuscripts the title of Abraham's work as given by Elias is كتاب المواعظ ("Book of Admonitions"), what, in turn, appears to be a rendering of Syriac ܟܬܒܐ ܕܡܬܪ̈ܝܢܘܬܐ. Such a retro-version, although well supported by the East-Syriac lexicographical tradition,[111] stands in conflict with ʿAbdīšōʿ's of Nisibis note which reads[112]: ܟܬܒܐ ܕܡܬܪܝܢܘܬܐ ("Book of Admonition") – thus introducing the difference in number. Since we have no other information on that particular work by Abraham, there are no sound grounds to prefer either option. There are, however, three observations to be noticed. First, the plural form is the constant feature of the Arabic text of the *Risāla* as attested by known manuscripts, which suggests that it should be regarded as already featuring in the autograph of Elias (and consequently, but with less plausibility, in the authentic text of Abraham) and not as a scribal error. Second, the difference may be due to corruption of the manuscript tradition of the "Catalogus librorum" of ʿAbdīšōʿ.[113] Third, the variant reading

sion of Isaac of Nineveh transmitted in four books, since the earliest mss date back to the end of the 13th c. (Graf, Geschichte, 436–442; Sabino Chialà, Dall'ascesi eremitica alla misericordia infinita. Ricerche su Isacco di Ninive e la sua fortuna, BRSLR 14, Firenze 2002, 336–338); an abridged version of Dadīšōʿ's "Commentary on the Paradise of Fathers" was translated in A.D. 1305 (see footnote 104).

110 E.g., the abovementioned Par. ar. 253, which partially depends on the "Paradise of the Father", dates back to the 14th c. (Gerard Troupeau, Catalogue des manuscrits arabes. Première partie. Manuscrits chrétiens. Tome I, n.os 1–323. Paris: Bibliothèque nationale, 1972, 212).

111 Rubens Duval (ed.), Lexicon syriacum auctore Hassano bar Bahlule. Tomus secundus, Parisiis 1901, col. 1163; Georg Hoffmann, Syrisch-arabische Glossen. Erster Band. Autographie einer Gothaischen Handschrift enthaltend Bar Ali's Lexikon von Alaf bis Mim, Kiel 1874, 261, no. 6752.

112 There is no critical edition of ʿAbdīšōʿ's important treatise. Therefore the relevant passage was checked in all available editions and translations (for all of them depend on different manuscripts): Ecchellensis, Tractatum continentem Catalogum Librorum Chaldaeorum, 92 (cf. footnote 40); Assemani, BOCV, 194; George Percy Badger, The Nestorians and their Rituals. Vol. 2, London 1852, 375; Yāwsep d-Bēt Qelāytā (ed.), Ktābā d-metqrē margānītā dʿal šrārā da-kreṭyānūtā da-ʿbīd l-mār(y) ʿbdīšōʿ mīṭrāpōlīṭā d-ṣōbā wad-armānyā, Mōṣul, 1924, 78; Yūsuf Habbi (ed.), Fihris al-muʾallifin, taʿlīf lʿAbd Īšūʿ al-Subāwī, Baġdād 1986, 97.

113 Such a possibility is confirmed by the fact that in the edition by Assemani one of the works attributed to Abraham has the title: ܕܪܫܐ ܕܥܡ ܝܗܘܕܝܐ (translated by Assemani: "disputatio cum Judæis", Assemani, ibid.), whereas in the edition by Ecchelensis it reads: ܕܪ̈ܫܐ ܕܠܩܒܠ ܝܗܘܕܝܐ (translated by Ecchelensis: "disputationes aduersus Iudæos", Ecchellensis, Tractatum

of the ms **C** (Vat. ar. 126)[114] جملة مواعيظه ("Corpus of Admonitions"), while being lexically different in the first member of the genetive construction, still confirms that most likely the plural form of the title of Abraham's text represent faithfully the original Syriac wording.

And finally, whichever variant of the title is authentic (in singular or in plural form), what is indisputable is that the evidence of Elias' *Risāla* enables us to maintain that the note of ʿAbdīšōʿ indicates the real title of Abraham's text and does not merely provide us with a descriptive name related to its genre of paraenetical literature.

4. Quality of the translation

Since it is quite probable that Elias used the original Syriac text of Abraham's work, it is inevitably important to deal with the issue of the quality of Elias' translation and thereby to evaluate how faithfully he renders the original wording. To get an impression of Elias' work as an interpreter, one could try to evaluate the quality of other quotations from the Syriac sources that were used in the *Risāla*. Regrettably, among the handful of quotations deriving from the Syriac texts, there is no one that could be taken as a specimen, since as was mentioned earlier, the quotations from the "Paradise of the Fathers" differ considerably from the published text,[115] while the other passages (like that from monastic canons, and from Denḥā the Logician) were either not identified or their original text is not extant.

For the reason just stated, one can take into account the following consideration of a general nature. *Prima facie* it should be remembered that Elias not only knew perfectly Syriac and Arabic and wrote in both languages, but he also studied both of them in detail and wrote a grammar of the Syriac language[116] and the Arabic-Syriac Lexicon *Kitāb al-tarǧumān.*[117] Thus Elias was certainly sufficiently trained and willing to produce a good-quality translation.

It is however worth stressing that Elias was translating his sources following the translation technique of his time. The domain of Arabic translations from Syriac is still waiting to be studied, but it goes without saying that in the time of Elias the practice of adjusting the quotations to the main narrative was a generally accepted one, and it was considered justifiable to handle the passage in such a way so that it might fit the context (and that may be at least a partial explanation of divergences

---

Continentem Catalogum Librorum Chaldaeorum, 93 [cf. footnote 40]).

114 The manuscript was considered by both Samir and Hau as the most reliable one.

115 See footnotes 14, 17, 18.

116 Richard James Horatio Gottheil, A treatise on Syriac grammar by Mâr(i) Eliâ of Ṣôbʰâ, Berlin and New York, 1887.

117 De Lagarde, Praetermissorum libri duo, 1–96 [edition] (cf. footnote 95); see also Stefan Weninger, Das ‚Übersetzerbuch' des Elias von Nisibis (10./11. Jh.) im Zusammenhang der syrischen und arabischen Lexikographie, in The World in a List of Words, ed. by Werner Hüllen, Lexicographica. Series Maior 58, Tübingen 1994, 55–66.

between quotations from the "Paradise of the Fathers" and the known text)[118]. Thus, we are not to exclude the possible editorial alterations introduced by Elias into the passage borrowed from Abraham's treatise.[119]

VII. Conclusion

The importance of the quotation is manifold. Let me mention only the main facets. First of all, it provides us with a quotation from the lost work by Abraham bar Dašandad which was otherwise known only from the "Catalogus auctorum". It thereby suggests that at least some works by Abraham listed in the "Catalogus auctorum" once indeed existed.[120] Second, it demonstrates that the classical East Syriac ascetic and mystical treatises (written in Syriac for the use within a monastic community in the 7th–8th c.) were still relevant in the new historical and theological situation the literary production of which is principally characterized by the apologetic approach. Third, it provides evidence to support a contention that a quest for excerpts from the Syriac ascetic and mystical works should not be limited to the Syriac sources only but ought to extend the field of possible sources by inclusion of the texts of Arabic Christian origin as well. And finally, one often comes across the statement that the nascent Muslim ascetic and mystical tradition was influenced by the Syriac ascetic and mystical tradition, but it is extremely difficult to find historical facts which could confirm it. The case of Elias *Risāla* – about which it is known that vizier Abū al-Qāsim Ibn ʿAlī al-Maġribī with whom Elias had a correspondence asked Elias to send him his refutation of al-Ǧāḥiẓ[121] – might reveal one particular

---

118 Although one should not neglect a possibility that Elias knew and used a different recension of the "Paradise of the Fathers".

119 A future study of the translation technique of Elias may well be assisted by the text of his "Chronicle", as yet unexplored in this respect, in which the majority of the passages are presented in the original Syriac and in Arabic translation. Also, the evaluation of Baethgen, who distinguished three persons working on the Arabic version (one being Elias himself), is worth carefully revising: Fragmente syrischer und arabischer Historiker, ed. and trans. by Friedrich Baethgen, AKM 8.3, Leipzig 1884, 6; cf. Witakowski, Elias Bar Shenaya's Chronicle, 225–226 (cf. footnote 11).

120 This issue is also touched upon in my "A List of East Syrian Ecclesiastical Authors in the "Book of Considerations on the Order of Church Services and Its Succession" of Abrāhām Šekwānā (A.D. 1849–1931)" to appear in the Proceedings of the Symposium Syriacum X Granada, 2008.

121 It is contained in the correspondence between Elias and the vizir which remains unpublished, for the passage in question see Hau, Brief über den Vorzug der Enthaltsamkeit, 13–14.

way in which the Syriac mystical tradition was able if not to influence current Muslim ascetic and mystical tradition,[122] then at least to impart and to make known its principals, ideas and values to searching Muslim contemporaries.

122 The issue is often considered as a kind of topos, but any treatment of it deals more with similar ideas, concepts and practices rather than with historical facts (due to the lack of the information), which would point to how it in fact was going on. See Ofer Livne-Kafri, Early Muslim ascetics and the world of Christian monasticism, in: Jerusalem Studies in Arabic and Islam 20 (1996), 105–129; Georg Günter Blum, Christlich-orientalische Mystik und Sufismus, in: III° Symposium Syriacum 1980. Les contacts du monde syriaque avec les autres cultures (Goslar 7–11 Septembre 1980), ed. by René Lavenant, OrChrA 221, Roma 1983, 261–271; Arthur Vööbus, History of Asceticism in the Syrian Orient. A Contribution to the History of Culture in the Near East. Vol. 3, CSCO.Sub 81, Louvain 1988, 428–432; Alexander Knysh, Islamic Mysticism. A Short History, Leiden 2000, 5–35; Arent Jan Wensinck, Bar Hebraeus's Book of the Dove. Together with some chapters from his Ethikon, Veröffentlichungen der De Goeje-Stiftung 4, Leyden 1919, xiii–cx; Brian E. Colless, Muslim Sufism and Syrian Christian Mysticism, in: Proceedings of the XIth Congress of AULA, Sydney 1967 [non vidi]; Serafim Seppälä, "In Speechless Ecstasy". Expression and Interpretation of Mystical Experience in Classical Syriac and Sufi Literature, Publications of the Institute for Asian and African Studies 2, Helsinki 2002, passim, esp. 26–36; Margaret Smith, Studies in Early Mysticism in the Near and Middle East, London 1931, passim, esp. 244–257; Chialà, Dall'ascesi eremitica alla misericordia infinita, 313–321 (cf. footnote 109).

The Place of Virgin Mary in the Ontology of Mystical Experience

Serafim Seppälä

Academic discussion on the mysticism of the Christian East is, and must be, based on certain premises and definitions of what mysticism is. The modern paradigm of mysticism is largely based on inter-religious studies in which the normative structures of mystical experience and mystical thought are abstracted from the religions of the Far East, as well as from certain Roman Catholic mystics, like Eckhardt, whose thoughts seem to fit easily into the pattern in question. The principal point of interest in the modern discussion on mysticism has been the private, psychological aspect of mystical experience. In the 20th century academic discussion, the prevalent trend was to marginalise the ontological and theological dimensions of mysticism into the category of interpretation; the interpretations were seen as secondary, even somewhat arbitrary in relation to the experience itself. In a closer look, however, this approach is extremely problematic, as S. Katz and others have more recently shown.[1]

In Eastern Christianity the approach to "mysticism" has traditionally been based on another kind of paradigm. Firstly, patristic and Orthodox authors generally are hesitant to focus the discussion on the private, psychological aspects of mystical experience. These are seen as consequences of and reactions to the mystical encounter rather than the actual *Ding an sich*: the experience is a psychological phenomenon, and as such it is by definition subjective and therefore somewhat accidental by its characteristics – even if caused by an encounter with the absolute. In other words, the psychological features of mystical experience are not the core of mysticism but merely subjective *reactions* to the mystical reality itself. (This is also the prevalent position in Roman Catholic approach to mysticism.)

Approach:	Traditional	Modern
Essential:	Mystical reality (The Uncreated)	Inner Experience
	↓	↓
Secondary:	Psychic experience	Interpretations
	↓	↓
	Discussion, interpretations	

1 "Mystical experience" is not a separate entity, but all experiencing is conditioned and penetrated by beliefs, expectations and intentions that are formed in accordance with one's own tradition. See e. g. Steven T. Katz, The 'Conservative' Character of Mysticism, in: Mysticism and Religious Traditions, ed. by Steven T. Katz, Oxford 1983, 3–60.

Secondly, in Orthodox Christianity mysticism is not considered as an extreme phenomenon in the margins of religious thought and practice, but rather the essence of all Orthodox theology, spirituality and liturgical life.[2] In other words, the same phenomena may be discussed in two modes, that of an outsider and that of the Church, and the choice of mode to some extent defines what mysticism is.

One potential problem caused by the situation is that the modern way of setting a universal paradigm of mysticism may fail to include certain aspects that are of importance for Eastern Christian mystics' spiritual life. Indeed, one such phenomenon is Virgin Mary, a subject of an enormous number of books.[3] There hardly is a case in the field of Christian theology with more divergent views. The same person is presented in the Catholic publications as the Mother of the Church, Heavenly Queen etc., and in non-Catholic books as a Virgin Goddess, a pagan remnant of some sort. It is astonishing that both approaches may even be backed with the very same source material, even in works of academic merit.[4] However, even in the Roman Catholic tradition, theological and philosophical works on mysticism usually do not touch upon mariology, even though mariological literature does contain ideas that deeply deal with mysticism.[5]

In the Eastern Orthodox tradition, much less has been recently written about Virgin Mary,[6] despite the fact that she is still seen as *Theotokos*, very much in the same

2 "The eastern tradition has never made a sharp distinction between mysticism and theology; between personal experience of the divine mysteries and the dogma affirmed by the Church." Vladimir Lossky, The Mystical Theology of the Eastern Church, London 1957, 8. Such an approach has an evident danger, both theoretical and practical: Naming all theology "mystical" may lead into a situation that no theology is mystical de facto.

3 The number of books on Mary seems to have surpassed 2.500. Cf. Jaroslav Pelikan, Mary Through the Centuries. Her Place in the History of Culture, New Haven/CT 1996, 225.

4 For example, Michael P. Carroll in his The Cult of the Virgin Mary. Psychological Origins argues that "there is little or no evidence that anything like the Mary cult existed during the first four centuries of the Christian Church" (Princeton 1986, 4), basing his view on the fact that the number of documentary evidence indicating the existence of such a cult is to be limited to four (Protoevangelium of James, apparition of Mary to Gregory the Wonderworker, Egyptian fragment of prayer to Mary and the existence of one feast of Mary). Hilda Graef, to name one, has defended the early veneration of Mary with the help of the very same material (Mary. A History of Doctrine and Devotion. Vol. 1: From the Beginning to the Eve of the Reformation, New York 1963). Even when disregarding the fact that Carroll neglects the patristic sources, it is quite amazing that the very same text material can be used in such a contrasting way by competent authors.

5 Virgin Mary is left unmentioned by such classics as Auguste Saudreau, The Mystical State. Its Nature and Phases, London 1924; Anselm Stolz, Theologie der Mystik, Regensburg 1936; Louis Dupré, The Other Dimension. A Search for the Meaning of Religious Attitudes, New York 1972; Jacques Maritain, Distinguer pour unir ou les degrés du savoir, Paris 1932.

6 The most remarkable publications are either popular readings or scholarly articles. The former include Alexander Schmemann, Celebration of Faith. Vol. 3: The Virgin Mary, Crestwood/NY 1995, and John Maximovitch, The Orthodox Veneration of Mary the Birthgiver of God, Platina/CA 1994. The latter include e. g. Kallistos Ware's, Mary Theotokos in the Orthodox tradi-

way as in the golden days of the 5th century. The presence of Mary in icons, liturgical hymns and prayers, also private prayers, is an obvious fact. There is no monastery in Eastern Christendom without strong visible and spiritual presence of Virgin Mary. Apparitions of the Mother of God are not rare (e.g. Coptic Egypt, Mt. Athos), and they have been experienced by the greatest theologians of mysticism, such as St Gregory Palamas,[7] as well as monastics of our time. All this, however, is often seen as some kind of random, detached phenomenon separate from the actual mystical theology. Obviously, there is a mystical reality here in need of certain doctrinal framework.

My aim in the following is to outline the place of Virgin Mary in the mystical thought of the Christian East in a way that does full justice to the modern as well as traditional approaches to mysticism. In the end I discuss some parallels with the position of Virgin Mary in Islam and Sufism. I start from the very kernel of the mystical theology in modern terms, the mystical experience.

Conception as Mystical Experience

If all Christian spirituality is mystical to some extent, as the Orthodox disposition claims, what then would be an *ultimate* mystical experience? The answer is given by the East Syrian mystic Isaac of Nineveh during an illuminating discussion on "overshadowing" (*maggenanutha*), a biblical term used by the East Syrian mystics, and analysed by S. Brock.[8]

For the East Syrian mystics, overshadowing is a general term for the mystical activity of divine origin. The basic sense is an exterior mystical divine activity of providence and protection (however, these do not concern us here).

---

tion, Wallington 1997; the same article has appeared also in Epiphany 9.2 (1989) and in Marianum 52 (1990).

7 Gregory Palamas had four personal experiences connected with the *Theotokos*, two in his childhood and two during his monastic years.

8 See Sebastian Brock, Maggnānūtā: a technical term in East Syrian spirituality and its background, in: Mélanges Antoine Guillaumont. Contributions à l'étude des christianismes orientaux. Avec une bibliographie du dédicataire, ed. by Patrick Cramer, COr 20, Genève 1988, 121–129. In spite of the "technical" character of the term, its semantic field is left very open. The only differentiation Isaac dares to make is that maggenānūtā is not 'knowledge' (cf. Brock, 122–123; Mar Isaacus Ninivita de perfectione religiosa, ed. by Paul Bedjan, Parisiis 1909, 160). Dadišoʿ of Qatar (Alphonse Mingana, Woodbrooke Studies. Christian Documents in Syriac, Arabic and Garshūni, Vol. 7: Early Christian Mystics, Cambridge 1934, 11a, 208; Dadišoʿ, Commentaire du Livre d'Abba Isaïe, 218) employs the same term twice, referring to the gifts of the Holy Spirit, and Simeon the Graceful (Mingana, 195b,315) once, obviously in the mystical sense. John of Dalyatha (Robert Beulay, La collection des lettres de Jean de Dalyatha, PO 39.3, Turnhout 1978, 13,2) exhorts: "Let the fragrance of your limbs waft like spices from the place where you lie by (means of) the maggenānūtā of the All-Holy." In brief, *maggenānūtā* is a general term for the activity of the Holy Spirit.

Maggenanutha may also indicate a secret operation, perhaps one taking place unconsciously, or a charismatic experience of more specific kind. The secret mystical activity, as understood by Isaac, basically is operation of the Holy Spirit. This operation is sanctifying by function and holistic by nature: it takes place in the whole person, in the physical as well as in the inner dimension. Isaac gives three biblical examples of *maggenanutha*: prophet Isaiah, St John, and Virgin Mary who was "overshadowed" by the Holy Spirit. Her case, St Isaac writes, has no parallel, "for it surpasses the natural order"; but still, it does belong to same category. According to the logic of St Isaac, Mary experienced in the absolute sense the same phenomenon what the mystics experience in part, the difference being quantitative rather than qualitative. This may sound surprising, but this is what Isaac seems to imply, and we must now investigate the question further. Is this just an etymological co-incidence or something remarkable?[9]

Mystical experience is basically a combination of the activity of the Holy Spirit and of the human reaction to it. Isaac describes mystic's experience with great detail in the same context:

> His spirit is drawn (away) in ecstasy and it opens into a sort of divine revelation. And as long as this influence is overshadowing the spirit, man is above the movements of psychic thoughts through participation of the Holy Spirit.[10]

Isaac seems to put very little emphasis on the mental, psychological phenomena in mystical experiencing. In the mystical experience man feels as though he rises above himself for a while, opening his personality and consciousness to the dimension beyond his normal mental activity. However, in the case of human beings even the strongest mystical experiences are subjective and limited – even though they may be experienced as being full and complete. All experiences are subjective by definition.

Now the extreme case of such an experience is Virgin Mary, whose total experience of the operation of the Holy Spirit may be called ultimate, or even "objective" in the sense that it obviously surpassed the sphere of subjective and its limitations. Therefore, according to St Isaac, what happened to Mary in the annunciation was not only an organic event with theological significance but a charismatic, mystical experience as well. It was definitely a charismatic experience in the absolute sense, with an ultimate ontological character, but its nature does not fundamentally differ from the charismatic encounters with the Holy Spirit as experienced by mystics and other Christians of all ages.[11] This is in a way obvious since all mystical encounters take place between the Holy Spirit and another human being.

---

9 Namely, St Isaac presents the matter under the umbrella concept of *maggenanutha*, which is a technical term derived from the verb *aggen*. The Syriac Bible uses the corresponding verb *aggen* of Mary's overshadowing. The connection is no arbitrary nor co-incidental since the phenomena belong to the same totality.

10 Isaac of Nineveh (ch. 54) in Bedjan, Perfectione Religiosa, 391. For the concept of *maggenanutha*, see Brock, Maggnānūtā, 122–123.

11 E. g., Basil the Great notes that Mary was full of Holy Spirit, and therefore Joseph was afraid,

This is a thought with enormous theological potential. The role of Mary in the *Theosis* of man is not only in being the means of the unification of divine and human in Christ, but she is also a perfect, ultimate example of a human being who is fully in God and God in her.

Illumination of Mary according to Ephrem the Syrian

In order to gain further insights to Mary's experience, we may turn to St Ephrem the Syrian († 373), who was in many ways a forerunner of mariology. His *Hymnen de Nativitate* contains various features that became prevalent in Byzantine and Catholic teaching on Mary from the 5th century on. In other words, St Ephrem was at least a hundred years or so ahead of his time in his understanding of Virgin Mary.

Ephrem praises the spirituality of Mary in a devotional way, and what is more interesting, he also portrays profoundly the way in which her high spiritual status was originated. This is the crucial question of Mariology. The effect of incarnation on the divinity and on the whole humankind has been discussed thoroughly in both patristic and modern theology, but what exactly was the effect of incarnation on Mary personally? Ephrem addresses his poetic admiration to Mary as follows:

> Inside your dwelling full of glory
> the shadows of dissoluteness[12] and desire
> were dispersed by the Saviour's rays.
> Spiritual (woman), all of you has become spiritual,[13]
> since you have given birth to the Spiritual (man).

In his poetry Ephrem hints that the sexual desire present in human being is – in some sense – originated in sexual conceiving. Therefore, it is interesting to see how he describes the conceiving of Christ. Ephrem says to Mary: "Your refined conception wipes and dissolves the impulsive desire from your members."[14] The conceiving of Christ fills Mary with holiness and purity, as if "washing" her with holy waves.[15]

Here we have one of St Ephrem's most important contributions to early mariology. He pays attention to the fact that incarnation was not only a physical occurrence but also a profound personal event with a mental and psychological dimension, not without deep spiritual and existential aspects as well. In other words, it was a – or, rather *the* mystical experience.

Homilia in sanctam Christi generationem 4, PG 31, 1465A.

12 ܪܦܝܘܬܐ The word also means, laxity, weakness.

13 ܟܠܟܝ ܕܪܘܚܐ ܗܘܝܬܝ The Syriac expression means literally: "all of you is (of the) Spirit."

14 Ephrem the Syrian, Hymnen de Nativitate, 28,6, in: Des Heiligen Ephraem des Syrers Hymnen de Nativitate, ed. and trans. by Edmund Beck, CSCO.S 82, Louvain 1959. More literally: "desirous impulse" (ܪܓܬ ܪܘܓܐ).

15 Ibid.

This is an extremely interesting aspect of incarnation. The divine *logos,* as it enters into Mary's womb, at the same time also is in some mystical sense projected into Mary's inner being. Ephrem's wording as such could be taken as indicating a normal imprinting of impressions into Mary's thoughts only, i. e. a natural psychological reaction expressed symbolically. If, however, we take into account Ephrem's ideas on Christ's illuminating and purifying effect on Mary, the outcome is clear. Mary has become a Christ-bearer entirely, not only physically but also in the immaterial sense. "Although He was begotten, indeed He was in you so that His brightness was entirely gazing out from your members."[16] Ephrem describes this unity in most beautiful terms, addressing to Mary: "Upon your beauty was spread His love, upon all of you He was stretched out."[17]

Consequently, Ephrem's Mary is a pneumatic character. Ephrem actually calls her "the Spiritual one", using the feminine form of the same word used in reference to Christ.[18] In the incarnation, Christ transforms the body and soul of Mary thoroughly.[19] This means that in Mary divinity has, as were, stamped itself onto humanity.[20] Divinity, however, is in a sense penetrating by nature, and therefore Mary's humanity is divinised.[21] Mary receives the seal of divinity into her own being. Here one might refer to St Athanasius' principle "God became man that man might become divinised" – if this did not happen in Mary, in whom then could it happen?

The consequences of Mary's illumination are manifold. Her womb becomes the definitive symbol of God's presence. Consequently, it may be understood in relation to other vessels of divine presence. Ephrem portrays a mystical connection between

---

16 This interesting sentence has caused differences of opinion in its interpretation. The editor of the text, Edmund Beck (a Roman Catholic), who also translated it into German, understood the word ܐܝܠܝܕ. as referring to the actual birth, but Kathleen E. McVey, who translated the text into English, understood it in the sense of "begotten", turning the basic idea more to the fact that Christ in His incarnation did not lose anything from His divinity. The expression as such, it seems to me, is open to both interpretations, which may well be Ephrem's original intention, for the verb of course means 'to be born', but the passive participle means basically 'to be in the state of having been born'. McVey's choice fits well in the total theological vision of Ephrem, but in this context I would still prefer Beck's interpretation.

17 Hymnen de Nativitate, 28,7. This crucial sentence happens to be among the most ambiguous ones. Above is McVey's translation. The expression in question (ܘܟܠ ܒܟܠܟܝ ܡܫܝܚ ܗܘܐ) is an interesting one indeed. The predicate ܡܫܝܚ may be an Aph'el participle of the verb ܫܘܚ, 'to melt', 'to cause to waste', indicating that Mary was completely consumed by the divine presence: "He was consuming (you) completely". More probably, however, ܡܫܝܚ is status absolutus of ܡܫܚ 'to anoint' – i. e. 'Messiah' – the idea being that Christ was anointed over Mary's whole being.

18 Hymnen de Nativitate, 28,4.

19 See Susan Ashbrook Harvey, On Mary's Voice. Gendered Words in Syriac Marian Tradition, in: The Cultural Turn in Late Ancient Studies. Gender, Asceticism, and Historiography, ed. by Dale B. Martin and Patricia Cox Miller, Durham/NC 2005, esp. 72.

20 The embryo "stamped (ܛܒܥ) Himself, as if by a signet" upon Mary's mind. Hymnen de Nativitate, 28,7. The 'mind' – ܬܪܥܝܬܐ.

21 "Today the Deity imprinted itself on humanity, so that humanity might also be cut into the seal of Deity." Hymnen de Nativitate, 1,99.

Mary's womb and the river Jordan. The water of Jordan became a womb of the divine word in a symbolical sense, but the water in Mary's concrete womb fashioned Him in the concrete reality: it "conceived Him in purity, bore him in chastity, made him ascend in glory".[22] In other words, the Jordan becomes a symbol referring to Mary. The same Christ came to the world from Mary's womb and arose from Jordan, radiating holiness. The parallel presented by Ephrem indirectly arises a question: If Christ did sanctify Jordan by merely entering into it, how much more did he sanctify Mary, in whom He dwelled and from whom He grew?

> Similarly, Christ was transfigured on the mountain with the divine Light, but in fact He was mystically shining forth the very same uncreated Light already in Mary's womb.[23]

Therefore, Ephrem may state that Mary is greater than Moses. Namely, Moses was illuminated by the light that shone and penetrated him from outside, but in the case of Mary the illuminating light shone from within.

> Moses gleamed with [divine] glory, because he saw the splendour briefly, how much more should the body wherein [Christ] resided gleam, and the river in which He was baptised?[24]

Mary is an abode of light, filled and illuminated by the divine light of Christ. "The Sun entered the womb, and in the height and depth His rays were dwelling."[25] Ephrem compares the case of Mary with an eye whose state of being is purified, strengthened, and illuminated when receiving sunlight.

> As though an eye the Light settled in Mary; it polished her mind, clarified her thought and made pure her understanding, causing her virginity to shine.[26]

What has been said above may cause some ecumenical turbulence. St Ephrem's stress on the purity and illumination of Mary may make him a bit uneasy reading for Roman Catholic audience, for he clearly is far from backing the dogma of immaculate conception.[27] The holiness and purity of Mary is unique and complete, but this seems to be rather *because of* incarnation than *vice versa*.

---

22 Hymnen de Ecclesia, 36,3. Des heiligen Ephraem des Syrers Hymnen de ecclesia, transl. by Edmund Beck, CSCO 199. English translation according to Sebastian P. Brock and George A. Kiraz, Ephrem the Syrian. Select Poems. Eastern Christian Texts 2, Provo/UT 2006, 71.

23 Ibid., 36,5. English translation according to Brock and Kiraz, 73.

24 Ibid., 36,7; Brock and Kiraz, 73.

25 Hymnen de Nativitate, 21,6.

26 Hymnen de Ecclesia, 36,2. Brock and Kiraz, 71.

27 For example, Ephrem's Mary is "redeemed" and even "baptised" by her son, Hymnen de Nativitate 16,10.

Virgin Mary and Universal Mysticism

What has been said above by Isaac and Ephrem is of significance for the understanding of the ontology of Christian mystical experience. If the mystical experience of Mary is ultimate, it is also paradigmatic. This idea was realised already by Origen, who in his discussion on Mary turned the perspective from the case of Mary to the mystical theology. The concrete development of the divine *Logos* in Mary's womb is a parallel phenomenon to the growth of *Logos* in the souls of Christians.[28] In other words, Mary's *body* is a kind of model and pattern of the *soul* of a Christian – a unique position indeed.

> Every uncorrupted and virginal soul that has been conceived of the Holy Spirit in order to give birth for the will of the Father, is Jesus' mother.[29]

The connection in question is not a homiletic trick but a deep ontological truth: A Christian or a mystic is dealing internally with the very same *Logos* that Mary did. This is exactly the fact mentioned above by Isaac of Nineveh. This, it seems to me, is an essential aspect of Christian mystical theology, even though often neglected. The basic setting of Mary's unique experience is in some mystical sense a universal calling.

Indeed, Origen presents some of his most lucid mystical teachings when commenting Mary's words "My soul magnifies the Lord". Origen remarks that the Lord as such cannot be subject to elevation or to diminution, but Christ is the image of Invisible Father, and it is man's calling to illuminate the image of this image in his inner being.

> ... each of us, by transforming our own soul into the image of Christ, reproduces an image of him, smaller or larger, sometimes hidden and dirty, but sometimes shining a luminous and corresponding to the original model.[30]

Origen was not only an outstanding theoretician but also a master of spiritual direction. In contemplating the inner dwelling of Christ in believers, Origen saw also the mariological aspect of the idea. The perfect one does not live for himself, but Christ lives in him, Origen reasons, and if Christ lives in him, then he will be spoken about to Mary: "Behold, your Son, Christ".[31] In this way the Christian mystic is presented to Mary, his spiritual mother.

The same theme was utilised by Gregory of Nyssa, who in his discourse on virginity opens the connection between the experience of Mary and the universal mystical experience.

---

28 Origen, Homiliae in Genesim 3,7 (PG 12).

29 Origen, Fragmenta e catenis in Matthaeum 281, in: Origenes Werke XII. Commentarius in Matthaeum III,1, ed. by Erich Klostermann and Ernst Benz, GCS 41.1, Leipzig 1941, 126.

30 Origen, In Lucam 8, c. 8 §8 (PG 13). Translation according to Luigi Gambero, Mary and the Fathers of the Church. The Blessed Virgin Mary in Patristic Thought, San Francisco 1999, 79.

31 Origen, Commentarii in evangelium Joannis 1,6, PG 14, 32B.

> What took place bodily in Mary, the inviolate Virgin, by the fullness of the divinity of Christ, which shone forth in that Virgin, the same will happen in every virginal soul that acts according to Logos (*kata logon*).[32]

I deliberately use the concept of *universal* mystical experience, due to the universalistic character of the Logos doctrine, which is not limited to the Church only. *Logos*, in Orthodox understanding, refers to the universal truth, and the particular manifestations of *logos*, the *logoi*, are universally present since and due to the creation. This divine indwelling in the created realm is by no means restricted to Christianity.

Ephrem also shows that the illumination experienced by Mary is something that spreads and is transmitted over and over again. In Ephrem's poetry, Mary herself says to the Jesus child that she has clothed herself in a robe of glory that is "enough for all".[33]

The idea of the mystical role of Mary, of course, is widespread and not new. It was utilised already by an early desert father, Abba Longinos.[34] It has also been prominently discussed by perhaps the greatest Byzantine mystic, Symeon the New Theologian. He even uses the term *Hieros gamos* to refer to Mary's marriage with God. Symeon argues that the same experience is repeated in the saints: they carry the divine *logos* inside them as if a baby is carried in the womb, and they are also consciously aware of it. Virgin Mary is a unique case, but all Christians are indeed called to share in her experience – and therefore also in its uniqueness.[35] All true and deep spirituality is based on the descent of the Holy Spirit, which is the source of mystical life, and in this Mary is the paradigmatic case.

The idea was common to many Church fathers from the East to the West. In the Latin tradition, it was championed, for example, by Ildephonsus of Toledo, whose *Libellus de virginitate perpetua sanctae Mariae* was one of the most influential Mariological writings in the early mediaeval West. "I pray you", he declared to the Holy Virgin, "that I might possess Jesus from that same Spirit by whom you gave birth to Jesus. Through that Spirit, through whom you your flesh conceived Jesus, may my soul accept Jesus." Ildephonsus developed the theme in detail, drawing parallels with Mary and believer in knowing Christ through the Holy Spirit, speak of him and adore him in the same Spirit.[36]

Not all modern authors on mysticism have missed this idea. Indeed, R. C. Zaehner closes his classic work on comparative mysticism by noting that God operates in the human soul, when it attains to the beatific vision, in the same way as God exists in Himself.

---

32 Gregory of Nyssa, De virginitate II, PG 46, 324B.

33 Ephrem the Syrian, Hymnen de Nativitate, 17,4.

34 PG 65, 257B.

35 Symeon the New Theologian, Discourse 1,9–10, trans. by C. J. de Catanzaro, New York 1980; St. Symeon the New Theologian. On the Mystical Life. The Ethical Discourses. Vol. 3, trans. by Alexander Golitzin, Crestwood/NY 1997, 93.

36 Ildephonsus of Toledo, Libellus de virginitate perpetua sanctae Mariae contra tres infideles, ch. 12 §12, PL 96, 106.

> As Christ was conceived in Mary's womb, so is He conceived in the receptive soul which thereby enters into the full life of the Trinity where it shares in the eternal outpouring of the Holy Ghost rejoicing for ever in His Being and his Thought.[37]

Mary as Mother of Asceticism

The role of Mary as the first fruit and paradigm of Christian spirituality, as shown by Origen, was due not only to her divine motherhood but also to her virginity.[38] This is also something of importance, not least because of the interrelatedness of asceticism and mysticism. Two different processes, that of the expansion of veneration of Mary and the emergence of monasticism, took place more or less simultaneously – but how exactly are these two phenomena related? The prevalent view seems to be that as the ideal of virginity became stronger and stronger, it finally became unavoidable to emphasize the perpetual virginity of Mary. The process, however, worked in the opposite direction as well. The appraisal of virginity was to no small extent connected with and caused by the admiration of Mary's virginity. This is clearly seen in how the fourth century Church fathers link the two themes in their homiletics. Mary, and her already existing veneration, is used as an inspiration for virginal life, hardly ever vice versa. This is quite remarkable since the preachers' interests represent actual historical situations.

The themes are also closely connected in the Hymns of Ephrem. He considers Virgin Mary as a mother of a new mode of existence, mother of all those leading virginal life, and especially of the female ones. Christ lived in Virgin Mary, and so does He live in all the other virginal women.[39] The female, almost feminist, perspective is of utmost importance. In the lullabies of *Hymnen de Nativitate*, Mary speaks asking women – sinners and pure ones alike – to wait for "my Beloved one to live in you".[40]

For a second example, we may note an interesting narrative solution from the *Hymnen de Nativitate* 28. The second verse is presented to Mary ("the head of angels salutes you"). The third verse, however, states that marriage is pure and "not accursed", even though in virginity there is more spiritual potentiality.[41] In the fourth verse Ephrem again continues her discourse to Mary, so that the remark about

---

37 Robert Charles Zaehner, Mysticism. Sacred and Profane. An Inquiry into some Varieties of Praeternatural Experience, Oxford 1957, Reprint 1971, 207.

38 Origen, Commentarius in Matthaeum 10,17, PG 13, 878.

39 E.g. "Within the seal You dwell even now within chaste women" (Ephrem the Syrian, Hymnen de Nativitate, 12,5); "Womankind possessed the evidence of virginity because of You" (ibid., 12,4).

40 Ibid., 17,8.

41 One must take in the consideration the possibility that the order of verses has been altered in the manuscript tradition here. The verse 28,2 is actually the same than 25,7.

the relationship of marriage and virginity remains in the middle of the praise of Mary, as a kind of comment to it. This may be taken as one small indicator of why the Virgin Mary came to be considered the mother of Christian asceticism.

Summit of Celestial Hierarchy

After the assumption of Mary had become a universally accepted topic between 5th and 7th centuries,[42] the role of Mary in the celestial hierarchy became a topic of theological reflection around late 7th and 8th centuries. This discussion in a way completed the position of Virgin Mary in the ontology of mystical experience.

In the Byzantine tradition, the leading hesychast and mystical theologian of the Middle Ages, St Gregory Palamas, discussed and developed the mariological aspect of mystical thought. He discussed the strength of the personal experience of Mary, the only one who "did not receive by measure".[43] The expression implies the same approach as that of St Isaac's, namely that it is the same mystical reality delivered to Mary in full and to other saints in part. Palamas also has views that parallel the ideas of St Ephrem on the illumination of Mary, who has "united her mind with God".[44] Palamas, however, applies more emphasis on the need to have been purified completely *before* the incarnation – not in immaculate birth, however, but in ascetic struggle!

In Gregory Palamas' time, the crucial position of Mary in the top of celestial hierarchy was taken for granted all over the Christian world. "She alone stands at the border between created and uncreated nature", Gregory Palamas declared.[45] The prominent position of Mary opens up the prospect of intercession, a concept that can be understood in two ways. In the practical sense intercession means simply praying for the other created beings. In the abstract sense, however, it may indicate that Mary is an ontological level of her own at the top of the created realm. Indeed, this very idea seems to be utilised by Gregory Palamas, who declares that "none of God's gifts can be bestowed on angels or men except through her".[46] Palamas clearly means more than Mary's role in the incarnation. With a slight Neo-Platonic tone he presents Mary as a being through whom the divine good is emanated into the world:

42 Stephen J. Shoemaker has recently published an outstanding study on the Assumption traditions: Ancient Traditions of the Virgin Mary's Dormition and Assumption, Oxford 2003.

43 Gregory Palamas, Homily 53,41 (Γρηγορίου τοῦ Παλαμᾶ. Ἅπαντα τὰ ἔργα 11. Ὁμιλίες 43–63, ed. by Παναγιώτης Κ. Χρήστου, Θεσσαλονίκη 1986; trans.: Mary the Mother of God. Sermons by Saint Gregory Palamas, ed. by Christopher Veniamin, South Canaan/PA 2005, 37.

44 Ibid., Homily 53,62.

45 Ibid., Homily 37,15 (Γρηγορίου τοῦ Παλαμᾶ. Ἅπαντα τὰ ἔργα 10. Ὁμιλίες 21–42, ed. by Παναγιώτης Κ. Χρήστου, Θεσσαλονίκη 1985).

46 Ibid., Homily 53,37.

> It is an eternal law in heaven that the lesser shall share by means of the greater in what lies beyond being. So as the Virgin Mother is incomparably greater than all, as many as will share in God will do so through her, and as many as will know God will acknowledge (or, know) her as the one who contained Him who cannot be contained.[47]

Therefore, it is in Mary that the human spirit becomes radiant with the presence of the divine spirit. She, as a divinised human being, is the leading representative of the created realm. Even the mystical influences are transmitted through her. "No one can come to God unless he is truly illuminated by her", Gregory Palamas declares.[48] Therefore, we may say that Virgin Mary has a unique place both in the practice of Christian spirituality, including mystical experiences, and in the theory of mysticism.

Virgin Mary in Islamic Mysticism

In our present context it is relevant to make also a few remarks on the position of Mary in Islam and Sufism. Even though Islam lacks the idea of incarnation, in the case of Mary the difference is much tinier as one might expect. Obviously, Mary has no status as a Mother of God, but she does have a unique status in Qur'an in which she even has a Surah of her own.

Mary of the Qur'an is purified by God and therefore pure by her body and soul, and in that sense sinless, as well as the mother of the word of God.[49] No other woman has been mentioned by name in the Qur'an, and it is not far-fetched to consider her the greatest women of all times also in Islamic standards. Indeed, in many authoritative sources Virgin Mary is named as the most solemn female creature in Islam. The next one in Islamic ranking might be Asya, the wife of Pharaoh, Khadija or Muhammad's daughter Fatima, depending on particular author's position. According to one *hadith*, there have been many perfect ones among males, but among women only two, Asya and Mary.[50] Another *hadith* considers Mary the best woman universally, Khadija (Muhammed's favourite wife) being the best woman of Muhammad's own community.[51]

---

47 Ibid., Homily 37,18, and a parallel in Homily 53,40 (trans.: Veniamin, Mary 37).

48 Ibid., Homily 37,15.

49 Purity of Mary is based on her miraculous childhood in the Jewish temple where she is presented by her parents at an early age, and where she miraculously received food from heaven. See Qur'an 3:33–47. The thematics roughly corresponds to the themes of Protevangelium of James. In Islamic exegesis, Mary was the only female child who ever was dedicated to the Temple.

50 Aliah Schleifer, Mary. The Blessed Virgin of Islam, Fons Vitae, Louisville/KY 1998, 79–81. The *hadith* in question seems to be authoritative. Sahīh al-Bukhārī 6:446, the complete text of which is in Ibn-Hajar, Fath al-bārī, Madina 1996.

51 Tafsir al-Tabari, 264. According to a tradition transmitted by al-Bukhari, al-Muslim and ad-

The unique position of Mary, it seems to me, has not been fully made use of in the Islamic mysticism – even though the archetype of the feminine has a place of its own in Sufism. The basic Sufi classics, such as al-Kalabadhi or al-Qušayri, do not refer to Mary at all. However, when Sufis do refer to her, the tone is all the more interesting. Sufis like al-ʿAbdārī (c. 14th century), agreed that Mary has reached perfection. The famous Persian poet ʿAttar († c. 1221) referred to the tradition that on the day of resurrection Mary will be the first one to enter paradise, aiming to prove that women have equal access to spirituality.[52]

Ibn ʿArabi (1165–1240) paid attention to the fact that Mary's strict morality was an immediate precondition of the miraculous conception. Namely, according to the Qur'anic narrative, Mary thought that the angel who appeared to her was a human being, yet she immediately refused in her mind the possibility of doing anything forbidden, even though the angel was a perfect one by his appearance. Therefore, it was this refusal that made her capable of receiving the divine word.[53]

Persian mystic Ruzbihan Baqli (1128–1209), however, gave another explanation, stressing that the angel's form was a representation of divine beauty, the revelation of which takes places constantly.[54] An early but less known Sufi, al-Tirmidhi (9th century), paid attention to the fact that Mary's heart was so pure that she immediately recognised the truthfulness of the divine words. God actually praised Mary because of the purity of her heart, al-Tirmidhī notes.[55]

Ibn ʿArabī considered Mary and her miraculous conception as a symbol of total receptivity of human nature to the activity of the Spirit.[56] In his theosophically orientated mystical speculations, Ibn 'Arabī developed the theme of the 'sophianic feminine', discussing especially on the mystery of her primordial creativity and createdness, both united in one being. Perhaps the sophianic feminine might be identified with Mary in some sense, but the exact relationship between the two would require

---

Dhahabi, Mary was the best woman of her time, Khadija of her time. See Schleifer, Mary the Blessed Virgin, 63.

52 Margaret Smith, Rābi'a the mystic and her fellow-saints in Islam. Cambridge 1928 (Reprint: Amsterdam 1974), 176; Farîd al-Dîn ʿAttar, Tadhkirât al-'awliyya, ed. by Reynold A. Nicholson, Persian historical texts 3.5, London 1905, I, 59 [in Persian]. See also Muhammad Ibn-al-Hājj al-ʿAbdārī, Al-madhal aš-šarʿ aš-šarīf, Al-Qahira 1960, II, 19.

53 Ibn al 'Arabi, The Bezels of Wisdom, trans. and introd. by Ralph W. J. Austin, The Classics of Western Spirituality, Mahwah/NJ 1980, chapter 15. According to Ibn 'Arabi, the body of Jesus was created out of the water in Mary's womb.

54 Carl W. Ernst, Ruzbihan Baqli. Mysticism and the Rhetoric of Sainthood in Persian Sufism, Curzon Sufi Series 4, Richmond/Surrey 1996, 73.

55 The Concept of Sainthood in Early Islamic Mysticism. Two Works by Al-Hakīm Al-Tirmidhī, trans. and introd. by Bernd Radtke and John O'Kane, Curzon Sufi Series, Richmond/Surrey 1996, 210. According to Al-Tirmidhī the words Mary heard under the palm tree (Qur'an 19:22–24) were neither angelic, nor Jesus', as they were taken by Islamic commentators (even though Jesus was still unborn at the moment) but divine, i. e. God's voice. Tirmidhī is quite alone with this view. Radtke and O'Kane, Concept of Sainthood, 162–163.

56 Ibn al 'Arabī, Bezels of Wisdom, ch. 20.

further study.[57] The feminine archetype is both a feminine projection of God, or rather, of the divine attributes, and an ideal projection of the human female. J. J. Elias has illustrated the setting with a following scheme:[58]

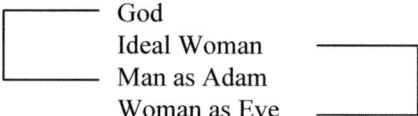

God
Ideal Woman
Man as Adam
Woman as Eve

The most famous Islamic author of all times, Rumi (1207–1273), has also reflected upon Mary in his poetry. He presented an interesting parallel: The speech of Adam – namely, the rationality of primordial man – was a ray of divine breath, as the speech of Jesus was derived from the spiritual beauty of Mary.[59] In this way, Mary could be presented as paradigmatic case of beauty. The idea of a 'new Eve', a central topic in patristic discussions on soteriology, is not far from this imagery.

Indeed, several Sufi authors have pondered on the mystery of Mary in an exceptionally deep and illuminating way. Ruzbihan Baqli, when commenting on Qur'an 19:16, praised Mary in relation to the whole Sufi cosmology and ontological levels contained therein. His presentation is in fact one of the most solemn pieces ever written about Mary:

> The essence of Mary is the essence of the holy *fitra* [primordial human nature]. And her essence was trained by 'the Real', by the light of intimacy. And in all of her respirations [in every breath], she was "possessed" (*majdhuba*) by the attribute of the closeness and intimacy to the Source of Divine Illumination. She became constantly in a state of spiritual vigilance (*murâqaba*) for the manifestation of the illumination of the World of Sovereignty (*jabarūt*), from the point of the rising place of spiritual orientation (*mašriq*) in the realm of the Kingdom (*malakūt*). And she withdrew from the world via spiritual resolve (*himma*) of the highest category, characterised by the light of the Unseen. And she approached the rising-palaces (*mašāriq*) of the Illumination of the Essence (*dhāt*), and she inhaled the Attributes – fra-

57 Ralph W. J. Austin, The Sophianic Feminine in Ibn 'Arabi and Rumi, In: The Heritage of Sufism. Vol. 1: Classical Persian Sufism from its Origins to Rumi (700–1300), ed. by Leonard Lewisohn, Oxford 1999, 240. The crucial text is the last chapter of Fusūs ak-hikam, parts three and four.

58 "In this scheme, the relationship of man as Adam to woman as Eve corresponds to that of God to the ideal woman or creative feminine." According to Elias, in the Sufi psyche there exist two "women", the sacred and the profane, that may be called "feminine" and "female". The feminine is glorified, female often trivialised. "The feminine is Maryam, Fatima, and the idealized beloved of mystical literature, remembered best as Layla." Jamal J. Elias, Female and Feminine in Islamic Mysticism, in: The Muslim World 78.3–4 (1988), 220. These interact in various ways.

59 Austin, Sophianic Feminine, 243 (quoting Rumi's Mathnawī, VI, 4549).

> grances from the Eternal world without beginning (*'ālam al-azal*). And the gift reached her – the communion with the Pre-Eternal (*azaliyya*).[60]

Most of Baqli's expressions here are reflections of Sufi doctrines on the primordial Essence of man, the paradigmatic case of which Mary is presented.

> And the Illumination of the 'witnessing of the Eternal' (*mušāhadat al-qidamiyya*) shone upon her. And she experienced the vision of the Illumination of the Manifestation of Eternity, Its Lights flashed, and Its Secrets reached her spirit (*rūh*), and her spirit became impregnated with the Divine Secret, and she became the bearer of the glorious word and the light of the Spirit of the Most High. And when her state became magnified with the reflection of the beauty of the Illumination of Eternity upon her, she concealed herself out of fear [of people] and withdrew [from them] with the 'bridgegroom' of the Reality (*al-haqīqa*).[61]

We may note here the presence of several expressions that have exact or close parallels with expressions of Christian authors, like the "bearer of the glorious word", as well as the bride of God, expressed indirectly by Baqlī.

Rūzbihān Baqlī actually managed to analyse the illumination of Mary with greater detail, as well as greater mystical depth, than most Christian theologians. Therefore, Rūzbihān is quite close to the Christian authors in many respects. His Mary is sanctified and illuminated *before* her miraculous pregnancy that would not have been possible except in the case of a pure creature. The emphasis differs somewhat from St Ephrem but parallels to that of Gregory Palamas.

In this way, Mary is a human light shining forth the light of divinity – also for Sufi eyes. Or to use the voice of A. Schmemann, perhaps the leading 20th century Orthodox theologian, Mary is "the highest and most perfect fruit of the Holy Spirit in the entire creation".[62]

---

60 Rūzbihān Baqlī, 'Arā'is al-bayān fī ḥaqā'iq al-Qur'ān, II,7. Translation according to Schleifer, Mary, 91 (translation by Alan Arthur Godlas is currently under preparation). Baqlī wrote both in Arabic and in Persian; for a detailed synopsis of his writings see Ernst, Ruzbihan, 151–159.

61 Baqlī, 'Arā'is II,7. Translation according to Schleifer, Mary, 92.

62 Schmemann, The Virgin Mary, 75 (cf. footnote 6).

The Vision of God as a Foretaste of Eternal Life According to Saint Gregory Palamas

Fadi A. Georgi

Introduction

The 14th century mystical writer Saint Gregory Palamas (1296–1359), Archbishop of Thessalonica, is considered one of the most remarkable porte paroles of the Orthodox Theology. He is the heir of the tradition of the Eastern Roman theology, nowadays known as the "Byzantine" tradition. This tradition, as the prominent Russian scholar Vladimir Lossky describes it, "has never made a sharp distinction between mysticism and theology, between personal experience of the divine mysteries and the dogma affirmed by the Church". It should rather be characterized as a "mystical theology" or as "a spirituality which expresses a doctrinal attitude."[1]

However, this fact was not easily established throughout the history of Eastern Christianity. On many occasions, it was put into question. The church synods and councils had to confront heresies that threatened the integrity of the faith and the spiritual experience of the community of the believers, i.e. its own existence and identity.[2] This was the case with the teachings of Saint Gregory Palamas, a monk of Mount Athos and, later, the archbishop of Thessalonica, who found himself, between 1338 and 1351, in a position of defending what was later called "the Hesychastic Spiritual Tradition."[3] Palamas aimed at clarifying both the doctrine of "the uncreated light" and the concept of "distinction in God between the incomprehensible and unattainable divine essence, and the communicated divine grace". His opponents were the intellectual elite of the "Byzantine Society", substituting empiri-

1 Vladimir Lossky, The Mystical Theology of the Eastern Church, Cambridge 1957, 7–8. See also Kallistos Ware, Tradition and Personnel Experience in Later Byzantine Theology, ECR 3 (1970), 131–141.

2 N. Ματσούκα,᾿Ορθοδοξία καί αἵρεσης τούς ἐκκλησιαστικούς συγγραφεῖς τοῦ Δ', Ε', ΣΤ' αἰώνα, Thessalonica [2]1992.

3 Hesychasm is one of the most representative trends in Eastern Orthodox spirituality. It is characterized mainly by the practice of the "Jesus prayer", in absolute stillness. Many studies have tried to analyse the roots and influences in the formation of this school of mysticism. We can mention among them: Pierre Adnès, "Hésychasme", DS 9 (1976), 381–399; Irénée Hausherr, L'Hésychasme: Etude de spiritualité, OCP 22 (1956), 5–40, 247–285. See also Kallistos Ware, The Debate about Palamism, ECR 9 (1977), 45– 63.

cal theology, based on mystical experience, with a rather speculative orthologistic system of thought.[4]

This debate between Palamas and his opponents was termed the “Hesychastic Controversy.”[5] As a result of the efforts he deployed in this Controversy, Palamas acquired a unique authoritative place in the Orthodox Church. He is considered the Theologian of the light[6] par excellence due to the central place in his teachings of the experience of the vision of the uncreated and divine light.[7]

The roots of the spiritual teachings of Saint Gregory Palamas can be traced back to the early spiritual tradition of Eastern Christianity as it evolved in ancient monastic centers like the Deserts of Egypt and Syria, the Lavra of Saint Saba in Palestine, the Monastery of Saint Catherine in Mount Sinai, and the Monastery of Stodion in Constantinople. As a result of this tradition, the hesychastic trend flourished in the 14th century in Mount Athos.[8] The writings of Saint Gregory abound in the richness and intensity of theological texts and concepts borrowed from Greek fathers of the Church such as Athanasios of Alexandria († 373), the Cappadocian Fathers (fourth century), John Chrysostom († 407), Cyril of Alexandria († 412), the Dionysian Corpus, Diadoque of Photice († before 474), Maximos the Confessor († 662), Anastasios the Synaite († 7th century), John of Damascus († between 754 and 787), Symeon the New Theologian († 1022), as well as from the Syrian Fathers like Ephrem the Syrian († 373) and the Ascetical treaties of Isaac of Nineveh († 7th century) and many other authoritative names.[9] Quotations of those fathers are weaved in carefully into his texts. They form an exceptionally rich and coherent theological mosaic, which defines the features and the identity of what Professor Jaroslav Pe-

4 Very interesting is the debate between John Romanides and John Meyendorff on the Identity of the opponents of Palamas, and on the essence of the Hesychastic Controversy. See John Romanides, Notes on the Palamite Controversy and Related Topics: Part I–II, GOTR 6 (1960–1961), 186–205; 9 (1963–1964), 225–270; and John Meyendorff, Introduction à l' étude de Grégoire Palamas, Paris 1959, and R. E. Synkevitch, Gregory Palamas, in: La théologie byzantine et sa tradition II (XIIIe–XIXe s.), CChr, ed. C. Conticello/V. Conticello, Turnhout 2002, 131–188. Sinckevitch's article is evidently one of the latest studies comprehending most of the results of the debates about the specific issue and other related notions.

5 J. Bois, Les débuts de la controverse hésychaste, EO 5 (1901–2), 352–362; John Meyendorff, Les débuts de la controverse hésychaste, Byz. 23 (1953), 87–120; Β. Χριστοφορίδη, Οι ησυχαστικής έριδες κατά το ΙΔ' αιώνα. Παρατηρητής, Thessalonica [2]1993.

6 Basile Krivocheïne, Grégoire Palamas ou Syméon le Nouveau Théologien, MEPREO 11 (1963), 205–210; Vladimir Lossky, The Vision of God, Crestwood/New York 1986.

7 P.-T. Camelot, Lumière: Etudes Patristiques, DS 9 (1976), 1149–1158; C. Veniamin, Divinae Consortes Naturae: Notes on the Centrality of the Thaborian Theophany in Saint Gregory Palamas, Κληρονομία 28 (1996), 85–103; Χ. Σταμούλη, Περὶ φωτὸς: Προσωπικὲς ἤ φυσικὲς ἐνέργειες; Συμβολὴ στὴ σύγχρονη περὶ 'Αγίας Τριάδος προβληματικὴ στὸν Ορθόδοξο χῶρο, Thessalonica 1999.

8 John Meyendorff, Saint Grégoire Palamas et la mystique orthodoxe, Paris 1959, 7–67.

9 George Florovsky, Saint Gregory Palamas and the Tradition of the Fathers, Collected Works 1, Belmont/Mass 1972, 118.

likan calls "the last flowering of Byzantine Orthodoxy"[10] in the Eastern Christian Empire, during the most critical historical period, preceding the fall of Constantinople.

Palamas himself affirms that the major theme of his theological writings and controversies is the divine light. "In this light", he says, "when Christ the Saviour, shone on Mount Thabor, he manifested the brightness and glory of the divine nature, through which God communes with creation and with man."[11]

The Theology of Light

Saint Gregory Palamas asserts that "the light of the Transfiguration of Christ precedes the existence of the material light of the Genesis of the world and the darkness which interrupts that created light." This eternal light "was, is, and shall be unto ages of ages."[12] Basing his theology on the patristic tradition that antedated him, mainly the teachings of Saint Basil of Caesarea († 379), he confirms that "all beings that existed before the foundation of the sensible and corruptible world, existed in the light, and that it was unlikely for the angels to have been in the darkness, but rather, they had a majestic presence in the light and enjoyed the spiritual beatitude." He characterizes this same light, revealed to the saints in prayer, as "the light of the future and perpetual age" and "our common hope"[13], clarifying that we should commune, from the present life, with the "heavenly light and the promise of the ultimate benedictions", and that "while the condemned shall be sent to the outer darkness, the righteous shall find comfort in this light that transcends this world."[14]

Palamas considers the redeeming work of Christ as the foundation of the theology of light. In this theological framework, the fall of Adam is represented as his separation from Beauty and Light and as the alienation from the divine "form" and the original destiny of humanity. Adam, before the transgression, partook of the divine radiance, which attired in splendor his bodily nakedness, rendering it incomparably beautiful. "Man rejected light, corrupted his resemblance to the highest light, and wore darkness as a tunic. But Christ, who is naturally good and merciful, condescended in his compassion, towards the fallen one, reviving him, and renewing His blackened Icon."[15] "The Logos of God, in his clemency, assumed the nature of

10 Jaroslav Pelikan, The Christian Tradition – A History of Development of Doctrine 2: The Spirit of Eastern Christendom, Chicago 1974, 252–254.

11 Ὑπὲρ τῶν ἱερῶς ἡσυχαζόντων Γ', 1,22, Συγγράμματα: Γρηγορίου τοῦ Παλαμᾶ Συγγράμματα, Ed. Π. Χρήστου, Κύρομανος 1,634.

12 Α' Κατὰ Γρηγορᾶ, 29, Συγγράμματα 4,252.

13 Πρὸς Δανιὴλ Αἴνου 18, Συγγράμματα 2,390; Δ' Λόγος Ἀντιρρητικός 18,49, Συγγράμματα 3, 277–278.

14 Κατὰ Γρηγορᾶ Α', 24, Συγγράμματα 4,249; Ὑπὲρ τῶν ἱερῶς ἡσυχαζόντων Γ', 1,39, Συγγράμματα 1,651–652; Basil of Ceasarea, Ὁμιλία εἰς τὴν ἑξαήμερον 2,5, PG 29, 40–41.

15 Λόγος Ἀποδεικτικός Β' 9, Συγγράμματα 1,85–86.

man which had become naked and deprived of divine radiance, due to the transgression of the commandment of God. He had mercy on the ugliness of this nature and revealed it to His disciples in its most shining form on mount Thabor."[16] Thus, He manifested the glory that human nature once had, and what man, living in the likeness of Jesus Christ, shall become, in the age to come.[17]

Saint Gregory's teaching about the mystical experience of illumination and deification of man is founded on the Christological definitions of the 4th and 6th ecumenical councils that were held in Chalcedon (451) and Constantinople (680–681) respectively.

According to the hesychast theologian, the divine "enlightened form of Christ, seen by his three disciples on Thabor, transcends heaven, precedes the existence of the created cosmos, and has no beginning to its existence". The manifested light of Christ "is the light of the age to come, the light that never sets and never ends, the archetypal beauty of the Logos of God, the radiance and glory of His divinity, which shines naturally from His divine nature and has become the glory common to the divine nature and the divinely-assumed human nature of Christ". This has been possible through Christ uniting in his one hypostasis (person) both divinity and humanity.[18]

Although this light is uncreated and divine, however, it should not be confused with the essence of God which remains inconceivable and beyond any form of human knowledge. It is distinguished from the divine essence as the "energy" common to the three persons of the Holy Divine Trinity.[19] This divine energy is granted to humanity by Christ as the grace of the Holy Spirit, through which, God is mani-

16 Daniel Rogich, Homily 34 of Saint Gregory Palamas: A Study of Palamas' Doctrine of the Transfiguration of Christ, GOTR 33 (1988), 149–152.

17 Κεφάλαια ἑκατὸν πεντήκοντα 66, Συγγράμματα 5,73.

18 Δ' Κατὰ Γρηγορᾶ 1, Συγγράμματα 4,341–342.

19 The theme of the simplicity of God and the distinction between essence and energy in the teaching of Palamas and in the Eastern Christian tradition in general has been the object of many debates. One can mention among the most representative studies: Paul Evdokimov, De la Nature et de la Grâce dans la Théologie de l'Orient, in: 1054-1954. L'Eglise et les Eglises 2, Chevetogne 1955, 171–195; Sébastien Guichardan, Le problème de la simplicité divine en Orient et en Occident aux XIVè et XVè siècles: Grégoire Palamas, Duns Scot, Georges Scholarios, Lyon 1933; Venance Grumel, Grégoire Palamas, Duns Scot et Georges Scholarios devant le problème de la simplicité divine, EO, 34 (1935), 84–96; Clement Lialine, The Theological Teaching of Gregory Palamas on Divine Simplicity, ECQ 6 (1946), 266–287; Lodewijk H. Grondijs, Le concept de Dieu chez Grégoire Palamas et la critique occidentale, in: Actes du Xè Congrés international d'Etudes Byzantines 1955, Istanbul 1957, 327–329; Georges Habra, The Source of the Doctrine of Gregory Palamas on the Divine Energies, ECQ 12 (1957–1958), 244–252, 294–303, 338–348; Leonidas Condos, The Essence-Energy-Structure of Saint Gregory Palamas, GOTR 12 (1967–68), 283–294; Christos Yannaras, The Distinction Between Essence and Energies and its Importance for Theology, SVSQ 19 (1975), 244; D. Coffey, The Palamite Doctrine of God: A New Perspective, SVTQ 32 (1988), 329–358.

fested in the bodies and souls of the saints. Hence this light is literally called "the Reign of God."[20]

The Eternal Reign and Glory of God

Desiring to describe the Light of divinity and deification, Palamas resorts to the narratives of the Transfiguration of Christ in the Synoptic Gospels[21], where Christ, six days after saying that "there be some standing here, which shall not taste of death, till they see the Son of man coming in his Reign", took with Him His three elected disciples and brought them up into Mount Thabor, and "his face did shine as the sun, and his garment was white as the light" and, since the disciples could not tolerate to look at this radiance, they fell down on their faces.[22] But they saw, as the Savior had promised, "the Reign of God, that divine and unutterable light."[23]

In the theological syllogism of Saint Gregory, the identification of the light of Transfiguration of Christ with the Reign and Glory of God is accentuated. Palamas describes the light as the "pure Reign of God" and the "benediction that transcends time", as "it would be absurd to believe that the Reign of God had a beginning and that it is limited by centuries and times."[24] He explains that the "Reign of God", His "simplicity", His "unlimitedness", His "authority", are "attributes of God" (προσόντα τοῦ Θεοῦ), are features that transcend time, and even though they are "eternal and co-eternal with God", they are not His nature, but proceed from His nature and are related to it.[25]

The Reign of God is not subject to the created realm, but is the unique Reign which is "ungovernable and invincible". It is "the inheritance of the saved ones."[26] This mystical light is "the divinity of God", "the beauty and radiance of the divine nature", "the natural ray and glory of Divinity", "the vision and delight of the saints in the unending age."[27] Being uncreated, it is not separated from the One God and the One Divinity, but is "distinguished from the divine essence as the glory and radiance of this essence."[28] This is why the uncreated divine "energy" together with the uncreated divine essence are considered One Divinity.[29]

---

20 Δ' Λόγος Ἀντιρρητικός 22,57, Συγγράμματα, 284; Maximos the Confessor, Κεφάλαια θεολογικὰ καὶ οἰκονομικὰ 2,88, PG 90,1168AB.

21 Mat 17:1; Mark 9:1; Luke 9:28.

22 See respectively Mat 17:2.6 and 16:28.

23 Κεφάλαια ἑκατὸν πεντήκοντα 146, Συγγράμματα 5,116.

24 Γ' Κατὰ Γρηγορα 25, Συγγάματα 4,335; Maximos the Confessor, Κεφάλαια θεολογικά 2,86, PG 90,1165AB.

25 Α' Κατὰ Γρηγορᾶ 29, Συγγράμματα 4,252.

26 Ὁμιλία ΛΔ', 12, Γρηγορίου τοῦ Παλαμᾶ Ὁμιλίες, Επ. Ψευτογκά Β., Κύρομανος, Επί ἔκδοση, 338.

27 Κεφάλαια ἑκατὸν πεντήκοντα 147, Συγγράμματα 5,256.

28 Ὑπὲρ τῶν ἱερῶς ἡσυχαζόντων Β', 3,66, Συγγράμματα 1,598–599.

29 Κεφάλαια ἑκατὸν πεντήκοντα 147, Συγγράμματα 5,256.

Palamas uses, throughout the theological controversies, a definitive eschatological language, attesting in the same time the uncreated and the common Trinitarian character of the light. He calls it "the holy, unsucceedable, unsetting, beginningless and eternal light, the beauty of the age to come and the glory of God the Father. The Son of God, in the end of time, shall come in the glory of the Father and of the Holy Spirit, since one is the glory of the Father and of the Son and of the Holy Spirit."[30]

Saint Gregory describes this fact in many linguistic forms. One can encounter in the texts of Saint Gregory expressions like the "... sensed and beyond-sense ... unapproachable, immaterial, deifying, eternal, radiance of the divine nature, the glory of divinity, the majesty of the heavenly reign" and "light of the world to come."[31] The light is called "light of the divine reign", "beauty of the future age", "glory of the divine nature."[32] It is described as "the most divine light ... uncreated ... true and eternal, not the inexpressible divine nature ..., but its enveloper ... true beauty and hyper-radiance to the saints, being shared and seen, now partially, but incessantly in the future age."[33] It is "the limpid and unsetting light"[34], termed "divinity" by the saints, "indescribable", "not only transcending the senses, but also transcending the intellect". Its perception by the eyes of the apostles can be only justified by the fact that "they acquired the power and the grace of the age to come."[35]

Mystical Experience as the Pledge of the Age to Come

Palamas argues that the experience of the uncreated light is common to the "theologians enlightened by the wisdom of God and to the angels." This light will be visible unto the ages and during the future state, and it radiates from Christ, who is called by the Holy Scriptures "the Father of the age to come." And as Christ revealed his divinity on Mount Thabor to his three chosen disciples[36], he shall also reveal it to all His saints, rendering them witnesses of His divinity, reign and glory. This revelation and theophany, will be continuous in the future age, for then, as Saint Paul teaches, "shall we ever be with the Lord."[37]

Thus, the pure-hearted perceive and taste eternal divine life even in this present age, assimilating through the vision of God, the uncreated deifying energy." "Because the saints do not only see, but they are also affected by the radiance of God." They are united to the divine energy, since "the energy of God and of the saints is

30 B' Λόγος 'Αντιρρητικός 7, Συγγράμματα 3,89.
31 Ὑπὲρ τῶν ἱερῶς ἡσυχαζόντων Γ', 1,22, Συγγράμματα 1,634.
32 Ibid. 1,635.
33 Δ' Κατὰ Γρηγορᾶ, Συγγράμματα 4,463.
34 B' Λόγος 'Αντιρρητικός 8, 24, Συγγράμματα 3,24.
35 Ibid. 3,10, 3,91–92.
36 Δ' Κατὰ Γρηγορᾶ 33, Συγγράμματα 4,358.
37 1Thess 4:17; Ὑπὲρ τῶν ἱερῶς ἡσυχαζόντων Γ', 1,22, Συγγράμματα 1,634.

one." The saints, united to the will, the energy and the radiance of the Holy Trinity, taste eternal life in the present time, becoming sons and heirs of God.[38]

Palamas clarifies that the uncreated light is the glory common to Christ and the saints who reach a "christomorphic" end.[39] In the last days, and as Christ will come in the glory of the Father, the saints shall also come in the same glory of the Father of Christ, and "they shall shine forth as the sun"[40] "and shall become light and contemplate light."

This vision has a prerequisite, which is the purity of the soul. In the present, however, the light "is revealed in pledge partially" to those who have overcome all things, impure and pure, through dispassion by means of pure prayer. In the future, the deification of "the sons of the resurrection"[41] takes place, as they are "co-eternalized and co-glorified through the communication of divine glory and radiance as it is granted to us (humans)."[42]

The pledges of this perfection of "the ones living according to Christ" are given in the present, candidly, to the saints of God, who have already partaken of the gifts of the age to come.[43] These saints are numerous to the extent that Saint Gregory declares that it would be impossible to list all those who received, as of now, the pledge of the anticipated gifts, and have attained that divine radiance and splendor.[44] In those, the light dwells eternally, as "the glory of divine nature", "the beauty of the future and perpetual age" and "the beginning-less and un-succeedable reign of God."[45]

Hence, such a spiritual vision, is indeed so great that it cannot be limited to place and time but transcends them, and becomes a foretaste of the future age, being a revelation of the divinity of Jesus Christ and His glory which shall be manifested permanently in His second coming. "He was transfigured ... manifesting a part of His Divinity and showing to them (the disciples) the inhabiting God."[46]

---

38 Πρὸς Γαβρᾶν 17, Συγγράμματα 2,344–345; Πρὸς Δαμιανόν 9, Συγγράμματα 2,465; Basil of Ceasarea, Περὶ Ἁγίου Πνεύματος, PG 52,826; Gregory the Theologian, Λόγος 28, PG 36, 29A.

39 Placide Deseille, "Gloire", DS 6 (1967), col. 421–463; Arthur Ramsey, The Glory of God and the Transfiguration of Christ, London 1967.

40 Mat 13:43.

41 Luke 20:36.

42 Ὑπὲρ τῶν ἱερῶς ἡσυχαζόντων Α' 3,28–30, Συγγράμματα 1,438–440; Dionysios the Areopagite, Περὶ θείων ὀνομάτων 1,4 PG 3,592 BC.

43 J. Behm, "ἀράβων", ThDNT 1,475.

44 Ὁμιλία ΙΣΤ', 40, Ὁμιλίες, 174.

45 Ὑπὲρ τῶν ἱερῶς ἡσυχαζόντων Β', 3,54, Συγγράμματα 1,586–587. Basil of Ceasarea, Ἑρμενεία εἰς 44 Ψαλμόν 5, PG 29,400C; John Chrysostom; Λόγον 21, Περὶ ἀρχῆς καὶ ἐξουσίας καὶ δόξης, PG 63,700.

46 Δ' Λόγος Ἀντιρρητικός 14,37, Συγγράμματα 3,267–268.

The Indefatigable Ascent

In the eternal and unending life, the knowledge and union of light does not stop or end, but increases continuously. It is the "light of Grace" as Palamas calls it, "which eternally and incessantly shall radiate around the saints in that beatific manner of the future age" as it radiantly surrounded the disciples during the transfiguration of Christ. The light will shine eternally and will then be seen perpetually.[47]

Saint Gregory Palamas indicates that the infinite progress of the saints, in the vision of God, in the future age, is similar to that of angels. He refers to "a desire and longing of those who attain this vision" which does not stop, because "the received grace drives them towards the greatest reception" and God "bestowing Himself is infinite and He grants generously and abundantly." The sons of the age to come advance in the vision of God, receiving "grace upon grace"[48] and they ascend "the indefatigable ascent."[49]

The continuous and uninterrupted knowledge of God as experienced by the angels and as shall be experienced by the saints in the age to come, is a continuous progress "in the most apparent vision in the unending age." It can be tasted by man in the present life, not only in the form of a yearning and beseeching, but also like the ascent of Moses to the most shining vision. By this vision, the saints see, beyond the capacities of vision, the light and God who is revealed inside it.[50]

This unceasing ascent is the substance of eternal life. St Gregory assures that the Church fathers refer to light, when they mention eternal life.[51] Because the vision of the uncreated light is not separated from the foretaste of eternal life, "that imperishable beauty, that unalterable and unlimited provision and glory and reign."[52] This vision grants eternal life and the reign that never ends.[53]

Palamas teaches that "this light and life is eternal" reminding his readers that, according to the Christian tradition, divine life is united to the deified man without being separated from God. This is why Saint Paul says "I live, yet not I, but Christ liveth in me"[54], and Saint Maximos the Confessor explains that man abides in this divine and perpetual life.[55]

The Archbishop of Thessalonica clarifies that the life and light, which the Holy Spirit grants to another person, are not separated from Him. Thus the Holy Spirit

---

47 Ὑπὲρ τῶν ἱερῶς ἡσυχαζόντων Β', 3,50, Συγγράμματα 1,582–583.

48 John 1:16.

49 Ὑπὲρ τῶν ἱερῶς ἡσυχαζόντων Β', 2,11, Συγγράμματα 1,517; Dionysios the Areopagite, Περὶ οὐρανίου ἱεραρχίας 42, PG 3,180A.

50 Ὑπὲρ τῶν ἱερῶς ἡσυχαζόντων Β', 3,56, Συγγράμματα 1,590; Gregory of Nyssa, Περὶ βίου Μωυσέως 2, PG 44,376 D–377 A.

51 Ὑπὲρ τῶν ἱερῶς ἡσυχαζόντων Γ', 1,39, Συγγράμματα 1,651.

52 Ὁμιλία ΙΒ', 15, Ὁμιλίες, 348.

53 Ὁμιλία ΚΓ΄ 10, Ὁμιλίες, 239.

54 Gal 2:20.

55 Ὑπὲρ τῶν ἱερῶς ἡσυχαζόντων Γ', 1,38, Συγγράμματα 1,651.

being himself Life, transmits life to those who participate in Him, and "they shall live a meet divine life and shall procure a heavenly life." This life is often called in the patristic literature "eternal and spiritual movement" and the one who acquires it, albeit "ashes and earth", shall become a saint.[56]

Light, Knowledge and Purity

According to Palamas, the mystical experience of the vision of light and the participation of the saints in the uncreated reality are beyond description in human limited language.[57] This is how he justifies the modes of expression in the Gospel, which place the beauty of the face and garments of the Lord, seen by the Apostles on Mount Thabor, beyond the whiteness of snow "so as no fuller on earth can white them."[58]

However, Palamas indicates that through the vision and experience of the union with the uncreated light, the apophatic way of knowing God is exceeded. This knowledge of the divine light is the unique knowledge which examines the depth of God, and does not prohibit his cognition. For through the uncreated light, not only does man proceed to the knowledge of God, but God Himself, draws near man and reveals Himself to him. In a fashion that exceeds the power of humans, the light allows them to see what transcends them. And just as the intellect, when it is united in an unutterable way with the senses, shows man symbolically and sensibly things that are perceivable, a similar thing happens when the senses and the intellect are united with the grace of the Holy Spirit, "they shall see the invisible light spiritually and are rendered similar to Him eternally."[59]

But man never sees the entirety of divinity. His perception of it is partial and it depends on the extent to which he made himself receptive of the grace of the Holy Spirit.[60] The vision of light is relative to the purity of the life led by the individual. Palamas explains that the light itself is "the radiance from thence to those who are purified in this present life, as they shall shine like the sun, and God himself will be present in them. These will be like gods and kings distributing the graces of the beatitude from thence."[61]

56 Ibid.

57 Kallistos Ware, God Hidden and Revealed: The Apophatic Way and the Essence-Energy Distinction, ECR 2 (1975), 125–136.

58 Mark 9:3; Ὁμιλία ΛΕ', 7, Ὁμιλίες, 344–345.

59 Ὑπὲρ τῶν ἱερῶς ἡσυχαζόντων Β΄, 3,50, Συγγράμματα 1,582–583.

60 Ὑπὲρ τῶν ἱερῶς ἡσυχαζόντων Α΄, 3,17, Συγγράμματα 1,427; Gregory of Nyssa, Ὁμιλία 4, PG 44,684.

61 Γ' Κατὰ Γρηγορᾶ 24, Συγγράμματα 4,335; Gregory the Theologian, Λόγος 40 εἰς τὸ ἅγιον Βάπτισμα, PG 36,365B.

Saint Gregory Palamas considers John the Baptist an exemplary prototype of the purity of life, who "whilst in his mother's womb, manifested, through the Holy spirit the perfection of the age to come."[62]

This relation between "purity" and the "Reign of God" is best illustrated, according to the hesychast theologian, by the life of the all-pure Mother of God[63], who "by renouncing every earthly relationship, retracted from mankind and chose the unseen mystical life, dwelling in the holy of holies. The 'All-holy' forwent all material bonds and elevated her intellect. And through prayer, she returned to her inner self and surpassed the throng of busy thoughts, eying in heaven the new unutterable path, which is the quietude of thoughts. And as she made her way to that path, which is not subject to the senses, she rose above creation and perceived, beyond Prophet Moses, the glory of God and His divine grace. Partaking of this vision, the 'Most Holy' became truly 'the radiant cloud of the living water' and the 'dawn of the mystic day.'"[64]

62 Ὁμιλία Μ΄, 4, Ὁμιλίες, 387–388.

63 Καληγόρου Ἰ., "Ἡ πρὸς τὴν Ὑπεραγίαν Θεοτόκον εὐλάβια τοῦ Ἁγίου Γρογορίου Παλαμᾶ", Χαριστήρια εἰς τιμήν τοῦ Μητροπολίτου Γερότος Χαλκηδόνος Μελίτωνος. Πατριαρχικόν Ἴδρουμα Πατερικῶν Μελετῶν, Thessaloniki 1977, 353–377.

64 Ὁμιλία ΝΓ', 59, Ὁμιλίες, 533–534.

Die Lichtmetaphysik im islamisch-gnostischen *Umm al-Kitāb* als Form der Mystik

Bärbel Beinhauer-Köhler

Zum Thema

„Mystik“ ist ein vielschichtiges Phänomen, das im Kern meist als religiöse Erfahrung der „Teilhabe“ am Transzendenten gefasst wird; darüber hinaus sind mystische Erfahrungen aufgrund der Natur dieses „Durchbruchs“ in eine nichtalltägliche Wirklichkeit über das Medium der Sprache nur gebrochen zu vermitteln. Gewöhnlich bedient sich die Mystik verschiedener sprachlicher Metaphern, narrativer Motive, Zeichen und Symbole, um diese Erfahrungsdimension zu veranschaulichen. In der christlichen sowie der islamischen Mystik, die hier beide gleichermaßen den Kontext zur Erarbeitung des Themas bilden, spielt das Bild des Lichts eine besondere Rolle.

Auch die sozialen Formen von Mystik sind vielfältig.[1] Augenscheinlich ist im frühen christlichen Mönchtum, aber auch im frühen Islam ein Rückzug aus der Welt; Mystiker sind im Islam als einsame oder in Gruppen wandernde Peripatetiker anzutreffen, ebenso wie in beiden Religionen eine Kultur von Ordensbildungen besteht, in denen vor allem gemeinschaftlich nach einem festen Regelwerk ein Lebensvollzug mit Offenheit zur religiösen Erfahrung versucht wird.

Im Islam ist diese Ordensbildung erst um das Jahr 1100 n. Chr. verstärkt zu beobachten.[2] Um so reizvoller ist es, eine Quelle zu untersuchen, die in ihren Wurzeln in die Zeit um 800 n. Chr. datiert. Diese entstammt einem Kontext, der aus islamisch-theologischer Perspektive, ebenso wie aus derjenigen der modernen wissenschaftlichen Rekonstruktion des Sufismus, bisher nicht der Tradition und dem Milieu der islamischen Mystik zugeordnet wurde. Dennoch spricht einiges dafür, das sogenannte *Umm al-Kitāb* der frühen häretischen Schia des Irak dem weiteren Kontext der Mystik zuzuweisen: aufgrund seiner Motivik und aufgrund der sozialen Struktur seiner Träger. Letztere war bereits Thema einer vorausgegangenen Untersu-

---

1 Dazu: Annemarie Schimmel, Mystische Dimensionen des Islam, München ²1992, 55f; Jürgen Wasim Frembgen, Die Reise zu Gott. Sufis und Derwische im Islam, München 2000; Martin Krause, Das Mönchtum in Ägypten, in: ders. (Hg.), Ägypten in spätantik-christlicher Zeit. Einführung in die koptische Kultur, Wiesbaden 1998, 149–174; Gawdat Gabra, Coptic Monasteries. Egypt's Monastic Art and Architecture, Kairo und New York 2002.

2 Schimmel, Mystische Dimensionen, 327.

chung,[3] sie wird einleitend kurz skizziert. Im Folgenden interessieren im *Umm al-Kitāb* schwerpunktmäßig die Symbolik und Metaphysik des Lichts und deren narrative Einbindung.

Hintergründe

Das *Umm al-Kitāb* war der zentrale sakrale Text einer Gruppe von Schiiten aus dem südlichen Mesopotamien aus der Zeit um 800 n. Chr., als die Schia selbst äußerst heterogene Züge aufwies und mit jedem Generationswechsel und sich ausdifferenzierenden Imamlinien neue Spaltungen einsetzten. Die großen Gruppen von Ismāʿīlīya und Imāmīya waren noch nicht etabliert, und es gab keinerlei theologische oder institutionelle Instanz, die die Entwicklung der religiösen Vorstellungen der Schiiten lenkte. Mesopotamien und die Region um das ehemalige sassanidische Seleukeia-Ktesiphon[4], in dessen Nähe erst um 750 n. Chr. die Gründung der abbasidischen Hauptstadt Bagdad erfolgte, war zudem ein religiös äußerst pluralistischer Raum. Heinz Halm, der das *Umm al-Kitāb* maßgeblich erschlossen hat, schildert dessen Bezüge zu den die heterodoxen Schiiten umgebenden z.T. häretisch-gnostischen Juden, nestorianischen Christen, Mandäern und Zoroastriern. Als kulturelle Strömung wird zudem der Hellenismus mit besonders seinem neuplatonischen Gedankengut greifbar. Die die Gruppe entscheidend prägende Religion war jedoch der Islam, in der Zeit um 800 n. Chr. mit einer sich etablierenden sunnitischen Theologie und in der Schia mit Vorstellungen vom abwesenden (*ġāʾib*) Imam, eng verknüpft mit eschatologisch-heilsgeschichtlichen Hoffnungen, sowie einsetzender weitreichender Verklärung der Heilsgestalten der Schia. In der Nähe der hier beleuchteten Region lagen nicht zufällig auch die schiitischen Heiligtümer Najaf und Kerbela.

In diesen Kreisen entstand das Werk, dessen Trägerschaft[5] als kleine Arkangemeinschaft erkennbar wird, die in der Hoffnung auf Erlösung Askese beispielsweise in Form von Sexualkontrolle betrieb. Vor allem die Männer – darauf weist zumindet das Genus der Terminologie, was nicht heißen muss, dass nicht auch Frauen eingeschlossen waren – bildeten eine geheime Gemeinschaft, die sicherlich nicht nach außen hin erkennbar war. Die als *ġulāt*, „Übertreiber", bezeichnete Gruppe wurde von der Orthodoxie des Vergehens des Polytheismus (*širk)* angeklagt. So pflegte man das geheime Wissen nach der Maßgabe der *taqīya*, der Geheimhaltung des eigenen Bekenntnisses, privat in kleinen Zirkeln, während man im Alltag

---

3 Bärbel Beinhauer-Köhler, Die Engelsturzmotive des „Umm al-Kitāb". Untersuchungen zur Trägerschaft eines synkretistischen Werkes der häretischen Schia, in: Christoph Auffarth, Loren Stuckenbruck (Hg.), The Fall of the Angels, Themes in biblical narrative 6, Leiden 2004, 161–175.

4 Maximilian Streck, Seleukia und Ktesiphon, in: Der Alte Orient 16, Leipzig 1917, 3f.

5 Beinhauer-Köhler, ebd.

seiner gewohnten Tätigkeit nachging. Halm findet für eine Vorläuferbewegung, die Viererschia (*kaisānīya*), einen Beleg für Anrufungen der Venus,[6] hinter denen sich eventuell ekstatische, der islamischen Mystik ähnliche Praktiken vermuten lassen, insofern als Gottesnamen in der Art eines *ḏikr* wiederholt rezitiert wurden. Für die Ġulāt selbst ist derartiges nicht konkret nachweisbar, da ihre religiöse Praxis weitestgehend unbekannt ist, Vergleichbares wäre jedoch denkbar. In die Nähe des Phänomens Mystik ist die Gruppe vor allem aus dem Grunde einzuordnen, als es sich um eine quietistische Form der Schia handelte, die sich keiner aktuellen Endzeithoffnung hingab, sondern dazu aufgerufen war, zunächst in ihrer „Bruderschaft" individuell einer spirituellen Erkenntnis (*'ilm,* gelegentlich auch *ma'rifa*) zuzustreben.[7] Zu ihren Grundpflichten gehörte ein Bekenntnis zur eigenen Gruppe, eine unbedingte Loyalität und der Gehorsam den Fortgeschrittenen (*'ālimān*) gegenüber, hier vermutlich aus politischen Notwendigkeiten geboren, aber im Effekt der Hierarchiebildung und Gruppenidentität sicherlich ebenfalls der Struktur von späteren Sufiorden ähnlich. In diesem Zusammenhang ist erwähnenswert, dass ein Schüler des berühmten frühen Mystikers al-Ḥasan al-Baṣrī (gest. 728), der für seinen Rückzug aus der Welt und eine asketisch orientierte Frömmigkeit bekannt ist, am Persischen Golf einen ersten Orden gegründet haben soll.[8] Dies bestärkt die hier vertretene These, dass bereits die soziale Form der Ġulāt in Verbindung zur islamischen Mystik und eventuell auch dem christlichen Mönchtum gestanden haben könnte. Vermutlich werden sich zudem alle diese frühen islamischen „Gottsucher" selbst weniger im Sinne unserer heutigen religionshistorischen Differenzierung entweder als Teil einer „konfessionellen Splittergruppe" oder einer mystischen Gemeinschaft wahrgenommen haben.

Erzählungen vom göttlichen Licht

Die zu untersuchende arabisch-persische Hauptquelle ist nach literargeschichtlicher Analyse Halms vielschichtig und weist Textfragmente aus unterschiedlichen Perioden auf, deren älteste auf die Zeit zwischen 750 und 800 n. Chr. zurückzudatieren sind. Das Werk entspricht von der Gattung her einer Apokalypse, es ist in einer Rahmenhandlung eine Vision, in der sich der 5. Imam Muḥammad al-Bāqir (gest. um 732 n. Chr.), der „Eröffner der Geheimnisse" *(bāqir al-'ilm),* seinem Anhänger Ǧābir al-Ǧu'fī aus Kufa[9] offenbart. Beschrieben wird die Entstehung des Kosmos, der, dem Neuplatonismus ähnlich, in zahlreichen Stufen vom „Erhabenen König", *al-malik-i ta'ālā*, ausgehend emaniert. Diese Entwicklung ist mit einem Verfallsprozess gleichzusetzen, bei dem ein Engelsturz eine entscheidende Rolle spielt. Der ent-

6 Heinz Halm, Die islamische Gnosis, Zürich und München 1982, 60f.
7 Beinhauer-Köhler, Die Engelsturzmotive, 173.
8 Schimmel, Mystische Dimensionen, 56.
9 Halm, Die islamische Gnosis, 96–112.

stehende Kosmos und die Erde sind somit, je weiter vom Ursprung entfernt desto mehr, zutiefst ambivalent – hier standen zoroastrische und manichäisch-gnostische Kosmogo- und Kosmologien Pate. Dem Menschen, der durch einen negativ konnotierten Leib und gottnahen Geist gekennzeichnet ist, obliegt es, sich für das ethisch Gute, ein Leben in Reinheit, absolute Loyalität mit der Gemeinschaft und zum verborgenen Imam zu entscheiden, um den individuellen Aufstieg zurück zum Erhabenen König zu ermöglichen.

Die sogenannte „Ǧābir-Apokalypse" ist in stilistischer Hinsicht ein Dokument, das zahlreiche narrative Motive des Volksislam aufweist. Auf den entstehenden Himmelssphären finden sich, ähnlich der bis heute lebendigen Ḥadīṯmotivik um Muḥammads Himmelsreise, diverse heilsgeschichtliche Gestalten, mythologische Tiere, gute und böse Engel, Geister, wundersame Bäume, Flüsse u.a. Was aber vor allem sämtliche Sphären durchzieht, ist das Licht, welches – hier passt unsere umgangssprachliche Wendung auch zum Stil der Quelle – in den „schillerndsten Farben" geschildert wird:

Mit Beginn der Schöpfung wird Gott als besondere Ausdifferenzierung des Lichts (*nūr*) gezeichnet:

> „Bevor es noch den Himmel, die Erde oder sonst ein Geschöpf gab, waren da fünf präexistente Lichter in fünf Farben gleich dem Regenbogen; aus deren Funkeln ging, gleich einer Sonne, Luft hervor, so daß, (so weit) auch Himmel und Erde ist, sublime Luft (vorhanden) war. Die fünf Lichter standen in dieser Luft, [82] und für alle Zeit erschien aus ihrer Mitte das Alleräußerste Licht (*nūr-e ghājet ol-ghājāt*) wie eine Lichtgestalt ... So also kreisen diese fünf Lichter auf dem göttlichen Thron zu Häupten der Gläubigen."[10]

Das göttliche Licht wird an dieser Stelle mittels des Terminus' *nūr-e ġāyet ol-ġāyāt*, „alleräußerstes Licht", zur Sprache gebracht. Es ist die Quelle des Lichts, das im Folgenden die Sphären durchzieht, welche die irdische Welt von Gott trennen. Das Licht geht von dem denkbar entferntesten Punkt aus, daher die Terminologie des „entfernten" Lichts. Dieses Licht ist gleichzeitig näher ausdifferenziert: Es spaltet sich bereits in der Region des Gottesthrons in fünf andere Lichter. In der weiteren Kosmologie wird erkennbar, dass diese für die fünf Heilsgestalten der Schia, Muḥammad, ʻAlī, Fāṭima, Ḥasan und Ḥusain, stehen. Im Zitat sind sie farbig, wie die verschiedenen Farben des Regenbogens, der Lichtkreis funkelt und strahlt aus wie die Sonne, und der Charakter dieses farbigen Lichtkreises wird darüber hinaus als immateriell und luftartig bezeichnet. Das Bild erinnert an eine Flamme mit ihrer Aureole und von dort ausgehenden Strahlen.

Im weiteren Verlauf der Apokalypse wird in parallelen Erzählsträngen die Entstehung des Kosmos geschildert. Immer noch in der älteren Textschicht erfahren die

10 In der arabisch-persischen Edition Wladimir Ivanow, Ummu'lkitāb, in: Der Islam 23 (1936), 1–136, hierzu 90f, in der dortigen Manuskriptzählung (im Folgenden MS) 82f; ins Deutsche übersetzt von Heinz Halm, Die islamische Gnosis, 145.

Leser, wie die Sphären des Himmels gestaltet sind. Die Sphären sind besonders durch Varianten von Licht gekennzeichnet:

> „Unter dieser Weißen Kuppel [d.i. die oberste Himmelssphäre, Anm. d. Verfn.] ist ein rubinroter Vorhang … Aus dem Alleräußersten Dīwān [d.i. ebenfalls die oberste Sphäre, Anm. d. Verfn.] waren 124 000 Lichter, vielfarbig wie der Regenbogen, in dem Weißen Meer erschienen, und (davon) sind 124 000 weiße Lichter in diesen Vorhang, der von rubinroter Farbe ist, herabgekommen; sagt Er doch: ‚Habt ihr denn nicht gesehen, wie Gott sieben Himmel geschaffen hat, in Schichten, und (wie er) den Mond als ein Licht und die Sonne [101] als eine Leuchte daran angebracht hat? Gott hat Euch aus der Erde entstehen lassen (wie) Pflanzen‘ (Koran 71,15–17), d.h. der Erhabene König hat in diesen Dīwānen so viele Lichter und Geister (*rūḥ*) [Anm. d. Verfn.] erschaffen und darin die Sonne und den Mond und die leuchtenden Bäume als Schmuck angebracht.
> Unter dieser Farbe ist ein weiterer Vorhang von der Farbe des Feuers … und wieder sind die 124 000 [102] Lichter aus dem rubinroten Vorhang in diesem Dīwān erschienen; sagt Er doch: ‚Licht über Licht. Gott führt seinem Lichte zu, wen er will. Und er prägt den Menschen die Gleichnisse‘ (Koran 24, 35). Dieses Licht hat man als feuerfarben geschildert. Das feuerfarbene Licht ist wie ein Ozean, bei dem der Glanz dieses Feuers (gleichsam) in einem weißen Kristall erglüht, der von Schönheit und Glanz sich weder beschreiben noch schildern läßt; und in diesem Dīwān sind so viele Lichter und Geister, daß es sich nicht schildern läßt.“[11]

Im Zitat werden zwei Sphären vorgestellt, wir erfahren, dass sich das Licht aus der höheren Sphäre immer in die niedere „ergießt“ bzw. in sie ausstrahlt: „… und wieder sind die 124 000 Lichter aus dem rubinroten Vorhang in diesem Dīwān erschienen“, heißt es z.B. von der feuerfarbenen Sphäre. Das Licht, das ganz oben noch fünffach gegliedert war, hat nun eine nahezu unendliche Anzahl von Ausdifferenzierungen erfahren, in die „124 000 Lichter“, in „so viele Lichter und Geister, dass es sich nicht schildern lässt“; man assoziiert unwillkürlich ganze Strahlenbündel oder ein Funkeln wie von Lichtreflexen, verstärkt durch die Erwähnung eines weißen Kristalls. Zudem werden Bilder eines unbegrenzten Lichtscheins erzeugt: Das feuerfarbene Licht erstreckt sich wie ein Ozean.

Dieses Bild des aus einer machtvollen Quelle gespeisten vielfältigen und gewaltig und weit ausstrahlenden Lichts, das sich in einer ersten Schilderung quasi in einem natürlichen Prozess in die unteren Sphären fortpflanzt, wird an anderer Stelle in einer Variante der Kosmogonie mit dem aktiven Schöpfungsvorgang verbunden:

> „Da ließ der Erhabene König einen Ruf nach rechts und einen Ruf nach links erschallen. Die beiden Rufe verwandelten sich in Strahlen, und die beiden

11 Ivanow, Ummu'kitāb, 86f; MS, 99–102; Halm, Die islamische Gnosis, 150f.

> Strahlen bestanden ganz aus Geistern, so vielen, daß sie in keiner Zahl noch Ziffer Platz gefunden hätten.“[12]

Aus dieser Schilderung lässt sich der weitere Verlauf des Schöpfungsprozesses erahnen. Die Lichter und Strahlen gewinnen zunehmend Materialität und büßen ihren lichten Charakter ein. Aus den Lichtern der ersten beiden Rufe wird u.a. ‘Azāzi’īl, der Demiurg und „gefallene“ Engel, der von Stufe zu Stufe in Richtung irdisches Dasein verstoßen wird und neue, ihm treue Anhängerschaften hervorbringt. Auf der Erde dann teilt sich die Menschheit in zwei Gattungen, die sich im Grad ihrer Lichtferne unterscheiden: die „Schatten“ (*aẓilla*), durch das Böse geprägte Gottferne und wie ‘Azāzi’īl Widersetzliche gegen Allah, und die „Schemen“ (*ašbāḥ*), potenziell gute Menschen, die sich um den Aufstieg zum göttlichen Licht bemühen.[13]

Nun kommt, in einer jüngeren Textschicht, die Soteriologie zum Tragen, die ihrerseits mit der Lichtsymbolik in Verbindung steht: Im Prozess der Erkenntnis, hier meist *‘ilm*, kommen in der Art einer „Inspiration“ „lichte“ Geistwesen, die das kosmische Drama von Beginn an mit prägen, zum Suchenden. Sie entstammen offensichtlich den anfänglich geschilderten Sphären und greifen nun nacheinander, dem Schöpfungsvorgang entgegengesetzt, in den Erkenntnisprozess ein: der „leuchtende Geist“, *rūḥ-e rūšanī*, aus dem mondfarbenen Vorhang, bis hin zum „größten Geist“, *rūh ol-akbar ol-kullī*, aus der weißen Kuppel. Dabei vollzieht sich die Erleuchtung:

> „Körper und Leib werden durch das Licht der Göttlichkeit hell und licht, d.h. durch die göttliche Epiphanie (*ẓohūr-e ilāhī*). Sagt Gott doch (Koran 39,22): ‚Ist denn einer, dem Gott die Brust für den Islam geweitet hat, so daß er [246] jetzt von seinem Herrn erleuchtet ist …‘.“[14]

Die erleuchteten Gnostiker werden im Rahmen dieses Konzepts mit dem Terminus *‘ālimān-e nūrānī*, „leuchtende Wissende“, tituliert.[15]

Die Lichtmetaphysik des *Umm al-Kitāb* im Kontext

Welches sind nun die Quellen dieser Lichtmetaphysik, die sich über Kosmogonie, Kosmologie und Soteriologie erstreckt? Zunächst einmal speist sich die häretisch-schiitische Variante sicherlich aus den Text durchziehenden koranischen Vorbildern: Mit dem bekannten und stark rezipierten Bild der schimmernden Lampe in der Nische aus Sure 24 ist ein Aspekt der extremschiitischen Vorstellungen vom göttlichen Licht vorgezeichnet. Mit dem kosmologischen Modell der gestaffelten Himmelssphären in Sure 71 übernimmt der Islam das verbreitete spätantike Weltbild mit neuplatonischen Anklängen, und auch bei den Ġulāt findet es sich wieder. Im Be-

12 Ivanow, Ummu’lkitāb, 82; MS, 122; Halm, Die islamische Gnosis, 156.
13 Ivanow, Ummu’lkitāb, 63; MS, 208; Halm, Die islamische Gnosis, 183.
14 Ivanow, Ummu’lkitāb, 56; MS, 245f; Halm, Die islamische Gnosis, 193.
15 Ivanow, Ummu’lkitāb, 57; MS, 239; Halm, Die islamische Gnosis, 191.

reich des Ḥadīṯ entstanden, schon früh belegt, etwa zeitgleich mit dem *Umm al-Kitāb*, narrative Motive, die von Heilsgestalten ein Licht ausgehen lassen, so in der *Sīra* das Licht, das vom Mutterleib ausstrahlt, als Āmina mit Muḥammad schwanger war.[16] Wir können also davon ausgehen, dass auch die häretischen Schiiten Mesopotamiens das offenbar beliebte Lichtmotiv aufgriffen, zumal auch Manichäer und Zoroastrier, die in der Region bis in die Abbasidenzeit hinein ansässig waren, diese Motivik in ihren strukturell analogen Kosmologien, assoziiert mit dem ethisch Guten, kannten.

Doch hier interessiert besonders die Möglichkeit, dass auch christliche und speziell mystische Vorbilder einflussgebend gewesen sein oder die christlichen Mystiker mit den frühen Schiiten einen gemeinsamen kulturellen Kontext gebildet haben könnten. Für die christliche Mystik und deren Rezeption des Lichts war sicherlich ihrerseits zunächst die Bibel prägend, man denke an das Johannesevangelium oder die auch in der Ikonentradition vielfach aufgegriffene Verklärungsgeschichte (Mt 17,2). Christliche Mystiker der Ostkirche schildern verschiedentlich ihre mystische Erfahrung als eine des göttlichen Lichts, so Symeon der Neue Theologe (949–1022) in Kleinasien:[17]

> „In meiner Zelle sitze ich bei Nacht, bei Tag. Die Liebe ist zugegen, auch wenn sie sich nicht zeigt, und man sie nicht erkennt. Und wenn sie außer allen Kreaturen ist und wenn sie wiederum in allen ist, sie ist ein Feuer, ein Glanz, wird Lichtnebel, wird zur Sonne gar. Als Feuer spendet sie der Seele Wärme, zündet an mein Herz, facht es zur Sehnsucht und zur Liebe seines Bildners an. Und bin ich hinlänglich entflammt, daß meine Seele brennt, umgibt sie gänzlich mich mit Lichtesstrahl, senkt Strahlenbündel mir in die Seele, und da sie meinen Geist erleuchtet und ihm Klarheit gibt, macht sie ihn fähig, Tiefen zu betrachten. Und dieses wars was eben ich des Leuchtens Blüte nannte. Da ich den Glanz erblickte, hat unglaublicher Jubel mich erfüllt."

Auch hier ist die Lichterfahrung eine äußerst vielfältige, die in vielen Details – Leuchten, Glanz, Lichtstrahl, Strahlenbündel – Parallelen zu den Lichtbeschreibungen des *Umm al-Kitāb* aufweist. Unterschiede liegen natürlich in den Eigenheiten der Gattungen begründet, hier die Schilderung einer mystischen Vision, dort die Schilderung einer Kosmologie, allerdings ebenfalls basierend auf einer Erzählung einer Vision, so der Rahmentext um den Imam al-Bāqir. Ein deutlicher Unterschied, und derjenige, der das *Umm al-Kitāb* sicher nur in den weiteren Kontext der Mystik einzuordnen lässt, ist der Faktor der Liebe, der für die christlichen Mystiker beson-

---

16 Ibn Hišām, as-Sīra an-nabawīya, hg. v. Walīd ibn Salāma, Ḫālid ibn Muḥammad ibn ʻUṯmān, 4 Teile in 2 Bd., Kairo 2001, hierzu I/1, 96; in Übersetzung Gernot Rotter, Ibn Isḥâq. Das Leben des Propheten, Stuttgart 1986, 28.

17 Ernst Benz, Die Vision. Erfahrungsformen und Bilderwelt, Stuttgart 1965, 330.

ders bedeutsam ist. Für die Trägerschaft des *Umm al-Kitāb* ist es dagegen die erlösungsrelevante Erkenntnis, die im Mittelpunkt steht.

In späterer Zeit wurden in der islamischen Mystik des Mittleren Ostens ganze Lichtmetaphysiken entworfen. Al-Ġazzālī (gest. 1111) griff in einer seiner prominentesten Schriften *Miškāt al-anwār* ebenfalls das koranische „Licht in der Nische" auf. Der Iraner al-Suhrawardī (gest. 1191) entwarf eine neuplatonisch-philosophisch orientierte „Lichtmetaphysik", ein Konzept einer göttlichen Lichtquelle, die das ganze Universum durchstrahlt, jedoch mit Abstand zum Ausgangspunkt immer schwächer wird. Dieses Konzept lässt sich in dieser Region verfolgen bis hin in die Neureligion der Bahā'ī, die im 19. Jahrhundert im Iran entstand und besonders ihren göttlichen Heilsbringern wie Bahā'ullāh („Das Leuchten Gottes"), mit sich abschwächender Intensität bei sekundären Heilsgestalten, göttliche Lichtanteile zuspricht.[18]

Schlussfolgerungen

Die auffällige Lichtsymbolik und -metaphysik des *Umm al-Kitāb* lässt annehmen, dass es neben diversen religiösen Traditionen unterschiedlicher Glaubensgemeinschaften auch aus der christlichen Mystik inspiriert gewesen sein könnte, die – auch wenn die konkreten Rezeptionsstränge nur erahnt werden können – im irakisch-iranischen Raum nicht zuletzt auf die islamische Mystik wirkte. Dass in Rezeptionsvorgängen um das *Umm al-Kitāb* die Mystik von Christen und Muslimen eine Rolle spielen könnte, ist ein neuer Gedanke, der bezüglich der inhaltlichen Parallelen von mystischer Lichterfahrung im orientalischen Christentum und im *Umm al-Kitāb* zusätzlich zu dieser ersten Skizze näher zu verfolgen wäre.

Die Annahme, dass die Trägerschaft des *Umm al-Kitāb* sozialhistorisch ein Verbindungsglied zwischen christlichen Mönchsorden des Orients und der später gängigen Ṭarīqa-Bildung islamischer Sufiorden darstellen würde, verstärkt diesen Gedanken. Und schließlich lebten die Träger des Werkes im gleichen geographischen Raum, in dem sich später islamische Beispiele für eine explizit der Mystik zuzuordnende Lichtmetaphysik finden. Es handelt sich ferner um den gleichen kulturellen und zeitliche Kontext, in welchem im Rahmen der Verehrung der schiitischen Imame eine volkstümliche narrative Tradition von Lichtwundern eine Blütezeit erlebte. Annemarie Schimmel belegt, dass die Texte Suhrawardīs in späterer Zeit besonders von Schiiten, die über die Vorstellungen über die Imame für Lichtmotive offen waren, rezipiert wurden. All dies spricht dafür, das *Umm al-Kitāb* als Teil des historischen Kontexts der Mystik in neuem Licht zu sehen.

18 Bärbel Beinhauer-Köhler, Züge der Hagiographie der Bahā'ī, ZRW 10 (2002), 3–17.

Metaphysics of light in the gnostic-islamic *Umm al-Kitāb* as a form of mystic

Summary

1. "Mystic" is a complex phenomenon. In its nucleus it is an experience of "Teilhabe", participating in the transcendent. One medium of mystical experience is language with its different signs, symbols, metaphors and narrative motifs. In the following context the symbol of light plays a prominent role.

The social patterns of mystic are complex too. There might be asceticism or peripatetic wanderers or social groups like orders that lead to mystical experience. In Islam Sufi-orders are a late phenomenon, generally speaking they occur around c. 1100. In this context it seems to be an interesting perspective to view a source of the heretical Shia, the *Umm al-Kitāb* of the so called Ġulāt of the 8th century, in the light of mystic and mystical contexts between Christianity and Islam.

2. The source developed in southern Mesopotamia at the beginning of the Abbasid period in a multi-religious milieu. Its protagonists came from the heretical Shia in a time before the today known Shii branches came to life. In the region around the former capital Seleuceia-Ktesiphon in early Islamic times still lived Mandaens, Zoroastrians, heretical-gnostical Jews, Nestorianic Christians, as well as hellenistic ideas with neoplatonic elements were quite popular. The major influence towards our group was the establishing Shia with its holy cities of Najaf and Kerbela'.

We know that the members of the group followed the concept of *taqīya* as they were accused by the orthodox majority of *širk*. They organized themselves as a secret brotherhood following strict rules of solidarity towards their imam or illuminated chiefs (*'ālimān*) and tried to realise bodily and sexual purity as steps to salvation. Probably they themselves didn't view their group either in the light of "mystics" or as "Shii sect". But from our perspective it seems to be interesting to analyse their beliefs and group-structure in the light of Muslim and Christian mystical concepts which would bring new light on their history that is normally viewed only in parameters of Shiism.

3. The *Umm al-kitāb* dates back to the time between c. 750 and 800. It is an apocalyptic vision of a Ǧābir al-Ǧu'fī from Kufa seeing the 5th Imam Muḥammad al-Bāqir who reveals cosmogonical and cosmological secrets: The universe emanates in a complicated process in several steps from *al-malik-i ta'ālā*. In this process also the evil element comes into existence and the human character is as a product of this process to be characterised as deeply ambivalent. Humans try to cultivate their intellect and moral potentials to find back to the "sublime king".

The narrative elements of the text are connected with folk-literature and living traditions of the Orient. It shows a colourful and picturesque language. The central motifs of the divine light are very rich and elaborated: The light is described as preexistant and essence of God, it is sublime and differs in five parts, identical with Muḥammad, 'Alī, Fāṭima, Ḥasan and Ḥusain.

When the cosmic spheres come into existence, the colours occour: The spheres are white, red, violette, green etc. Every sphere is a universe of its own, shining and shimmering by hundreds of thousands rays of light.

On earth the light is pale, as far away from its ultimate source. There are two groups of beings: The shadows (*aẓilla*) and the scemes (*ašbāḥ*), the former utterly against God and following its counterpart, the latter ambivalent and able to salvation. This is possible, if one cultivates its soul and the good entities (*arwāḥ*) from the upper spheres support the searcher towards *ma'rifa* or '*ilm*.

4. Searching for influences to this motifs, the first idea is Sura 24, *an-nūr*, "the light": God is characterised as a shimmering lamp in a niche. The Qur'an knows also the cosmic concept of celestial spheres. As well as the Sunna, e.g. in the Sīra, the prophet's biography tells about a light shining from Mekka to Medina when his mother was pregnant. Other oriental religions knew light-motifs as well, like the Manichaens and Zoroastrians, associating the light with the good side of the universe and the good God in an ethical sense.

It is an interesting question if there might have been Christian and especially mystical influences as well. My only source is the later Simeon the New Theologian (949–1022) from Turkey with his famous visions of light. The light he describes also differs in its shape and intensity like the many variants in the Shii source. But there is also a big difference: Simeon describes an experience and an analogy of light and feelings of love. For the Mesopotamian heretical Shiites love plays no prominent role in their pattern of salvation.

5. Apart from that, the parallels of the metaphors and narrative motifs of light between this text and examples of mystic in oriental cultures are striking. It seems to be worthwile to analyse a broader context of Christian and Islamic mystics as a possible influence towards the early heretical Shia, moreover as later Muslim mystics show very similar metaphysical concepts of light like al-Suhrawardī or work on the idea of God as a lamp (*miškāt al-anwār*) like al-Ġazzālī while especially Imāmī Shiites receipt mystical ideas of light too and there is an ongoing exchange between Shia and mystics. The fact that the later Sufi-orders would have a predecessor in our Shiite group and a possible background in the Christian monastic tradition would support this thesis.

Reflecting Divine Light: *al-Khidr* as an Embodiment of God's Mercy (*raḥma*)

Irfan A. Omar

Bernard McGinn, who wrote extensively on aspects of Christian mysticism acknowledged that to define mysticism is a problematic task. Mysticism is a controversial dimension of religious practice and thus may be seen through the lens of a variety of categories or frameworks rather than a single one. Thus he notes three general ways of viewing mysticism. Firstly, as part of religion; secondly, as a way of life; and, thirdly, as a process of communicating the inner experience of the presence of the divine.[1] The subject of this essay may be located primarily in Islamic mystical thought, or more appropriately in Sufi writings. In as much as al-Khidr (Khidr) lies within the realm of Sufism, it would be apt to say that he has been received in all the three different ways within the Islamicate tradition.[2] Khidr has been viewed as one who is at once connected to the Quranic text, the exegesis, the hadith (the prophetic tradition), the *Qiṣaṣ al-anbiyā'* (stories of prophets), massive Sufi literature, as well as various folk traditions, many of which remain fluid and ever changing. The Khidr phenomenon and its associated traditions have taken up such a huge space within the Islamicate traditions and cultures that it is impossible to do justice to this topic in such a short essay. Therefore, here I will primarily focus on the religious/mystical understanding of Khidr's role and how it may be connected with the symbolism of "light" and spiritual or inward "illumination" which many Sufis claim to have received through him.[3]

---

1 Bernard McGinn, The Foundations of Mysticism: The Presence of God: A History of Western Christian Mysticism, Vol. 1, New York 1991, xvff.

2 Islamicate is a comprehensive term that embraces the variety and richness of Islam and Muslim civilizations generated since the rise of Muslim empires in the eight century. The term was first introduced by the noted scholar of Islam, Professor Marshall Hodgson. He viewed it as something referring not only to the religion of Islam but also and perhaps more importantly "...to the social and cultural complex historically associated with Islam and the Muslims, both among Muslims themselves and even when found among non-Muslims." Marshall G.S. Hodgson, The Venture of Islam: Conscience and History in World Civilization, Vol. 1, Chicago 1974, 59.

3 This is not to be equated with illumination of the mind alone but rather with a kind of spiritual realization that is more inclusive of one's totality of being. In religious discourse this occurs as a result of piety on the part of the seeker and imparting of grace on the part of God.

I. *Khidr*: Origins and Meanings

Khidr is the legendary figure mentioned in the Qur'an in *Surat al-Kahf* (18:60–82). These verses primarily deal with an allegorical story about Moses – who is recognized as an influential and important prophet in the Qur'an – and a mysterious spiritual person, later identified with Khidr. The main thrust of the Quranic story is that the scope of knowledge is so vast that no one besides God may ever be able to acquire even a minute portion of it. There are individuals to whom God has given some of this knowledge and prophets such as Moses, Jesus and Muhammad are certainly considered among these individuals. However, God also gives from his knowledge to those who have traversed the spiritual path (*ṭarīqah*) – these are the so-called "friends of God" (*awliyā*, sing. *walī*) or the saints, who are given *ma'ārifah* (knowledge of God or of the spiritual, hence "hidden" world, *al-'ālam al-ghayb*). They have received this knowledge because of their exceptional rigor and piety and because God grants knowledge and wisdom "to whomever He will."[4] One such person is Khidr who is known in the Qur'an only as "one of Our [i.e. God's] servants – a man to whom We had granted Our Mercy and whom We had given knowledge of Our own."[5] The supreme symbolism of the Moses-Khidr story is that divine knowledge may be received in the form of "law" or revelation (as Moses did) or as mystical, intuitive knowledge (as was given to Khidr). These two forms of knowledge are complementary and neither is above the other; hence Moses' journey in search of this servant of God (Khidr) so he can learn something in addition to the knowledge he already received from God as a prophet.[6]

The name "al-Khidr" is given to him by the early interpreters of the Qur'an (*mufassirūn*) who thought of him as a person who by his very presence revives, regenerates, and makes things green, hence the Arabic, al-Khidr, which means the "Green One". Although this quality of "greening" or making things come "alive" remains at the center of his identity, in different parts of the Islamic world, Khidr is also known as Khwajah Khizir, Pir Badar, Raja Kidar, Abul Abbas, and Hang Tuah which relate to Khidr's multiple roles as a guide, teacher, and even as a "savior" of sort and who is venerated widely as a saint.[7] From the very beginning Khidr was seen as someone who could not be contained within a single tradition or be confined to a single region in terms of his popular manifestations. In the flowering of the

---

4 Qur'an 2:269a, translation by M.A.S. Abdel Haleem, The Qur'an: A new translation, Oxford 2004, 31.

5 Qur'an 18:65, ibid., 187.

6 Irfan A. Omar, "Khiḍr in the Islamic Tradition", The Muslim World 83 (1993), 279–94. For a succinct account of Moses' meeting with Khidr and their interaction see Anthony H. Johns, "Moses in the Qur'an: Finite and Infinite Dimensions of Prophecy," in: Robert B. Crotty (ed.), The Charles Strong Lectures 1972–1984, Leiden 1987.

7 Some of these names are attempts to link Khidr with a particular era and place; others such as "Khwajah," "Pir," and "Raja" are honorific titles that show an elevated status in spiritual and mythical receptions of Khidr.

Islamic civilization he quite literally became part of many cultures and traditions simultaneously. After all, he is by profession a wanderer – always on the move – and much like Elijah of the Biblical tradition, seeking to help those in distress and those in need of advice. Khidr is said to appear in "green" or even in a "white" cloak. In *Saḥīḥ al-Bukhārī* we find a report of the Prophet: "He was named al-Khiḍr because he sat upon barren land and when he did, it became green with vegetation."[8] The greening of a patch of barren land (*farwa*) referred to by several early Muslim scholars implies making the land fertile and in its allegorical sense may also mean rejuvenation of the human spirit, something which Khidr came to be identified with in later traditions. In the present context one might ask, "what nationality does Khidr belong to?" or "what is his ethnic identity?" and "where does he live?," "does he still exist," and so on. However, these are questions that cannot be dealt with in any literal sense, because Khidr belongs to that category of Islamic/religious literature which is known as the "imaginal" or that which pertains to the world of images (*mundus imaginalis*).[9] Of course, these questions would be considered absurd in the realm of rational assessments of the story of Khidr where it may be viewed as a mere myth. It is futile to seek verification of such stories; however asking such questions may help us understand the various dimensions of the Khidr tradition which has played a major role in Muslim social, cultural, and spiritual life for many centuries. In a postmodern understanding, Khidr perhaps has no particular nationality or ethnicity; he is neither old nor young. We can even say that he continues to "exist" – even as irrational as it may sound – because countless people claim to have "known" him and have had some form of interaction with him.

Nevertheless, early *tafsīr* literature (exegesis) provides a variety of answers to the kinds of questions raised above. An enormous wealth of details pertaining to his name, genealogy, appearances, origins and status is found there. For example, al-Baghdadi (d. 1324) in his work *Tafsīr al-khāzin* reports that Khidr's real name was "Baliya bin Malkan," while al-Nawawi refers to him as "Abul Abbas" which he says was his nick name.[10] According to Tha'labi (d. 1036), he lives on an island from

8 See Ṣaḥīḥ al-Bukhārī, hadith no: IV.23.614. Ṣaḥīḥ al-Bukhārī, named after its compiler, is one of the most authoritative hadith collections; Muslims regard it as one of the foremost textual resources in interpreting the Qur'an.

9 In Sufi cosmology there is a so-called "world of images" (*'ālam al-amthāl*) which lies in between (as the *isthmus*, or *barzakh*) the other two spheres of "existence" as it were, the "world of spirits" (*'ālam al-rūḥ*) and the "world of matter" (*'ālam al-khalq*). The world of images plays an important role in connecting the other two in that it allows ordinary yet pious human beings to possess the ability (by the leave of God) to perform or witness miraculous things. Those who are advanced in their journey on the path to God (*ṭarīqah*), God may enable them to have such powers. Stories of meeting with Khidr and other "miraculous acts" are generally explained to have been taking place in the imaginal realm – or the world of images. This may be compared to "dream imagery." An example of one such claim is made by Ibn 'Arabi, who experienced several miraculous appearances of Khidr.

10 See 'Ala al-din al-Baghdadi, Tafsīr al-khāzin: Lubāb al ta'wīl fī ma'an al-tanzīl, Beirut n.d., 205; Ahmad Ibn Hajar al-Asqalani, Al-Zahr al-Nadīr fī nabā al-Khaḍir, Beirut 1988, 25.

which he protects sailors; he is the guardian of the sea, etc.[11] Others have suggested places such as the Nile delta and other such places where two bodies of water converge. Other places where Khidr is discussed extensively are the historical sources, where various narratives of the story are found. These are Muhammad Jarir al-Tabari's *al-Tarīkh*; the hagiographical literature known as the *Qiṣaṣ al-anbiyā'*; Sufi literature and the biographies of Sufis which are often filled with reports of their meeting with Khidr; and, finally in a variety of folk literature in various languages. As far as accounts of meeting with Khidr are concerned, we have numerous reports by Sufis, scholars, and even non-Muslims who have come in contact with the Islamicate cultures. Carl Jung, the influential psychiatrist and author, wrote in his autobiography that he dreamt of Khidr several times and then goes on to elaborate the symbolism of these dream images connecting them to other events in his life. Jung in fact made significant use of the figure of Khidr in his writings and identified him as one of the archetypes.[12] He also used the Khidr-Moses parable to teach his patients the "importance of accepting paradoxes."[13] There are countless others throughout Muslim history who consider Khidr to be "alive" and stories of him appearing to people are given as evidence of such claims. Among the many personal accounts of meetings with Khidr, Muhyiddin Ibn 'Arabi (d. 1240), the famous Spanish Sufi may have left one of the most intricate reports concerning his meeting the mysterious saint. Ibn 'Arabi writes that while he was on the port of Tunis, Khidr appeared to him as if coming from over the water but he was not wet, and then he proceeded towards a distant light house reaching it while taking only a few steps.[14] Ibn 'Arabi also wrote of praying with Khidr.[15]

Generally, in Islamic religious literature, Khidr is seen as *walī*, (saint) as well as a *nabī* (prophet), although there is a considerable difference of opinion about this in official Islam. Many scholars and exegetes throughout Muslim history regarded Khidr as prophet since he seemed to fulfill the criteria for being one; that is, he has received knowledge from God and has been referred to as a "mercy" from God. Others questioned whether the modality of knowledge and its purpose can be considered equivalent to that given to prophet Moses since Moses was also a bearer of divine law (*rasūl*).[16] These scholars would be more comfortable accepting Khidr as

---

11 Abu Ishaq Ahmad al-Tha'labi, Qiṣaṣ al-anbiyā' al-musammā 'Arā'is al-majālis, Beirut n.d., 197.

12 Carl Gustav Jung, Four Archetypes: Mother, Rebirth, Spirit, Trickster, translation by R.F.C. Hull, London 2003.

13 Mohammed Shallan, Some Parallels between Sufi Practices and the Path of Individuation, in: J. Marvin Spiegelman, et. al. (eds.) Sufism, Islam and Jungian Psychology, Scottsdale/AZ 1991, 91.

14 Muhyiddin Ibn 'Arabi, Al-Futūḥāt al-makkiyah, Cairo 1911; rep. Beirut n.d., Vol. 1, 86.

15 Peter L. Wilson, The Green Man: The Trickster Figure in Sufism, Gnosis, Spring 1991, 23.

16 See Omar, Khiḍr in the Islamic Tradition, 284–86. While the debate over whether Khidr was a prophet or not continued for centuries, Reynold A. Nicholson in his Studies in Islamic Mysticism (Cambridge: 1921) brought an additional nuance to bear on this discussion. He argued that perhaps the kind of prophecy Khidr held was that of "saintship" or (*nubuwwatu'l wilāya*)

an important saint but not as a prophet.[17] Contemporary orthodox religious understandings of Khidr seldom venture beyond the literal interpretation of the verses in question. In contrast, the mystical and popular views of Khidr are often embellished by allegorical and metaphorical interpretations. One might say the former is primarily concerned with an "Islamic" view of Khidr, while the latter would most certainly fall under the purview of the Islamicate tradition. Therefore, when it is noted that Khidr, from the start seemed larger than life figure who could not be contained within one religious tradition, it also alludes to the fact that before assuming an Islamicate persona, some aspects of the character which embodies Khidr existed in different forms and was known by different names. Similarly as a result of Islam's influence, other pre-Islamic legends adopted variations of his name substituting it with existing figures in those legends. Thus as the Khidr's Quranic narrative Islamizes some pre-Islamic ideas; these same ideas were recycled in older legends adding newer elements to them. For example, in some Indian legends the patron of sailors is known as "Khwajah Khizr," even though these legends have existed long before Islam came onto the scene. There the name, "Khwaja Khizr," appears to be a later substitution for an earlier figure that fulfilled the role of a guide and protector deity for the sailors of that region.[18]

The earliest scholarly discussions of Khidr trace the Quranic narrative to three sources: the Alexandar romance, the epic of Gligamesh, and the story of the wandering Elijah.

Since becoming part of the Islamicate tradition, Khidr legend has assumed numerous manifestations and as a result continues to grow. The story of Khidr has played a particularly important role in folklore and popular mysticism as they developed in several Muslim societies. As a mystical figure, Khidr has had an enormous impact on various dimensions of Sufi thought and practice. Among some prominent Sufis he is regarded as the spiritual teacher who continues to guide those who do not have an earthly teacher.[19] As noted above, my focus in this paper is on religious and

---

whereas that of Moses' status as a prophet and a lawgiver was that of "institution" (*nubuwwatu'l tashrī'*).

17 Some modern Qur'an interpreters have a more radical reassessment of the Quranic verse that is regarded as referring to Khidr. There is however, a general consensus amongst most classical scholars regarding the verse in question (18:65: "... one of Our [i.e. God's] servants – a man to whom We had granted Our Mercy...") that the "servant" mentioned is the same person later identified in the hadith as Khidr. These modern writers, most notably, Sayyid Qutb, argue that the "servant" mentioned in 18:65 should not be identified as Khidr since there is no Quranic evidence. See Sayyid Qutb, English translation by Adil Salahi, In the Shade of the Qur'an, Fi Ẓilāl al-Qur'an, Vol. 11, London 2007.

18 Ananda K. Coomaraswamy, Khwājā Khaḍir and the Fountain of Life in the Tradition of Persian and Mughal Art, in: Ars Islamica 1 (1994), 173; cf. Irfan A. Omar The Symbol of Immortality: Some Popular Images of Khiḍr in the Orient, in: Islamic Culture 74 (2000), 33–51.

19 The central Asian Sufism contains a group known as Uwaysis, named after a contemporary of Prophet Muhammad who converted to Islam without ever meeting him thus establishing a model of following a teacher who is distant or invisible yet present and available to the followers. Uwaysis regard Khidr as their guide as a "hidden" master. Annemarie Schimmel, And Mu-

mystical understandings of the symbolism represented by Khidr. I will not address the role Khidr plays in popular piety and mythic folklore. Here I am particularly interested in one consideration of Khidr's story, namely, "how does Khidr's 'presence' constitute an act of mercy on the part of God?" and, following this lead I ask, "what does this presence and his being a symbol of divine compassion say about the characteristics endowed within the figure of Khidr with respect to the motif of light and spiritual illumination?"

II. *Khidr*: A Symbol of Mercy from God

Khidr symbolizes divine mercy (*raḥma*) here on earth which is dispensed through his presence and actions. The Qur'an describes Khidr as one of God's special servants to whom God had given both his mercy and his knowledge.[20] Since Khidr is seen as a "repository" of divine knowledge on earth, he is seen as playing a role of a mediator between God and human beings who are on the path and seek divine proximity (*qurb*). However, Khidr is a recipient of God's mercy in the same breath as he is a recipient of God's knowledge; here mercy and knowledge are synonymous. Furthermore, both God's mercy and his knowledge are meant for all servants of God, in essence for all of creation. Khidr here becomes part of a chain through which *raḥma* of God reaches a worshipper and a seeker of *qurb*.[21] The notion of *raḥma* appears many times in the Qur'an. For example, Q. 43:32 speaks of God's prophets as "... the ones who share out ... Lord's grace" as against the wealthy and powerful who might be more inclined to misuse their power to maintain their wealth. Thus the role of the prophets is deemed to be that of being "protectors" of the masses and in full accordance with and to realize God's will on earth. The prophets dispense mercy because God has granted them certain powers, charisma, resources and so on to do so. Thus, in Islamic worldview all prophets and messengers are viewed as symbols of God's mercy; they are guides to the path to God; they are also known to announce warning of the impending wrath of God for those who cause *fitna* (anarchy and social unrest). Being the bearers of the knowledge of and from God, they represent God's concern for the creation. God is most often invoked as "most merciful" (*Al-Rahmān*) and "most compassionate" (*Al-Rahīm*). The Quranic usage of the term *raḥma* referring to Khidr's knowledge, as granted by God, resonates with other appearances of that term in the Qur'an. Besides Q. 43:32 it may be noted that in Q. 21:107, the Qur'an, while referring to Prophet Muhammad says, "It was only as a mercy that We sent you [Prophet] to all people" (*raḥmat al-l'il*

---

hammad is His Messenger: The Veneration of the Prophet in Islamic Piety, Chapel Hill 1985, 22.

20 Paraphrasing Q. 18:65.

21 Of course, this also raises a number of theological questions as to the viability of the notion of a mediator in orthodox Islam which would fall outside of the scope of the present study.

'ālamīn).[22] Here again the usage of the term *raḥma* denotes the sending of prophets as "mercy" from God. Quranic verse 18:65b thus points to the fact that this symbol of mercy, i.e. Khidr, is as such because he is given certain knowledge, knowledge from God. These two ideas converge in this verse enabling one to deduce that Khidr has an elevated status in the Qur'an, that of being a prophet who, by virtue of being endowed with divine knowledge, is a representative of the mercy of God. [23] Furthermore, to possess divine knowledge is a quality that is often also claimed by saints (*awliyā*). Khidr is thus both a prophet and a saint as has been identified by numerous persons who have "encountered" Khidr as well as scholars.

I have argued that Khidr is an embodiment of God's mercy because of the knowledge he has been given by God. This is how he is viewed in terms of his role and function in Muslim cultures as well as depicted by the scholars and commentators of the Qur'an. This allows one to speak about the probability of an intimate link between Khidr's knowledge and his charism, i.e. between his divine mandate and his ability to perform "miraculous" and "magical" acts of healing for the sick and to provide guidance for those who have lost their way. It is these acts or the believability of Khidr's ability to perform such acts which have transformed him into a popular figure among the masses and made him a sought out teacher by the Sufis and the like. Here I am also suggesting that Khidr's role as a depository of divine knowledge makes him a person who reflects divine light (*al-nūr*) in the metaphoric sense of light as the source of spiritual countenance (*jalāl* or *tajallī*). Such interpretation of Khidr is primarily to be found in Sufism, the mystical dimension of Islam, where Khidr lends himself to a host of allegorical roles. Below I will address some of the textual and historical connections that may be considered in support of this thesis.

III. Gnosis as Light

Khidr is someone who is said to possess gnosis, the one on whom God had bestowed mercy and given knowledge from God (Q. 18:65). Gnosis is defined in the following words. "If gnosis were to take visible shape, all who looked thereon would die at the sight of its beauty and loveliness and goodness and grace, and every brightness would become dark beside the splendour thereof."[24] This idea of distinguishing between worldly brightness and divine splendor makes it plain that there is a kind of illumination of the soul which happens as a result of becoming a recipient of divine knowledge. This notion of "inward illumination" is found in many religious traditions from Indic to Western religions. Islamic mystical discourse is no exception and one can find the term in many Muslim mystical accounts from early in the ninth century. Illumination (*kashf* or unveiling) of the mysteries of *'ālam al-ghayb* has

22 Translation by Abdel Haleem, The Qur'an: A new translation, 317, 208.
23 For a general treatment of this issue, see Omar, Khiḍr in the Islamic Tradition, 279–291.
24 An unnamed mystic quoted in Reynold A. Nicholson, The Mystics of Islam, London 1989, 7.

been sought by mystics from all walks of life and was promoted by individual Sufis as well as some schools of Sufi practice since the 9th century. One of the schools which deals with the theme of "light" and illumination, having to do with *ma'ārifah* or spiritual knowledge, is known as al-Ishraqiyyah, the philosophy of illumination, which was founded by Shihabuddin Yahya Suhrawardi (d. 1191).[25] In the words of Henry Corbin, the foremost commentator on Islamic mystical traditions in the West, Suhrawardi was seminal in bringing out the "oriental" dimension of Islamic wisdom – a dimension without which, by implication, the western or semitic aspects of Islam would remain incomplete. What Corbin means is that Suhrawardi among others sought to maintain the unity of philosophy and mystical experience, which would not be the case in the West.[26] At the same time Corbin identifies the extra-Islamic elements within the "theosophy of Light" (*ḥikmat al-Ishrāq*) related to ancient Persian ideas prevalent prior to Islam. Nevertheless, the "light-infused ontology"[27] of the Suhrawardi seemed to have influenced a number of major Muslim thinkers who in turn opened new frontiers for perceiving the notion of light in Islamic mystical discourse.

The notion of divine knowledge as "light" and its symbolic meanings arose as a result of trying to interpret the so called "Light verse" which appears in the Qur'an 24:35 (*Surat al-Nūr*) where it speaks of a "lamp" which reflects divine light:

> God is the Light of the heavens and earth. His Light is like this: there is a niche, and in it a lamp, the lamp inside a glass, a glass like a glittering star, fuelled from a blessed olive tree from neither east nor west, whose oil almost gives light even when no fire touches it – light upon light. God guides whoever He will to his Light; God draws such comparisons for people; God has full knowledge of everything.[28]

Taking their cue from this allegorical narrative many mystical interpreters of the Qur'an theorized about the symbolism of the lamp and its light. The expression "mystical lamp" became extremely popular in Sufism and was understood as an "illuminating device" that gives the Sufi his/her enigmatic and extraordinary status compared with other human beings. The idea of a lamp lit with the "blazing fire" of divine love symbolizes higher station (*maqām*) held by individuals as a result of their knowledge and wisdom. The "lamp" is said to reside at the core of this person's being (*al-qalb*) which is where one connects with God as it were. Among the many Sufis, al-Ghazali (d. 1111) wrote a famous treatise (*Mishkāt al-anwār*) about the mystical lamp that "burns in his heart" and warms his soul.[29] For al-Ghazali, the

---

25 J. Spencer Trimingham, The Sufi Orders in Islam, with a new foreword by John Voll, New York and Oxford 1998, 140–41.

26 Henry Corbin, Creative Imagination in the Ṣūfism of Ibn 'Arabī, Princeton/NJ 1969, 20–21.

27 Ian Richard Netton, Allāh Transcendant: Studies in the Structure and Semiotics of Islamic Philosophy, Theology, and Cosmology, London and New York 1989, 157.

28 Translation by Abdel Haleem, The Qur'an: A new translation, 223.

29 M. Asín Palacios, La Espiritualidad de Algazel y su sentido cristiano, Madrid 1934–41, 371.

lamp signifies the archetypes or most beautiful names of God.[30] Numerous other references to the lamp are to be found in mystical writings.[31] Another famous Muslim mystic Ibn 'Arabi, mentioned above considers "niche" (*mishkāt*) as an outer cloak of the heart to protect from passions (*ahwā'*); the glass within it represents the heart even as it is transparent allowing the light to shine through because it (the heart) has attained the level of purity and has been enabled to reflect divine radiance.[32] Ibn 'Arabi regards the "lights" (*anwār*, sing. *nūr*) as the "Divine Sayings which appear in the 'niche' of the Prophet [Muhammad], who manifests the glory and beauty of these lights exactly as they are in reality."[33] The light motif is used in a variety of ways in the Islamic tradition. Many scholars and mystics have alluded to the notion of light as an allegory for mystical insight and as a precursor to religious experience. Ibn 'Arabi has an interesting anecdote which seems to represent such an experience. He reports that in 1198 C.E. as he prayed in Azhar mosque, located in the city of Fez, he had an extraordinary experience:

> I saw a light that seemed to illuminate what was before me, despite the fact that I had lost all sense of front and back, it being as if I had no back at all. Indeed during this vision I had no sense of direction whatever, my sense of vision being, so to speak, spherical in its scope, I recognized my spatial position only as hypothesis, not as reality.[34]

Ibn 'Arabi by relating this experience claimed to have reached what he calls "the Station of Light."[35] In this vision of reality, for Ibn 'Arabi at least, the "normal coordinates of space and time are suspended and become mere hypothetical."[36] What is at stake here is the very idea of how we understand reality. Ibn 'Arabi asserts that human beings exist at the crossroads of two kinds of reality: one that is not really a reality as such – this worldly reality; and the other, a reality that connects human beings, and them alone, to God. This dimension is part of the spiritual "inheritance" from God given to human beings who are God's vicegerents (Q. 2:30).

---

30 Q. 7:180; Abu Hamid Muhammad al-Ghazali, Mishkāt Al-anwār: The Niche for Lights, translation by W.H.T. Gairdner, London 1924.

31 For example: "When God kindles that lamp in the heart of His servant, it burns fiercely in the crevices of his heart [and] he is lighted by it", in A. J. Arberry, Sufism: An Account of the Mystics of Islam, Mineola/NY 2002, 50; and "...while the inner lamp of jewels is still alight, hasten to trim its wick and provide it with oil," in Idries Shah, The Sufis, New York 1990, 146.

32 Ibn 'Arabi, Futūḥāt al-makkiyah, Vol. 1, 434.

33 Muḥyīddīn Ibn 'Arabī, Divine Sayings: Mishkāt al-anwār, trans. Stephen Hirtenstein and Martin Notcutt, Oxford 2005, 12.

34 Muhyiddin Ibn 'Arabi, Sufis of Andalusia: 'Rūḥ al-quds' and 'al-Durrah al-fākhirah' of Ibn 'Arabī, trans. with introduction and notes by R.W.J. Austin, London 1971, 30.

35 Stephen Hirtenstein and Michael Tiernan (eds.), Muhyiddin Ibn 'Arabī: A Commemorative Volume, Shaftesbury 1993, 55. Cf. Adam Dupre and Peter Young (eds.) The Life and Influence of Ibn 'Arabi, Proceedings of the First Annual Symposium of the Muhyiddin Ibn 'Arabi Society, Durham University, April 1984.

36 Peter Coates, Ibn 'Arabi and Modern Thought, Oxford 2002, 164.

Whether human beings are able to visualize, actualize, and realize this inheritance within their lifetime or not is another matter. Light for Ibn 'Arabi is "synonymous with knowledge of God and knowledge of the Unity of Being."[37] In many of his writings, Ibn 'Arabi speaks of "those illuminated ones" referring to other Sufi masters and *awliyā* (plural of *walī* – saint). He also believed that the *qalb* (spiritual heart or intellect which the Sufis identify as the organ that lies at the core of one's being) is the place where God dwells and the seeker should "illumine it with the lamps of the celestial and divine virtues ..."[38] Similarly, al-Ghazali in his *Ihyā 'ulūm al-dīn* (*Revival of the religious sciences*) speaks of those whom the uncreated light illumines with its brilliance.[39] Al-Ghazali also has his own "highly developed light metaphysics" where he identifies illumination as the third degree of *tawhīd*.[40] This light motif is also expressed in terms of veils and the separation through them between divine reality and the world of matter. Thus we find a description within Sufi thought of the path from darkness to light which involves "seventy-thousand veils" and at least half of these are said to be the "veils of light."[41] The goal of the seeker is to become "refined" by going through each of these veils until the seeker (*sālik*) has attained the freedom from the "taint of darkness" and "the freedom of light from darkness means the self-consciousness of light as light."[42] The unveiling of each of these invisible barriers is equivalent to illuminating the spiritual self to a degree which was otherwise experiencing darkness, which equals ignorance.

The connection between light and gnosis is made by numerous Muslim thinkers and mystics. The light is also seen as the light of certainty (*al-yaqīn*). Without this light one remains in the state of ambiguity insofar as one's faith is concerned. Thus, *nūr* within a believer's heart (*al-qalb*) allows him/her to "see" what is not visible to the naked eye. Hence a believer who is endowed with "light" of certainty is said to have attained the *r'uyāt al qalb* (visitation of the heart) and through which the believer is endowed with extraordinary powers of discernment (*firāsah*). Thus notions such as inward illumination and spiritual light (*al-nūr*) can be said to represent the divine knowledge and the wisdom that accompanies such knowledge.[43]

---

37 Ibid. 133.

38 M. Asín Palacios, El-Islam cristianizado, Madrid [2]1981 [1931], 423.

39 Abu Hamid al-Ghazali, Ihyā 'ulūm al-dīn, Delhi 1933.

40 Annemarie Schimmel, Mystical Dimensions of Islam, Chapel Hill 1975, 96.

41 Attributed to W.H.T. Gairdner in Nicholson, The Mystics of Islam, 15–16.

42 Muhammad Iqbal, The Development of Metaphysics in Persia: A Contribution to the History of Muslim Philosophy, Whitefish/MT 2005, 116.

43 Nicholson, The Mystics of Islam, 51.

IV. *Khidr's* Knowledge as a Conduit for Experiencing Divine Light (*al-Nūr*)

In his work on the symbolism of the role played by Khidr, Patrick Franke speaks of the idea of "sacralization of spaces in the traditional world of Islam"[44] as well as about the notion of "encountering Khidr."[45] This latter work deals with accounts of the Sufis' meetings with Khidr which allowed them to claim special spiritual status and confirmed their being on a mystical path. This is a process which I regard as the 'sacralization of being' or of experience in the sense that it is through an encounter with Khidr that many have come to be regarded as saints. Meeting with Khidr somehow became the norm in the Sufi experience and Franke has collected some accounts by Sufis who claim to have met Khidr and have thus gained what is variously called mystical insights, secret knowledge, divine mysteries, and so on.[46] This shows two things simultaneously. First, it shows that Khidr's high spiritual status allowed the mystically inclined to gain a spiritual status within their own contexts and for their own purposes, be they interested in pursuit of divine proximity or in asserting their right as inheritors of spiritual authority and attaining the role of a Sufi master. The first denotes a purely spiritual quest and the second perhaps a more politically tainted quest for power and control of an institution or group. As Franke notes, Khidr was almost always "instrumentalized as a symbol of religious authorization."[47] Second, by the very nature of such accounts and their proliferation, Khidr gains universal appeal and his veneration grows steadily. This explains the wide dissemination of the Khidr legend in the predominantly Muslim regions. Franke attests to the fact that his collection of Sufi accounts of meeting with Khidr allowed him to map out the "general historical phenomenology of the veneration of this figure within the Islamic world."[48]

Just as Khidr has been used to transform profane space into a sacred one (this is what Franke's work tries to show) it can be noted that the Khidr symbol has also been used to transform individuals – according to Sufis, their souls – journeying from the inner darkness of ignorance to attaining knowledge of and proximity with God and thus achieving the station of light. If we apply this analysis to the story of Khidr, two aspects of Khidr's being seem to converge: a manifestation of God's

---

44 Patrick Franke, Khidr in Istanbul: Observations on the Symbolic Construction of Sacred Spaces in Traditional Islam, in: On Archeology of Sainthood and Local Spirituality in Islam: Past and Present Crossroads of Events and Ideas, Yearbook of the Sociology of Islam, ed. Georg Stauth, Bielefeld 2004, 45.

45 Patrick Franke's doctoral dissertation which he later published as Begegnung mit Khidr: Quellenstudien zum Imaginären im traditionellen Islam, Beirut and Stuttgart 2000.

46 Franke notes that as part of his doctoral dissertation which was on the subject of al-Khidr, he collected one hundred and fifty texts from various times and regions; See Franke, Khidr in Istanbul, 45; Cf. Begegnung mit Khidr.

47 Ibid., 48.

48 Ibid., 45.

mercy (*raḥma*) and a reflection of divine light (*al-nūr*). Khidr's knowledge is primarily esoteric (*'ilm al-bāṭin*) and thus his being a conduit to divine knowledge can be viewed as his being a dispenser of divine light simultaneously, since God in Islam is both the "source of all knowledge" (*Al-'Alīm; Al-Khabīr*) as well as "source of esoteric light" (*Al-Nūr*). Khidr makes divine knowledge manifest for Moses in the Quranic episode and thus he brings him to "light," as it were, from being in the "dark" about the true reality of things and events.[49] It may be noted that Khidr's role as a prophet can be maintained within the classical understanding of Quranic interpretation and other religious literature, while his role as a revealer of "divine light" is mainly developed and continues in the Islamic mystical tradition.

V. Conclusion

Inasmuch as Khidr is seen as a repository of divine knowledge and the initiator of those who seek divine proximity, i.e., those who are on the path, it may be argued that Khidr functions as an illuminator of the souls, as it were. For these two are allegories that may be considered two sides of the same coin. As guardian of the symbolic lamps that illuminate every corner of the *qalb* (heart) of the seeker, Khidr remains a servant of God like every other human being. Khidr does the spiritual service for other seekers on behalf of God or by the leave of God, as noted by Sufis of all rank and every school, for the last thing they wish to do is to create an intermediary between a seeker and the divine that is not reconcilable with Islamic monotheism.

Another interesting dimension of Khidr is that he is a great leveler of rank, a remover of distinctions based on worldly privilege. While he bestows spiritual status or rank, he does so indiscriminately; thus he appears and helps all not just the *al-khāṣṣa* (the spiritual elite or the accomplished Sufis.[50] The elitist idea that gnosis can be achieved only by the elect is contrary to how Sufism is blended in Muslim life and religion in the Islamic world. Khidr as a popular figure can be said to be the most 'accessible saint' in universal Islam. His availability to one and all counters the claim that only the elect may know the divine or have the ability and the means to

---

49 The Quranic episode refers to Moses' encounter with Khidr as related in Q 18:65–82 where Moses experiences three acts by Khidr which Moses finds reprehensible in that they seem to violate the "law". Moses' objections thus compel Khidr to explain the hidden meanings or mystery behind each act which when seen in their entirety do not seem objectionable. The object of the story seems to be to convey the immensity of knowledge and the levels through which it is received from God. While Moses was given the shari'a or the law (exoteric knowledge), Khidr was endowed with 'ilm ladunnī or the knowledge of the unseen world (esoteric knowledge).

50 According to popular belief, Khidr appears to anyone who calls his name and seeks help from him. In mystical traditions such as that of the Uwaysis of Central Asia; he is the physically absent teacher of those who put their trust in him and are willing to toil on the path (see note 19 above).

seek *ma'ārifah*. Inasmuch as Khidr touches the lives of human beings, even if it is imaginary to the rationalist, he allows the common person to feel this direct relationship with the unseen and transcendent God, making this God immanent and active in their lives. This is the hope that religious beliefs ultimately are designed to deliver and in the story and symbolism of Khidr it seems this goal may have been achieved for many. Finally, miracles or *mu'jizāt* which come as a result of the knowledge of the unseen (*'ilm al-ghayb*) are not due to personal abilities but are granted by God; this is as true of Moses and other prophets as much as it is of Khidr. Even though in popular piety much good is often credited to his own doing, Khidr of the Qur'an operates like the Christ of the Qur'an in that the special acts they are able to perform are achieved by the leave of God. They are granted these powers in the moment of their execution by the grace of God so as to allow the dispensation of divine mercy through a medium which does not transgress the boundaries of orthodox Islam. Thus, just as Muhammad is said to have the power to mediate on behalf his followers on the day of judgment, the Khidr legend allows the same kind of mediation through Khidr with one key difference; it is imminently available to a sincere seeker. It must be noted, however, that in popular piety, many Muslims call on Prophet Muhammad for a variety of similar reasons, including honoring the Prophet with words of praise in order to seek God's blessings.

Rationalists often decry any claims of truth made on behalf of mystical traditions, regarding these as superstitions. However, many mystics thought of such knowledge as not only within the realm of certitude but as accompanied with a sort of "inner light" which is its own evidence.[51] No outside evidence is sought or is seen as necessary because it is a subjective and experiential truth and no amount of reasoning against it would either be able to strengthen or weaken such claims. Thus, the two forms of "knowledge" seem to be on two different tracks, almost parallel to each other.[52] Similarly one can see two parallel paths travelled by Khidr and Moses; the former is on the path of an *experience of being given* the knowledge instantaneously and immediately, while the latter is on the path of *witnessing to a revelatory event* which is comparable to the divine mandate received by other prophets such as Abraham, Noah, Jesus and Muhammad. Here, too, the dialectic is invoked between the orthodoxy of the path of Moses and the mystical sublimity of the path of Khidr.

51 It must be added that the proponents of this idea would acknowledge the need for necessary prerequisites for one to be able to perceive this inner experience or "light." William James would call this conditioning of the self, a realization of trust in God's presence resulting in an "unaccountable feeling of safety", in: The Varieties of Religious Experience: A Study in Human Nature, London 1905, 285.

52 This idea is drawn from Nicholson, The Mystics of Islam, 114.

In these two figures, the law and the experience, the *ẓāhir* and the *bāṭin*, the hidden and the manifest are differentiated, or as one might argue, differentiated so as to show an even deeper course of their convergence.[53]

53 This is indeed what many scholars and mystics hold to be true because they see mysticism as an integral part of their orthodox practice. In Islamic legalistic writings much has been made of the contrast between "law" and "experience" or the sharī'ah and the ṭarīqah; in fact they are two sides of the same coin. Law requires one to practice the faith diligently but the final aim remains the attainment of the love of God and the certainty (*al-yaqīn*) of the eternal life with God in the hereafter (*al-ākhirah*) while still in this world. Thus, both aspects of faith are necessary for complete realization of God.

The Shortest Way to God is (through) Love

Ramazan Muslu

The divine love is like a huge ocean;
there is no definition of love or of its borders.
(Seyyid Nizamoglu)

Introduction

According to Islam, Adam, said to be created as a best mould,[1] is a vicegerent (*khalīfa*) of God.[2] This means that He is the Owner, the supreme creator of the universe and man is created from the similar qualities as His Master. He says in the Quran "I have breathed into him of My Spirit."[3] This implies that man has two sides: one belongs to the world, and the other belongs to the divine. God is said to have created man in His form[4] and this shows that a human being is different from His other creations. Man is a combination of body and spirit and has been entrusted with both wisdom and the ability to recognise wisdom.[5] Man is different from animals according to the philosophers; man is explained as *hayvān-ı nātiq* i.e. man with wisdom. According to the Islamic mystics man is a lover (*hayvān-ı āshiq*).

In this paper I will try to present the way to love and its peculiarities as the Sufis interpret it with reference to Hujwīrī (d. 1077), Najmaddin al-Kubrā (d. 1221) and specially Mawlānā Jalāl al-dīn al-Rūmī (d. 1273). My purpose is to understand the subject according to the views of the historians, the intellectuals and the academics. Love is something as vast as an ocean und thus I feel that it is impossible to speak about real love properly, much less define it. Further more, it is well known that the explanation of love is not love alone, because love is a feeling (*hāl*), and feelings are never mere words (*qāl*). In Sufi tradition, this constraint is stated briefly in these words: "the one who doesn't taste, doesn't know." So how are we now going to find out how we might reach the heights of loving God and what are the ways by which we can reach Him?

1 Qur'ān 95:4.
2 Qur'ān 2:30.
3 Qur'ān 15:29; 38:72.
4 Bukhārī, "Istīzān", 1; Muslim, "Birr", 115.
5 The verse says that: "Surely We offered the trust to the heavens and the earth and the mountains, but they refused to bear it because they were afraid of it. Yet man took it up; surely he is unjust, ignorant." (Qur'ān 33:72).

The ways of reaching the great heights to God

In the Sufis books, it is written generally that the ways to God are according to the number of creatures' breath, meaning that the ways to reach God are uncountable. A question then comes to mind; are these ways similar or different? In another words, does every man reach God at the same time and in the same manner? According to the historical research, the dervishes have completed the spiritual training in different times according to their individual characteristics. Najmaddīn al-Kubrā, who is the founder of Kubrawiyya order, classifies the ways to God, in three main groups: Akhyār, Abrār, and Shuttār.

The way of Akhyār is the path of piety (*zuhd*), and consists of being without doubts (*varā*), and full of devotion (*taqwā*). It includes a fear of displeasing God and yet hoping that He will love us. It includes ibādah meaning worship. The basic tenets of Akhyār are, prayers, fasting, reciting the Qur'an, and of course, remembrance of God. It is also called as the way of Ābids and Zāhids. It is necessary to spend much time in ibādah or worship in order to reach to God. For that reason, there are few men who reach their objective through Akhyār.

The way of Abrār is the path of self exertion (*Mujāhada*), of abstinence (*Riyāzah*) and of purification (*Tasfiya*). In Abrār, it is necessary to not separate from sincerity (*Ihlās*) and Truth and remain straightforward in relations between men and Truth (*Haqq*). The essential teaching of this order is to uproot the bad habits, and replace them with good habits. There are more men who reach their objective by this order than by the way of Akhyār.

The way of Shuttār is the path of excessive love, ecstasy (*Jazba*) and rapture. This way, according to the Sufis, is the shortest way to God. It is established on death, when one accepts denials willingly, i.e. to die voluntarily before the known death. In other words, this means that while still living in this world; abandon all the bodily and worldly desires. The voluntary death is the main basis of the some Sufi orders, like Kubrawiyya and Mavlawiyya.[6] The principle of voluntarily death (dieing of one's ego) is aimed to take away the love of this world. This aim is emphasised by the remembrance of death and one ponders on the consequences of death (*tafakkur-i mawt, tazakkur-i mawt*), and "ties oneself by remembering the death" (*rābita-i mawt*), making man ready to accept death. He awaits the meeting of His Lord with pleasure as his final goal. He remembers Allah and dies with the words of oneness (*tawhīd*) on his lips; i.e. there is no God but Allah.

The principle of the voluntary desire of death is mentioned in the Sufis' books as of ten, hundred or thousand stations and stages.[7] For example, ten stages are: (1)

---

6 Najmaddīn al-Kubrā, Usūl al-'Ashara: Tasavvufī Hayat (Prepared by Mustafa Kara), Istanbul 1980, 33–43; Mehmet Ali Ayni, Tasavvuf Tarihi, 193; Ismail Hakkı Izmirli, Yeni Ilm-i Kelām, Vol. I, 155; Māhir Iz, Tasavvuf: Mahiyeti, Buyukleri ve Tarikatlar (Prepared by M. Ertugrul Duzdag), Istanbul 1990, 175; Selcuk Eraydin, Tasavvufī ve Edebi Yazilar, Istanbul 1997, 86.

7 See for the stations and stages: al-Ansārī, Manāzil al-Sāirīn; al-Baqlī, Maşrab al-Arvāh; Anqa-

repentance (*tawba*), (2) piety or renunciation (*zuhd*), (3) reliance (*tawakkul*), (4) contentment or satisfaction (*kanāah*), (5) to live alone at a particular period (*uzlah*), (6) to continue the remembrance (*dhikr*), (7) the submission (taslīmiyyah), (8) inclination towards God (*tawajjuh*), (9) contemplation of Divine Nearness (*murāqabah*), and (10) contentment after accepting Allah's ways (*ridhā*).

The concept of love

The love of God for the servant is described in the Sufi tradition as annihilation for the beloved, in the Beloved. Real love, therefore cannot be described or understood, or defined easily.[8] At the same time, there is nothing clearer and more certain than love in the heart of the lover. As long as the lover feels and understands the concept of love, there is no need to explain it. Rūmī explains it in his poem: "Whenever I have to explain the concept of love, I feel repentant as I become influenced by love. My pen moves over the paper, and the pen would not dare to write but splits."[9] For example explanation of love is like a donkey stuck in the mud. This means that the wisdom reaches its borders and one is not able to explain what love is.

In order to understand the concept of love, we have to elaborate upon the concepts of 'ishq majāzī and 'ishq ilāhī', which is known as the real love. The first one, which is 'ishq Majāzi, is related to the material world and body love, like the love between male and female. But the real love, 'ishq Haqīqī, is the love which is felt towards God. In other words, the metaphorical love is transient and, therefore, fleeting. However, the real love is eternal and infinite. [10]

It should be noted that metaphorical or transient love is not an empty one as long as it is not stained and contaminated with the desires of the flesh. It is also believed that this type of love can be a bridge to real love. And on the other hand, the love toward the beautiful is not the love toward the person, but it is the love towards the beauty that the person is created with. The amazing beauty of the beautiful is a reflection of the beauty of the Creator, His art, His power, and His majesty. To be amazed and stunned by such beauty opens the way to real love. Rūmī says:

ravī, Minhāc al-Fuqarā.

8 Süleyman Derin, Love in Sufism, Istanbul 2008, 13.

9 In other words: "Whatsoever I say in exposition and explanation of love, when I come to Love (itself) I am ashamed of that (explanation). Although the commentary of the tongue makes (all) clear, yet tongueless love is clearer. Whilst the pen was making haste in writing, it split upon itself as soon as it came to Love. In expounding it (Love), the intellect lay down (helplessly) like an ass in the mire: It was love (alone) that uttered the explanation of Love and loverhood." See, Mathnawī, Vol. I, no. 112–115.

10 Sefik Can, Fundamentals of Rūmī's Thought: A Mevlevi Sufi Perspective, ed. and tr. by Zeki Saritoprak and Cuneyd Eroglu, New Jersey 2004, 149.

> "Whether Love be from this (earthly) side or from that (heavenly) side, in the end it leads us yonder."[11]

After briefly mentioning the concept of transient love (*'ishq Majāzī*), we have to elaborate upon the concept of real love (*'ishq Haqīqī*). Therefore, the question needs to be answered. How can we human beings love God, who is not seen, not known, and not understood thoroughly?

In fact, God's Messenger, Prophet Muhammad, referring to this ambiguity, says: "O Lord, we have not understood You, as You are supposed to be." The Prophet of Islam, despite his closeness to God, confesses that he has not understood God as He (the Almighty) merits. Therefore, for the majority of people it is hard to understand, what love really is?[12]

In order to love God, first of all, we have to feel His existence within our conscience, and within our reason. The Creator of this universe has hidden Himself behind His works, and has made His works as a veil for Himself. We can not see Him, but his works are obvious. Everything has been beautifully created. The world is ruled by unchangeable rules. The Creator is majestic and unique. Rūmī, in one of his poems, prays to the Lord as follows:

> "O Lord who gives life to my life, lift the veil off from your Face! O You who joins me in my grief and my problems! O My Lord, wherever I am, You are with me! O Beloved who is with me in the night! O the one who hears my supplications all the time! O My Lord who has sent the fire of love to all atoms of my body! You are exalted from all shapes and all bodies, and you are purer than all spirits. You have no image or shape, but you are the magnet of all my shapes. All my existence runs toward You and annihilates itself in You."[13]

As Rūmī mentioned in the above poem, we can think of the nature of God, which is beyond any shape or image. The Prophet of Islam commended his community not to reflect excessively on how God came into being (*zaat*), for we will never understand that. We can understand God by means of His beautiful Names and attributes, and we can feel Him through His art and His manifestations.

We of course, feel God according to our level of understanding and also according to the grace given by God to us. Without His grace and bounty, we can not find a way towards Him. Therefore, man understands God through God. Everything manifests His power and His art is evident in all spheres.[14]

Rūmī says, "All those who live on the earth eat and drink, move and travel. All our bodies are in fact a shadow. The reality of our existence is beyond the limit of this body." In other words beyond the body the rooh or the soul remains. The Tur-

---

11 Mathnawī, Vol. I, no. 111.
12 Sefik Can, Fundamentals of Rūmī's Thought, 153.
13 Ibid., 154.
14 Ibid., 154–155.

kish poet and mystic, Yūnus Amra says, "There is an 'I' in me beyond me." It is said in Sufi tradition; God said "I wanted to be known, therefore, I have created mankind." The desire to be known is hidden in the concept of love. God does not need to be known and loved, but He loves to be known and loved.[15]

Those human beings, who lower themselves from the level of humanity to the level of animals and don't have senses beyond the biological five senses, are the ones who deny the love of God or any relationship with God Almighty.[16]

One way to love God is to give thanks to God because He has given us everything that makes our life beautiful and our world beautiful. He has given us what he has not given to any other creation: the wisdom and the will to choose. Therefore, to not love God considering His unlimited bounties, is to be ungrateful. In fact, there is a need in mankind for love and faith. The person who has abandoned this need of spiritual love becomes ungrateful, not only to God, but also to all the creation.

This lack of love creates emptiness in one's spirit, in one's soul and makes us feel that we are missing something important. Thinking of this seriously, one will understand that there is a strong relationship between God the Creator, and man His servant. Usually we take refuge in God when we are in despair, when we grieve, or when we face a disaster. The Qur'an says, "He (Allah) is closer to you than your jugular vein."[17] Solace then comes in seeking help and refuge in difficult times because we know that Allah says He is so close to us and knows our grief and knows how we feel.

Accepting God therefore, is a natural phenomenon. Those who remember God frequently, work for humanity, do good deeds and commit their actions honestly regardless of the nature of their duty, and who pray to God excessively are the happy people who have reached this level of closeness to God.[18]

God is not something material. Therefore, closeness to Him should not be understood in a material and physical sense. This closeness has nothing to do with space and distance. The closeness is through the senses, love, and attributes. As the verse suggests, "I have blown into him (Adam) a part of my spirit."[19] Man, who has become the reflection of this verse, is therefore close to God. The verse says, "Surely, we have made you a vicegerent on the earth."[20] Therefore this special relationship between man and God exists. It is actually God, who has given man superiority over all other creatures. After all we do have God Almighty's rooh or spirit in all of us, hence our closeness.

Rūmī says, the situation of a man who feels alone in this life and has been left by all of his friends, says: "Don't feel alone. There is a hidden one here, inside you."[21]

---

15 Ibid., 155.
16 Ibid.
17 Qur'ān 16:55.
18 Sefik Can, Fundamentals of Rūmī's Thought, 156.
19 Qur'ān 15:29.
20 Qur'ān 26:38.
21 Muhammad b. Muhammmad b. Husayn Mevlana Jalal al-Din Rūmī, Dīvān-i Kabīr, tr. Bedi-

The One who Rūmī is referring to is the One who cannot fit within the heavens and the earth because of His majesty, but can fit into the heart of a believer because the heart of a believer can be larger than the universe as long as it is connected to God.

In the other poem, Rūmī says: "There is another soul in your soul. You seek for that soul. In the mountain of your body, there is a highly valuable element. You seek for the mine of that element. O mystic, you, who looks around, if you search for Him. Don't look for Him outside. For Him, look inside."[22]

The soul, the spirit or the rūh which has come to us from Him, make us look for Him. The search for the soul, therefore becomes the search for understanding God. To understand God is to love God. But what is love of God in the heart of the servant? This is a feeling of the servant and cannot be described in words. It is a subtle, joyful, a pure sense. This leads us humans to exalt God over everything, to seek for His pleasure before everything. When he fulfills his duties to God, he finds relaxation in his inner self. Therefore, those who are friends of God and feel friendship with God, live in a state of purity. They ritually wash themselves which is called ablution, not only at times of five daily prayers, but those who are friends of God, always think of Him and keep pure inside and outside with their piety as well as with ablutions and wash themselves frequently. They remember Him in their hearts, they feel Him in their inner sense, and they work hard and are excited to please Him and to meet Him. The servant, thus, will find God's power, His beauty and harmony in everything and in every event and will be amazed to discover God's bounties. When people smell a beautiful flower's fragrance, they see the beauty and the art of God. When people eat fruits, they think of the Creator who has given these lovely fruits from the soil and they are amazed by the bounties of God that have been given to them and therefore thank Allah in gratitude.

Those of us who travel towards God, have to believe in the ultimate justice of God. If and when we see injustice in society, we believe that sooner or later, His justice will prevail, here in this world as well as in the hereafter.[23] A firm believer knows that he has to meet and face His Lord on the Day of Judgment. All actions of our life are recorded and will be revealed to us. Each person will then know how much good he earned or how much of evil has he accumulated. A firm believer believes that God is a just God and we all will be judged according to our deeds.

Sufis' definition of love

I want to give you a few examples of love as it has been defined by the Sufis. However, first I should make it clear that the answers, which were given to the question

uzzaman Furuzanfar, Danishgah-i Tehran, 1377/1957, Vol. I, no. 188.

22 Sefik Can, Fundamentals of Rūmī's Thought, 157.

23 Ibid.

of what love is, are relative. A particular lover replies to the question, according to his spiritual level and his views. I think that this is the reason for the different definitions of real love.

'Abdullah al-Tustarī (d. 896) says: "Love consists in embracing acts of obedience and in avoiding acts of disobedience."[24] Hujwīrī explains this definition like this: "a man performs the commands of his beloved more easily in proportion to the strength of love he holds in his heart.

On the other hand, some people say that man can attain such degree of love without obedience to the commands. It is pure heresy as I feel, to suggest that one can abdicate one's religious duties or divine commands and still claim to love Allah. A believer cannot be a believer if he does not follow the commands of Allah and his prophets. Even prophet Muhammad was not made exempt from the commands of Allah; He followed them rigorously, and if one such person was granted relief from the requirements then why not all people?

The case of persons, who are overcome with rapture (*maghlūb*) and those who are mentally deficient (*ma'tūh*) is different. It is possible, however, that God in His love should bring man to such a degree that he has no trouble in following the commands of Allah and his religious duties, because the more he loves Allah, the easier obedience becomes. The Prophet, Peace be upon him, said: "Verily, a veil is drawn over my heart, and I ask forgiveness of God seventy times daily." He asked to be forgiven for his actions as he thought that his actions were not worthy of God's acceptance. Though he was the most pious of the pious he kept asking for forgiveness."[25]

Junayd al-Baghdādī (d. 909), one of the important Sufis in the early period, says: "Love is an inclination of the heart." Kalābāzī (d. 990) explains this definition like this: "Love is inclination of heart; of a servant of God and that it belongs to Him."[26] And Shiblī (d. 945) says: "Love is called as a "*mahabbat*" because it obliterates from the heart everything except the beloved."[27]

Abu'l-Qāsim al-Qushayrī (d. 1072) says: "Love is the effacement of the lover's attributes and the establishment of the Beloved's essence."[28] Hujwīrī says that since the Beloved is subsistent (*bāqī*) and the lover is annihilated (*fānī*) the jealously of love requires that the lover should make the subsistence of the Beloved absolute by negating himself, and he cannot negate his own attributes except by affirming the essence of the Beloved. No lover can stand by his own attributes, for in that case he would not need the Beloved's beauty; but when he knows that his life depends on the Beloved's beauty, he necessarily seeks to annihilate his own attributes, which

24 Ali b. Uthmān al-Jullābī al-Hujwīrī, The Kashf al-Mahjūb: The Oldest Persian Treatise on Sufism, translated: Reynold A. Nicholson, Darul-Ishaat, Karachi 1990, 311.

25 Hujwīrī, The Kashf al-Mahjūb, 312.

26 Kalābāzī, al-Ta'arruf: Dogus Devrinde Tasavvuf (prepared by Suleyman Uludag), Istanbul 1992, 161.

27 Hujwīrī, The Kashf al-Mahjūb, 305.

28 Ibid., 311.

veil him from his Beloved; and thus in love for his Beloved he becomes an enemy to himself.[29]

According to Hujwīrī, for the heart love is like food or nourishment. The heart, which has no love, is empty, ruined and destroyed.[30]

These definitions of the Divine love are mentioned here: the inclination of the servant's heart towards God; the obliteration of everything from the heart except the beloved; the effacement of the lover's attributes and the establishment of the Beloved is the essence.

From love (*mahabbat*) to the excessive love (*'ishq*)

It is said that there are two stages of love in early period of the Sufi training. The first one is fear (*hawf*) or grief (*huzn*) which is represented by Hasan al-Basrī (d. 728). The second one is love, which is represented by Rābia' al-'Adaviyya (d. 801). The way which is represented by Hasan al-Basrī is not well known or acclaimed. However, the second one given by Rābia' has spread among the Sufis, and has been a major understanding of Sufi thought.

Historically, love in the beginning is called *muhabbat.* This term of *mahabbat* is used in the Qur'an and the Sunnah. God says: "O believers, whosoever among you apostatize from their religion; God will assuredly bring in their stead a people whom He will love and who will love Him."[31] And He also said: "Some men take idols beside God and love them as they love God, but the believers love God best."[32] And the other verse says to the Prophet (*Pbuh*): "(O Messenger), tell people: 'If you indeed love Allah, follow me, and Allah will love you and will forgive you your sins. Allah is All-Forgiving, All-Compassionate."[33] The last verse explains that to love and to obey the Prophet are obligatory for the believers.

And He also said: "God loves to meet those who love to meet Him, and dislikes meeting those who dislike meeting Him."

And said again: "When God loves a man He says to Gabriel, 'O Gabriel, I love such and such a one, so do you love him'; then Gabriel loves him and says to dwellers in Heaven, 'God loves such and such o one' and they love him too; then he bestows on him favour in the earth, so that he is loved by the inhabitants of the earth; and as it happens with regard to love, so does it happen with regard to hate."

---

29 Ibid., 311. Hujwīrī also says: "It is well known that the last words of Husayn b. Mansūr (al-Hallāj) on the scaffold were "It is enough for the lover that he should make the One single." See same page.

30 Hujwīrī, The Kasf al-Mahjūb: Hakikat Bilgisi (translated into Turkish by Suleyman Uludag), Istanbul 1982, 448–449. (This passage is not translated into English by Reynold A. Nicholson).

31 Qur'ān 5:59.

32 Qur'ān 2:160.

33 Āl-i Imrān, 3:31.

The term of *'ishq* is not mentioned in the Qur'an clearly. According to Ibn al-'Arabi (d. 1240) there is a slight mention in the Qur'an of 'ishq, as ashadd-i hubb. God says: "But those who (truly) believe, they love Allah more than all else."[34]

Up till the twelfth century, Sufis prefer to use term of *mahabbatullah,* that is *love of God,* rather than *'ishqullah*, which is excessive love for God. This term (*'ishqullah*) became widespread after Ahmad al-Ghazzālī (d. 1126), Ibn al-Fārid (d. 1235)[35], Fahraddīn al-Irāqī (d. 1289) and especially Mawlānā Jalāl al-dīn al-Rūmī. According to the record of Ibn al-Jawzī (d. 1201), the first time that this term has been used was by Abū Hussein al-Nūrī (d. 908), who said: "I loved God excessively."[36]

Hujwīrī summarizes the discussion. He says: "There is much controversy about Ishq or excessive love, among the Shaikhs. Some Sūfīs hold that excessive love towards God is allowable, but that it does not proceed from God. Such love, they say, is the attribute of one, who is debarred from his beloved, and Man is debarred from God, but God is not debarred from Man. Therefore Man may love God excessively, but the term is not applicable to Allah. Others, again, take the view that God cannot be the object of Man's excessive love, because such love involves passing beyond limits. The modernists assert that excessive love, in this world and the next, is properly applied only to the desire of attaining the essence, and inasmuch as the essence of God is not attainable, the term (*'ishq*) is not rightly used in reference to Man's love towards God, although the terms "love" (*mahabbat*) and "pure love" (*safwat*) are correct.

Man feels love towards God, because God through His attributes and actions, is a gracious benefactor to His friends. Allah's manifestations of love are seen in Jacob. The father of Joseph was absorbed in love for his son, from whom he was separated. He had lost his eyesight because of too much weeping, but when he touched and smelt his son's shirt his eyesight returned. Zulaykhā was ready to die on account of her excessive love for Joseph; her eyes were not opened until she was united with him, according to Hujwīrī. It has been said that excessive love is applicable to God also, since God gives the power of excessive love.[37]

Intellect (wisdom) and excessive Love

According to Sufi thought, the pace with which man travels with his intellect is limited, but becomes limitless with excessive love or real love. In other words, when the intellect (*'aql*) or wisdom is insufficient, the excessive love starts. In reality, love is an attribute of God. Allegorically, it can be related to the servant. The Qur'an

34 Qur'ān 2:165.

35 See for more Derin Suleyman, Love in Sufism, 201–226

36 Ibn al-Jawzī, Telbīsu Iblīs, Beirut 1992, 153; Tasavvuf Ilmine Dair Kuseyrī Risalesi, translated into Turkish by Suleyman Uludag, 500 (footnote 160).

37 Hujwīrī, The Kashf al-Mahjūb, 310.

says: "He loves His servants. They love Him."[38] Love is a state of experience that cannot be explained in words. There is no doubt that as a result of knowing God, finding him in our hearts through the utmost efforts and long contemplations, prayers, good deeds, and help to others, one will be able, even at the lowest level, to feel the secrets of the existence of God. Through this discovery, the person may reach a higher level of spiritual taste and can feel an indescribable joy of the spirit. Therefore, one can say that the spiritual enjoyment that comes from knowing and loving God is beyond all pleasures. The goal of all lovers of Allah, is to reach that higher level. Here lies the spiritual flavour that few can feel. It has been said that those who feel this state and have reached this level have annihilated their wants and they have no grief at all. Their hearts have become busy with spiritual flavour. Even if they are thrown into fire, they will have no feeling of fire because of their utmost joyfulness that they have been experiencing, in loving God. Even if all of paradise were offered to them, they would not even glance in the direction of paradise for the joy that they have, is even greater than paradise.[39] Rūmī describes the state of such mystics in the following poem:

> "O My Lord who is my rest of my soul when I am in grief. O My Lord who is the treasure of my spirit when I suffer hunger and poverty. What the imagination cannot attain, and understanding and reason cannot reach, since all beauties come from You to my spirit, You are my Pole Star. My Lord, because of Your grace and bounty I look down on the worldly things. How can this transient world's richness and wealth deceive me? My Lord, through Your utmost generosity if You give me countless properties and You put before me all Your hidden treasures, I will prostrate from my inner most being and put my face on the ground and say, "My Lord, for me, Your love is worthier than all of this."[40]

It is possible that the Man may only reach to God through real love. There is no physical closeness when the term of "ultimate union" (*vuslat*) is used. It is intended that this concept (*vuslat*) spiritual closeness which the Man obtains it with his sixth sense, i.e. his inner eyes which is called the "eyes of the heart," or "basīrah". There are thousands of veils between Man and God. But the Man, who reaches the real love, sees everything in the cosmos as a revelation of his Beloved.

To love the Prophet

All Muslims love dearly their Prophet. In fact, not only Rūmī, but all saints have love and respect for the Prophet of Islam. Moreover, they love not only the Prophet

---

38 Qur'ān 5:54.
39 Sefik Can, Fundamentals of Rūmī's Thought, 158–159.
40 Dīvān-i Kabīr, Vol. I, no. 207.

of Islam, but all messengers of God. Rūmī has a special place in his heart for the Prophet of Islam because the Prophet proposed a high standard of ethical conduct for humankind, such as freeing slaves and caring for the poor. There is no other historical personality like Muhammad who brought freedom to the slaves and the lower classes. Therefore not only Muslim saints but philosophers like Thomas Carlyle and the German poet Goethe have fallen in love with Prophet Muhammad because of his service to humanity throughout his life. They have expressed their reverence for Muhammad, peace and blessings be upon him, in their books. Very recently, Michael Hart has written a book[41] about the hundred most influential historical personalities and ranked Muhammad (*Pbuh*) as number one.[42]

Rūmī in remembrance to the Prophet says: "We hear all the time the voice of divine love from right and left. With the influence of this voice we are ascending to the heavens. Who has the capacity of watching us? Before coming to this world we were in heaven. We were friends of the angels. There is real homeland, and we will return to it. How distant are the pure pearls of the divine and the dirty world of this soil. Without thinking of your honour, you came to this lower world. Pick up your properties and tie up your burden. This place is not ours. We have to migrate. This young desire is our friend. Sacrificing the soul is our job. And the head of our caravan is Mustafa, the Prophet, of whom the whole universe is proud. Mustafa, peace and blessing be upon him, is so high a being that the moon did not dare to see his face and split."[43] And he says in another poem: "Our prophet's way is the way of love. We are the children of love, and our mother is love."[44]

Rūmī is concerned with the love, love of humanity and the love of God. Because he witnesses Allah's manifestation in every thing. Rumi ignored the mistakes of people and was kind and tolerant towards everybody. Rūmī's love for the prophet was enhanced by the fact that our prophet always behaved with utmost humility and with tolerance. Not only towards all human beings, but towards his most cruel enemies, also. The well-known title of Prophet Muhammad is Habib Allah or the Beloved of God. The Prophet is the ideal model of all human beings. Therefore, Rumi's love for the Prophet is based on this principle. In his famous poem, Rūmī says:

> "I am the servant of the Qur'an as long as I live. And I am the soil where the foot of Muhammad stepped."[45]

---

41 See Michael H. Hart, The 100: A Ranking of the Most Influential Persons in History, New York 1992.

42 Sefik Can, Fundamentals of Rūmī's Thought, 159–160.

43 Dīvān-i Kabīr, Vol. I, 212 (no. 463).

44 Ibid., Vol. II, 1270 (no. 57).

45 Ibid., Vol. II, 1387 (no. 1331).

Rūmī's thoughts about the excessive love (*'ishq*)

Mawlānā Jalāladdīn al-Rūmī is one of the important representatives of excessive love for Allah. In his books, there are a lot of explanations regarding the Divine love and the excessive love in which he has drowned his soul.

Rūmī notices that the Love is the doctor of spiritual ills and of suffering and pain: "Rejoice, O Love that is our sweetest passion, physician of our many illnessses!"[46]

According to him, mankind soars to the skies via Love. Rūmī says: "Through love the earthly body soared to the skies: the mountain began to dance and became nimble."[47] "Love inspired Mount Sinai, O lover, (so that) Sinai (was made) drunk and Moses fell in a swoon."[48] Rūmī gıves the example of divine love as a ship, on which the believers boards. He says: "Love is a ship for the elect: Seldom is calamity (the result); for the most part it is deliverance."[49]

Rūmī praises the eye which weeps for God and calls the tears as pearls. He says: "Oh, happy the eye that is weeping for His sake! Oh, fortunate the heart! that is scared/burnt for His sake."[50] "The tears which people shed for His sake are pearls and people think they are tears."[51]

According to him, the light of God illuminates mankind and the light of man who doesn't love, blinds the eyes. Rūmī says: "The reflexion of the servant of God is wholly luminous; the reflexion of the stranger (to God) is wholly blindness. Know every one's reflexion: See (it plainly), O my soul. (Then) ever sit beside those whom thou desirest."[52]

Rūmī advises to work and to strive for obtaining the love of God and plunge oneself in the ocean of love. He says: "He that is drowned in God, wishes to be more drowned, (while) his spirit (is tossed) up and down like the waves of the sea, (Asking) "Is the bottom of the sea more delightful, or the top? Is His (the Beloved's) arrow more fascinating, or the shield?"[53]

According to him, a lover is a loved man at the same time. Rūmī says: "Whomsoever thou didst deem to be a lover, regard (him) as the loved one, for relatively he

46 Mathnawī, Vol. I, no. 23.

47 Ibid., Vol. I, no. 25. There is a sign to the verse of surah 7th: "And when Moses came at our appointment and his Lord spoke to him, he said: 'O my Lord! Reveal Yourself to me, that I may look upon You!' He replied: 'Never can you see Me. However, behold this mount; if it remains firm in its place, only then will you be able to see Me.' And as soon as his Lord unveiled His glory to the mount, He crushed it into fine dust, and Moses fell down in a swoon. And when he recovered, he said: 'Glory be to You! To You I turn in repentance, and I am the foremost among those who believer" (Qur'an 7:143).

48 Ibid., Vol. I, no. 26.

49 Ibid., Vol. IV, no. 1406.

50 Ibid., Vol. I, no. 818.

51 Ibid., Vol. I, no. 1780.

52 Ibid., Vol. III, no. 3253–54.

53 Ibid., Vol. I, no. 1745–46.

is both this and that. If they are thirsty and seek water from the world, (yet) water also seeks those that are thirsty. Inasmuch as He is (thy) lover, be silent: as when He pulls your ear, be thou (all) ear."[54]

Conclusion

Mawlānā Jalāl al-din al-Rūmī, says about the man who doesn't comprehend value of Divine love, he is like the bird which has no wings. He doesn't go anywhere or fly anywhere. The traveller of Truth, knows the value of Divine love, should pass stages and stations for arriving to their home and original country, i.e. the Divine world or the Akhirat. Coming close to Truth is endless and infinite. Sufi, whichever stage and station he is in, should go on by the Divine love without hesitating. Firstly, he should acknowledge himself and recognize his truth and his place. Where does he stand in the cosmos? He is acquainted with God and ultimate union with Him, when he achieves this knowledge and recognition. The more he has patience and endurance, the more quickly he goes on to the way to Divine love.

Finally, Rūmī, in the beginning of his Mathnawi, says, "Someone asked me, 'What is love?' And I told him when you become like me you will understand."[55]

---

54 Ibid., Vol. I, no. 1740–42.
55 Ibid., Vol. II, (foreword); Dīvān-i Kabīr, Vol. II, 1015 (no. 2733).

Autorenverzeichnis

Dr. Bärbel Beinhauer-Köhler, Professorin für Religionsgeschichte, Fachbereich Evangelische Theologie, Philipps-Universität Marburg

Dr. Sebastian P. Brock, formerly Reader in Syriac Studies, Faculty of Oriental Studies, Professorial Fellow of Wolfson College, University of Oxford/UK

Till Engelmann, Doktorand, Theologische Fakultät, Georg-August-Universität Göttingen

Dr. Fadi Georgi, Assistant Professor of Dogmatic Theology, St. John of Damascus Institute of Theology, University of Balamand/Lebanon

Dr. Sidney H. Griffith, Professor, Department of Semitic and Egyptian Languages and Literatures, The Catholic University of America, Washington DC/USA

Dr. Martin Heimgartner, Privatdozent für Kirchengeschichte, Theologische Fakultät, Martin-Luther-Universität Halle-Wittenberg

Dr. Grigory Kessel, Wissenschaftlicher Mitarbeiter im Fachgebiet Ostkirchengeschichte, Fachbereich Evangelische Theologie, Philipps-Universität Marburg

Dr. Ramazan Muslu, Associate Professor of Sufism, Faculty of Theology, Sakarya University/Turkey

Dr. Irfan A. Omar, Associate Professor, Department of Theology, Marquette University, Milwaukee WI/USA

Dr. Karl Pinggéra, Professor für Kirchengeschichte, Fachbereich Evangelische Theologie, Philipps-Universität Marburg

Dr. Gerrit J. Reinink, Professor, formerly Senior Lecturer of Syriac and Aramaic Studies, University of Groningen/Netherlands

Dr. Serafim Seppälä, Professor of Systematic Theology and Patristics, Faculty of Theology, University of Joensuu/Finland

Dr. Dr. h.c. Martin Tamcke, Professor für Ökumenische Theologie und Orientalische Kirchen- und Missionsgeschichte, Theologische Fakutät, Georg-August-Universität Göttingen

Dr. Herman G. B. Teule, Professor of Eastern Christianity, Institute of Eastern Christian Studies, Radboud University Nijmegen/Netherlands, and Faculty of Theology, Katholieke Universiteit Leuven/Belgium